P9-DFK-936

THE POISONED TONGUE

A Documentary History
of American Racism
and Prejudice

BY STANLEY FELDSTEIN

As Author
ONCE A SLAVE
The Slaves' View of Slavery

As Editor
THE POISONED TONGUE
A Documentary History of American Racism
and Prejudice

THE POISONED TONGUE

A Documentary History
of American Racism
and Prejudice

Edited by
Stanley Feldstein

William Morrow & Company, Inc. New York   1972

Copyright © 1971 by Stanley Feldstein

All rights reserved. No part of this book may be
reproduced or utilized in any form or by any means,
electronic or mechanical, including photocopying,
recording or by any information storage and
retrieval system, without permission in writing from
the Publisher. Inquiries should be addressed to
William Morrow and Company, Inc.,
105 Madison Ave., New York, N.Y. 10016.

Printed in the United States of America.
Library of Congress Catalog Card Number 76–166349

For two, who have meant so much,

Thomas Payne Govan
Jane Davis Govan

ACKNOWLEDGMENTS

In the course of researching and editing this book, I incurred numerous debts and obligations. Librarians, colleagues and friends were most generous with their time, advice and encouragement. Chiefly, my indebtedness to Dr. Lawrence Costello of Nassau Community College and the New York City Board of Education is great. His unique understanding and familiarity with the material in this manuscript, and his important contributions to the sections on American nativism, were essential to the completion of this study.

I would also like to thank Professor David Reimers of New York University for encouraging me to research the problem of American racism, and Professor Thomas P. Govan of the University of Oregon for contributing so much time and unrivaled historical insights. I am also grateful to James Landis and Joslyn Pine of William Morrow & Company for the confidence they have shown in me and for their excellent editorial assistance. And, to Jim Reisman, my thanks for his legal advice.

To my friends, colleagues and family: Mrs. Evelyn Costello, Harold and Marion Siegel, Bernard Koven, Mrs. Jane Davis Govan, Ted and Lenore Jacobs, Paul Bernstein, Arnold Ratner, Robert and Shirley Feldstein, Peter Goodman, Robert Gruber, Martin Cane, Reuben Kravitz and Samuel Forsheit, my thanks and everlasting appreciation.

Lastly, I wish to pay special tribute to three people who have made my task so much easier: Roberta Robins and Susan Feldstein, who performed the prodigious feat of researching, typing and proofreading the book; and Mr. Leonard Leibowitz, who in the midst of his law practice found time to contribute his excellent editorial talents.

The research for this study was facilitated by many library

staffs. I am particularly grateful to Mr. Mortimer Kass of the Anti-Defamation League of the B'nai B'rith, Mr. Harry Alderman, Librarian for the American Jewish Committee, Joseph Schwarz and Robert Slevin of the New York Historical Society, the staffs of the Library of Congress, the New York Public Library, the Brooklyn Public Library, the Schomburg Collection of the New York Public Library, the South Carolina Historical Society, the South Caroliniana Library, the General Library of the University of California at Berkeley, the New York University Library, the Columbia University Library, the Massachusetts Historical Society, and the General Library of the University of Oregon at Eugene.

And, as a father, I recognize my greatest obligations to my daughter Eileen and my son Louis Mark for their patience, understanding, and love.

Stanley Feldstein
New York City
June, 1971

CONTENTS

INTRODUCTION

For several decades historians have been investigating the reasons for American inter-group hostility. For the most part, these scholars have suggested that class conflict inspired by material gain was the primary motivation for the racial and ethnic "warfare" that was so inextricably a part of the nation's past and present. Upon initial consideration, this explanation seems plausible, and has consequently been accepted by many. But beyond this supposition, the impact and significance of America's racist heritage has remained somewhat unexplored. Taking into account the violence of the civil rights movement, the rejection of integration by the white majority and the bitter racial exchanges of present-day America, it is difficult to admit mere economic struggle as the basis of the nation's racial crisis.

If the conflicts between the nation's racial and ethnic groups emanated fundamentally from economic causes, a nation so abundantly wealthy as the United States should have within its power the ability to share some of that prosperity in order to engender a society which is not forced to live in manic fear and hatred of its racial minorities. Economic solutions then, which have in the past been successfully utilized in the United States to resolve other problems, could conceivably have "bought" racial peace. This has not happened, and is not likely to. Thus, one must look elsewhere for the roots underlying the racism that permeates our society.

In actuality, the causes of racial conflict in the American past and present stem from fear and transcend the defense of one's economic security. Therefore, one should explore other areas besides economic motivation for a deeper understanding of the basis of our hatred, why we still fear, and more importantly, why we refuse to allow those we consider to be "outcasts" an opportunity to participate fully in all areas of society.

In 1968, the full-fledged existence and significance of racism
in American life was formally confirmed with the publication
of the Report of the United States Commission on Civil Disorder. Through what is commonly called the Kerner Report,
we were officially informed for the first time in our history that
we are a racist society. After investigating America's racist institutions, practices and attitudes, the Commission concluded
that the "nation is moving toward two separate societies,
one black, one white—separate and unequal." Moreover, it
charged that separatism was created by "white racism" which
bears the onus for the explosive mixture which has been accumulating in our cities since World War II.

Although I am in agreement with the spirit of the Report,
I take issue with its statement that the accumulation of racial
discord dated from 1945 and arose solely from our urban centers. From the racist ideologies imbedded in the historical material presented in this volume, it becomes apparent that racial
intolerance in America has existed since the very inception of
English colonization, and has subsequently grown with this
nation as an integral part of its society for the past four centuries. Thus, since the roots of racial antagonism reach deeply
into our past, it is necessary to undertake a more thorough and
extensive investigation in order to fully comprehend the central
domestic issue of mid-twentieth-century America: racism.

In preparing this study it was necessary to present not only
the assaults on specifically racial groups, but also those directed
against the ethnic minorities that experienced the sharp bite
of American bigotry. Thus, a broad definition of racism has
been adopted. This definition was supplied by *The Dictionary
of Social Sciences* (1964),[1] which denotes racism as "the doctrine that there is a connection between racial and cultural
traits, and that some races are inherently superior to others."
It further states that "racism indiscriminately includes such
non-biological grouping as religious sects, nations, linguistic
groups, and cultural groups under the concept of race, and
can be regarded as a particularly virulent form of ethnocentrism." With this definition as guideline, there is sufficient jus-

[1] *The Dictionary of the Social Sciences,* Julius Gould and William L.
Kolb, eds. (New York, 1964), p. 571.

tification for the inclusion in this study of the ideologies of racists and nativists as directed against America's several racial and ethnic minorities.

Racism has been intrinsic to this nation since its colonial beginnings. It was inherited from the first European settlers, who had deeply rooted racist attitudes. From the first landing of the British in North America, racist and nativist ideology was permitted to flourish in the midst of an allegedly democratic society. Through the years, the style and rhetoric of racism have evolved from blatantly overt to more subtle and discreet forms, the latter being especially characteristic of America today.

America's literature of hatred testifies to the paradox that existed in the nation. The hostility contained in the defenses of Negro slavery, the almost systematic presentation of blacks as subhuman, the anti-Indian literature of the nineteenth century, the fear of the Asian "yellow peril," and the influential nativist movements of our past serve as an infamous "tribute" to those who asserted that America was an egalitarian society.

The so-called racial inferiority of the blacks has been the prime target of American racism. Motivated by economic gain and an anti-black ideology, the latter having its origin in the first British contact with black Africa, whites brought blacks to America as slaves; they then justified their actions by evolving myths that portrayed Negroes as something other than a creation of God. As slavery became an American institution, vindication for it ranged from acceptance of the theory of innate black inferiority to biblical substantiation and approval, and supplied the nation with its foundation for anti-black sentiment. Even after the Emancipation Proclamation, blacks continued to be subjugated on the basis of an ideology which deemed them a threat to the white race. Surrounded by the white-inspired fears of miscegenation, mongrelization and Africanization, the blacks were shut out from American society by a systematic campaign which included black codes, segregation, threats and violence. This trend continued well into the twentieth century. And it is only today that blacks, buttressed by legal measures and a growing awareness and appreciation of their own cultural identity, are beginning to partake of the

American dream of equality. Perhaps within this century the black man will achieve his full birthright.

From the beginning, the Indian represented an obstacle to the advancing white civilization. Dismissed as nonhuman by some and dreaded by most, Indians were removed to the West, subjected to genocide, and finally imprisoned on reservations. This was justified in the name of a "superior white civilization," in the process of bringing its beneficent qualities to an untamed land.

Nativism has been second only to racism as a negative force in American history. As a form of ethnic superiority, nativism manifested itself as American hostility to nearly all foreign-born persons, and thus antedated even racism. Nativism found some of its leading advocates among the nation's founding fathers; these included Benjamin Franklin, Thomas Jefferson and Alexander Hamilton, who favored the natural growth of population rather than immigration as a means of increasing the number of the country's inhabitants.

Like racism, nativism has been endemic in the United States; but unlike the ubiquitous nature of the former, nativism's most virulent form has appeared in certain definitive periods. From the 1820's to the 1850's, the great waves of immigrants who entered the country included many Irish. Consequently, during these decades nativism was primarily anti-Catholic. Those who opposed immigration argued that the Irish immigrants were undesirable because they were poor, violent, untutored in the ways of democracy, and a source of unfair labor competition for native workers. But most significant of all was their Catholicism.

In the latter part of the nineteenth and early twentieth centuries, when the main sources of immigration were southern and eastern Europe, the arguments against a free immigration policy were no longer exclusively religious, but included political and cultural objections as well. These immigrants, Italians, Poles, and Russians (mostly Jews), came from areas which had little or no familiarity with democratic institutions; and their language and customs made their assimilation far more difficult than that of the earlier immigrants'. Even more offensive to Americans were the Orientals, who nativists insisted represented the lowest elements in their societies and threatened to destroy the native workers' standard of living. In the twentieth century, inspired by racism and alarmed by Japanese imperialism, Japanese-Americans were considered potential fifth columnists and were herded into prison camps.

Like the racist, the nativist of the past eighty years has drawn upon scientific and pseudoscientific findings to support his prejudices. He has exalted the immigrant of Anglo-Saxon or Teutonic background as superior to all others, and in Social Darwinism he found a convenient rationale for verifying the supremacy of Anglo-Saxon institutions. Nativism finally received full official recognition in the restrictive legislation of the 1920's. Although the Immigration Act of 1964 removed most of the nativist aspects of our immigration law, hostile attitudes toward foreigners persist strongly to this day; this is evidenced by the inferior treatment of, and regard for, Mexican-Americans and Puerto Ricans.

Thus, the racist rhetoric and actions of the past have endured. The defense against the "black encroachment" into traditionally white-dominated areas of housing, employment and government, and the elevation of property rights above human rights indicate that racism is still firmly entrenched in this nation's culture. The contemporary attacks on "open housing" legislation, and the euphemism "welfare cheater" for an individual who is black or Puerto Rican are examples of current embodiments of America's traditional racial hostility. Today, however, the one basic difference is subtlety; the racist feels somewhat uncomfortable about being exposed or identified as such. Nevertheless, although the rhetoric has changed, the motives for racial antagonism have remained the same.

After an investigation of the various documents pertaining to American racist and nativist ideology, many of which are contained herein, certain conclusions may be drawn. Foremost is the observation that the practice of both racism and nativism are abiding themes in the American experience. Moreover, racism is as significant to the cultural, political, and social development of the United States as is the evolution of the alleged equality this nation offered to the oppressed millions who migrated to its shores.

In addition, several subsidiary conclusions may be advanced:

(1) The contradiction between *professed* American ideals and the reality of racism and nativism has caused many critics to express disappointment over America's lost opportunity to become a nation devoid of the ancient hatreds that have plagued the world for so many centuries.

(2) Racism has existed among all groups. Even the victims of racism have on occasion become the perpetrators. Witness the attitudes of the Irish-Catholic immigrants of the nineteenth century, themselves once the victims of nativist attacks, toward the abolition of slavery and subsequent attempts to bring blacks into the mainstream of American life. A more recent manifestation of this phenomenon is the emergence of professed anti-Semitism among some of the more militant black power groups of today, e.g., the Black Panthers.

(3) Despite the Kerner Commission Report, and although most Americans practice and/or harbor racist feelings, they stubbornly refuse to accept the fact that racism is an integral part of their institutions and society. Most have been able to quell their own consciences by rationalizing out of existence the treatment of others. For example, some of the loudest voices in the 1950's condemning the segregation laws of the South became most disruptive in their opposition when integration was attempted in the more northerly white communities.

(4) Although racism has been a pervasive theme throughout American history, it has peaked or crested under certain demographic, economic, or psychological conditions. With the emancipation of blacks in the 1860's, the predominantly white areas of the North reacted as though they were gripped by an impending destruction of their culture by the "massive hordes" of ex-slaves who were moving into their communities. This same fear struck the nation with the Asian immigration to the Pacific coast, the Irish and German Catholic immigration in the 1840's, and occurred most recently with the presence of a strong and fearless civil rights movement, and the more frightening development of black power. One may even predict that the next wave of fear in the white community will come with the emergence in the 1970's of the American Indian and the Chicano (Mexican-American). Both groups appear to be re-

peating the patterns of demands established by their predecessors, and the white backlash appears to be following likewise its familiar pattern.

(5) Racism, more than class conflict, has been a determining factor in the nation's development, especially when it involves color. While there were racial assaults against the Irish, Germans, Jews, Slavs, and Italians, their whiteness allowed them to escape intensive persecution within two or three generations. Indeed, members of most of these groups eventually joined the ranks of the racists. Thus, to many nonnative Americans, assimilation meant, and still means, absorbing the racist scheme of America.

The avowed purpose of this collection is to trace the historical development, through primary sources, of racist thought in the United States. The study spans the period from the first English contact with black Africa to the present racial crisis. In addition, it is an attempt to lead the student of the American past to an understanding of the intensity and significance of racism, nativism and ethnocentrism in America's history; and to account for racism as a veritable institution in the American way of life.

The book follows a chronological order. Moreover, each chapter, which is generally devoted to a selective time period, is further divided to include in separate sections the racial or ethnic groups most affected by the racial assaults. Each of the book's seven sections begins with an introduction which enables the reader to place the selected document in its historical perspective. It explores the racial themes that were most ostensible during the period and identifies the groups that were confronted with overt racial hostility. And to crystallize the significance of the selection, a brief explanation of it precedes each document. In order that the reader be given an opportunity to decide for himself, I have chosen in most cases not to inject interpretation into any of the introductions or explanations.

The documents presented were chosen because they reflect what I consider to be a broad range of racist and nativist thought. They comprise both the writings of some of the more prominent figures of the American past, such as Thomas Jefferson, and the sentiments of the average American. Among the material included are selections from newspapers, magazines, speeches, books, laws, and letters.

Because of the vast amount of material available, I culled only those sources which I believe to be the most significant and most accurately representative. Not seeking to present sources with which many are already familiar, e.g. Madison Grant's *The Passing of the Great Race* (1916), I have attempted to use documents which are not so easily accessible or well-known to the layman. Unfortunately, because of the requirements that limit this collection to an acceptable length, it was impossible to reprint many documents which I felt were as significant as those that are included. However, these would be, in the main, repetitious. As a result of these omissions, the reader will discover certain time gaps in each section, and will occasionally come across documents clustered around a few specific years. Nevertheless, the several selections chosen to represent the ideology of a period actually embody the thinking of an entire era.

In addition, the reader will note that several of the selections are not racist but anti-racist. In presenting these anti-racist attitudes there is a threefold purpose: (1) to make the reader aware that there was opposition to racism in this country by individuals and organizations; (2) to indicate that the anti-racist material discloses as much about racism in the nation as other documents; and (3) to reveal the existence of a vanguard, small in number, who recognized the paradox of thought and action in this country. The relative scarcity of anti-racist documents is due, of course, to the avowed intention of the book as a documentary history of racism and prejudice.

The difficulty of presenting a complete documentary account of racism is unquestionable. In the book, each section and its subdivisions should have at least a volume devoted to it. And possibly, the most important consequence of this study will be to develop motivation for additional research into this vital area.

Finally, this collection is by no means an attempt to besmirch the American past or to depict the American as a merciless racist, preoccupied with making life miserable for others. Certainly, racism is not solely an American trait, but characterizes all nations and all peoples. Moreover, the efforts to eliminate this "disease" were constantly in progress throughout American history, and sometimes achieved success. Unfortunately, though, the nation is still comparatively young and has yet to reach the juncture when all groups can be free of bigoted assaults. Although a critic of American racial hostility, I write in the firm belief that this nation is stronger than the hate that many Americans harbor. And that one day all Americans will accept and practice the egalitarian ideology which was for so many years embraced by only a relatively small segment of our population.

PART 1

The Genesis of American Racism From Exploration Through the Colonial Decades, 1550-1750

INTRODUCTION

In commenting on slavery in America, the French general and traveler Marquis de Chastellux observed in 1780: "Sufficient attention has not been paid to the difference between slavery, such as we have kept it in our colonies, and slavery as it was generally established among the ancients. A white slave, in ancient times, had no other cause of humiliation than his present lot; if he was freed, he could mix straightway with free men and become their equal. . . . But in the present case, it is not only the slave who is beneath his master; it is the Negro who is beneath the white man. No act of enfranchisement can efface this unfortunate distinction." Two major factors helped to create the basic difference between classical slavery and slavery in America: the European, particularly English, attitude toward Africans, and the institutionalization of American slavery as a cultural and economic vested interest.

The attitudes of English colonists toward Negroes were conditioned by the English pre-colonial views of Africans. Long before they came to the New World, Englishmen regarded African blacks in a totally negative and denigrating light and as uniquely different from all other peoples. First, Negroes were set apart by their blackness; Englishmen, more than most Europeans, invested the Negroes' color with a "special meaning." Blackness was synonymous with filth, foulness, and evil. In addition, the Africans came from a continent that was inextricably linked with heathenism, and their customs and beliefs relegated them to the cultural level of savages. Moreover, the theory that Africans were related to the ape, and the common notion that blacks were particularly lustful had popular currency in Elizabethan times.

Despite their deep-rooted prejudices against blacks, the English came to the New World without any preconceived

plan for establishing black slavery in America nor were they
involved in the early slave trade. The Portuguese and Spaniards
pioneered in the slave trade; their explorations and trade with
the coast of West Africa had given them primacy in the traf-
ficking of blacks. In 1562, however, the English sea captain,
John Hawkins, broke the Spanish-Portuguese monopoly by
transporting slaves from Portuguese Africa to Spanish America. English activity in the trade grew slowly at first, but by
the latter part of the seventeenth century the English-chartered
Royal African Company was the largest single enterprise in
the slave trade. The War of the Spanish Succession rewarded
the English with the very desirable *Asiento*—a thirty-year
monopoly over the slave trade with the Spanish colonies. Although two-thirds of all slaves brought by English ships to the
New World went to foreign colonies, a goodly number were
consigned to the English colonies.

Historians have noted repeatedly that the first Negroes
brought to the English colonies—the twenty blacks who landed
in a Dutch man-of-war in 1619 in Virginia—did not arrive as
slaves. In fact, the position of the earliest blacks in Virginia
appears to have been similar to that of indentured servants.
Between 1640 and 1660, however, important changes occurred
with regard to the status of blacks in Virginia and the other
colonies which reduced them legally to slaves. By 1700, the
Negroes of all colonies were treated by custom and law as distinct from Englishmen.

While the basic attitude of Englishmen toward Africans
made the acceptance of black slavery possible, economic conditions in the colonies helped to produce the transformation
of "servants" into chattels. The English colonists had observed
how the Spaniards and Portuguese had met their labor problems by using slaves. The labor requirements for the tending
of large staple crops made the use of black slave gangs practicable, particularly in the southern colonies. In New England,
where there was no special need for slave labor, the practice
of slavery evolved from the notions of captivity and punishment.

The racial aspect of American slavery was partially demon-

strated by certain taboos related to the "peculiar institution."
The white man's approach to sexual relations with blacks was
ambivalent; his desires would bring him into intimate contact
with blacks, but his fear of social stigma would cause him to
reject the fruits of such a liaison. In almost all colonies, the
offspring of interracial relations were illegitimate, and there
were legal prohibitions on marriage between the races. In most
countries the term mulatto denoted something other than slave
and often carried some rank and even acceptance in white
society. In the English colonies, however, the term was synonymous with Negro and hence, almost always, with slave. John
Woolman, usually recognized as the founder of the Quaker
anti-slavery movement, noted that the white children born of
the lowest parents could never be destined for a lifetime of
slavery. Woolman saw American slavery and race as insep-
arable. Judge Samuel Sewall of Boston protested vigorously
against slavery and the slave trade, and yet he could not foresee
white and black blood ever mixing.

Two significant mid-eighteenth-century movements, the
Great Awakening and the rise of rational thought, which might
have had application in the freeing of the slaves, resulted
instead in a tightening of the strictures on the blacks. The
religious revival of the 1740's brought many slaves into the
ranks of Christianity and aided the eighteenth-century humanitarian movement. Yet while blacks might be accepted on a
spiritual level, their skin color continued to isolate them socially. And since heathenism was no longer a negative attribute
in the black stereotype, other objections were found in order
to bar Negroes from participation in the white community.
Similarly, while the rationalism of the Enlightenment served
to free many white men, it was used to tighten the reins on
the blacks. One of the most important scientific activities of the
eighteenth-century intellectual revolution was the pioneering
effort in the classification of animal and plant species. Attempts
to classify humans on the basis of racial characteristics were
distorted by racists who sought to place Negroes in a subhuman
category and reinforce the age-old myth relating the black man
to the ape.

The Second Voyage of John Hawkins, 1564–1565

In the middle of the sixteenth century, the African slave trade had been flourishing between Portuguese Africa and Spanish America. Both nations held a tight monopoly on the transportation of "human cargo." In 1564 an English sea captain, John Hawkins, broke the exclusive Spanish-Portuguese control over the infamous trade.

While sailing to the Canary Islands, Hawkins conceived a plan to capture Africans and sell them as slaves to Spanish America. He acquired a cargo of blacks on the Guinea coast and shortly thereafter sold his "merchandise" to an eager Spanish market on the island of Hispaniola. His first two voyages were financially successful, but on his third trip, Hawkins met with disaster at San Juan de Ulua. Here, the Spaniards seized his ships and subsequently brought his crew before the Inquisition.

Despite the successful voyages of Hawkins, it was not until 1631 that a company was chartered in England to compete seriously in the slave trade. And finally, by the second half of the seventeenth century, the slave trade became an important factor in the English mercantile economy.

Master John Hawkins with the *Jesus* of Lubek, a shippe of 700, and the *Salomon* a shippe of 140, the *Tiger* a barke of 50, and the *Swallow* of 30, tunnes, being all well furnished with men to the number of one hundreth three score and tenne, as also with ordinance and victuall requisite for such a voyage, departed out of Plymmouth the 18 day of October, in the yeere of our Lord 1564.

Here we stayed but one night, and part of the day: for the 7 of December wee came away, in that pretending to have

Source: [1] Richard Hakluyt, *The Principal Navigations, Voyages, Traffiques and Discoveries of the English Nation* (New York & London, 1926), pp. 12–13, 17–22, 25–29.

taken Negros there perforce, the *Mynions* men gave them there to understand of our coming, and our pretence, wherefore they did avoyde the snares we had layd for them. In this place the two shippes riding, the two Barkes, with their boates, went into an Island of the Sapies, called La Formio, to see if they could take any of them, and there landed to the number of 80 in armour, and espying certaine made to them, but they fled in such order into the woods, that it booted them not to follow: so going on their way forward till they came to a river, which they could not passe over, they espied on the otherside two men, who with their bowes and arrowes shot terribly at them. Whereupon we discharged certain harquebuzes to them againe, but the ignorant people wayed it not, because they knewe not the danger thereof; but used a marveilous crying in their flight with leaping and turning their tayles, that it was most strange to see, and gave us great pleasure to beholde them. At the last, one being hurt with a harquebuz upon the thigh, looked upon his wound and wist not howe it came, because hee could not see the pellet. Here Master Hawkins perceiving not good to be done amongst them, because we could not finde their townes, and also not knowing how to goe into Rio grande, for want of a Pilote, which was the very occasion of our coming thither: and finding so many sholes, feared with our great ships to goe in, and therefore departed on our pretended way to the Idols.

In this Island we stayed certaine daies, going every day on shore to take the Inhabitants, with burning and spoiling their townes, who before were Sapies, and were conquered by the Samboses, Inhabitants beyond Sierra Leona . . . These inhabitants have diverse of the Sapies, which they tooke in the warres as their slaves, whome onely they kept to till the ground, in that they neighter have the knowledge thereof, not yet will worke themselves, of whome wee tooke many in that place, but of the Samboses none at all, for they fled into the maine . . . The two and twentieth the Captaine went into the River, called Callowsa, with the two Barkes, and the *Johns* Pinnesse, and the *Salmonons* boate, leaving at anker in the Rivers mouth the two shippes, the River being twenty leagues in, where the Portugals roade: hee came thither the five and twentieth, and dispatched his businesse, and so returned with two Caravels, leaden with Negros. The 27, the Captaine was advertised by the Portugals of a towne of the Negros called Bymba, being in the way as they returned, where was not onely great quantities of golde, but also that there were not above fortie men, and an hundred women and children in the Towne, so that if hee would give the adventure upon the same, hee might gette an hundredth slaves: with the which tydings hee being gladde, bacuse the Portugals shoulde not thinke him to bee of so base a courage, but that hee durst give them that, and greater attempts: and being thereunto also the more provoked with the prosperous successe hee had in other Islands adjacent, where he had put them all to flight, and taken in one boate twentie together, determined to stay before the Towne three or foure houres, to see what hee could doe: and thereupon prepared his men in armour and wapon together, to the number of fortie men well appointed, having to their guides certaine Portugals, in a boat, who brought some of them to their death: wee landing boat after boat, and divers of our men scattering themselves, contrary to the Captaines will, by one or two in a company, for the hope that they had to finde golde in their houses, ransacking the same, in the meane time the Negros came upon them, and hurte many being thus scattered, whereas if five or sixe had bene together, they had bene able, as their companions did, to give the overthrow to 40 of them, and being driven downe to take their boates were followed so hardly by a route of Negros, who by that tooke courage to pursue them to their boates, that not onely some of them, but others standing on shore, not looking for any such matter by meanes that the Negros did flee at the first, and our companie remained in the towne, were suddenly so set upon that some with great hurt recovered their boates; othersome not able to recover the same, tooke the water, and perished by meanes of the oaze. While this was doing, the Captaine who with a dosen men, went through the towne, returned, finding 200 Negros at the waters side, shooting at them in the boates, and cutting them in pieces which were drowned in the water, at whose coming, they ranne all away: so he entered his boates, and before he could put off from the shore they returned againe, and shot very fiercely and hurt divers of them. Thus wee returned backe some what discomforted, although the Captaine in a singular wise manner carried himselfe, with countenance very cheerefull outwardly, as though hee did little weigh the death of his men, nor yet the great hurt of the rest, although his heart inwardly was broken in pieces for it; done to this end, that the Portugals being with him, should not presume to resist against him, nor take occasion to put him to further displeasure or hinderance for the death of our men: having gotten by our going ten Negros, and lost seven of our best men, whereof M. Field Captaine of the *Salomon*, was one, and we had 27 of our men hurt.

The 28 they came to their ships, the *Jesus*, and the *Salomon*, and the 30 departed from thence to Taggarin . . . sojourning at Taggarin, the *Swallow* went up the river about her trafficke, where they saw great townes of the Negros, and Canoas, that had threescore men in piece: there they understood by the Portugals, of a great battell betweene them of Sierra Leona side, and them of Taggarin: they of Sierra Leona, had prepared three hundred Canoas to invade the other. The time was appointed not past sixe days after our departure from thence, which we would have seene, to the intent we might have taken some of them, had it not bene for the death and sickenesse of our men, which came by the contagiousnes of the place, which made us to make hast away.

The 18 of Januarie [1565] at night, wee departed from Taggarin, being bound for the West Indies, before which departure certaine of the *Salomons* men went on shore to fill water in the night, and as they came on shore with their boat being ready to leape on land, one of them espied an Negro in a white coate, standing upon a rocke, being ready to have received them when they came on shore, having in sight of his fellowes also eight or nine, some in one place leaping out, and some in another, but they hid themselves straight againe; whereupon our men doubting they had bene a great companie, and sought to have taken them at more advantage, as God would, departed to their ships, not thinking there had bene such a mischiefe pretended toward them, as then was in deede. Which the next day we understood of a Portugal that came downe to us, who had trafficked with the Negros, by whom hee understood that the king of Sierra Leona had made all the power hee could, to take some of us, partly for the desire he had to see what kinde of people we were, that had spoiled his people at the Idols, whereof he had newes before our coming, and as I judge also, upon other occasions provoked by the Tangomangos, but sure we were that the armie was come down, by meanes that in the evening wee saw such a monstrous fire, made by the watring place, that before was not seene, which fire is the only marke for the Tangomangos to know where their armie is alwayes. If these men had come downe in the evening, they had done us great displeasure, for that wee were on shore filling water: but God, who worketh all things for the best, would not have it so, and by him we escaped without danger, his name be praysed for it.

The 29 of this same moneth we departed with all our shippes from Sierra Leona, towardes the West Indies, and for the space of eighteene dayes, we were becalmed, having nowe and then contrary windes, and some Ternados, amongst the same calme, which happened to us very ill, beeing but reasonably watered, for so great a companie of Negros, and our selves, which pinched us all, and that which was worst, put us in such feare that many never thought to have reached to the Indies, without great death of Negros, and of themselves: but the Almightie God, who never suffereth his elect to perish, sent us the sixteenth of Februarie, the ordinary Brise, which is the Northwest winde, which never left us, till wee came to an Island of the Canybals, called Dominica, where wee arrived the ninth of March, upon a Saturday: and because it was the most desolate place in all the Island, we could see no Canybals, but some of their houses where they dwelled, and as it should seeme forsooke the place for want of fresh water, for wee could find none there but raine water, and such as fell from the hilles, and remained as a puddle in the dale, whereof wee filled for our Negros.

The tenth day at night, we departed from thence, and the fifteenth had sight of nine Islands, called the Testigos: and the sixteeth of an Island, called Margarita, where wee were entertayned by the Alcade, and had both Beeves and sheepe given us, for the refreshing of our men: but the Governour of the Island, would neither come to speake with our Captaine, neither yet given him any licence to trafficke: and to displease us the more, whereas wee had hired a Pilote to have gone with us, they would not onely not suffer him to goe with us, but also sent word by a Caravel out of hand, to Santo Domingo, to the Vice-roy, who doeth represent the kings person, of our arrivall in those partes, which had like to have turned us to great displeasure, by the meanes that the same Vice-roy did send word to Cape de la Vela, and to other places along the coast, commanding them that by the vertue of his authoritie, and by the obedience that they owe to their Prince, no man should trafficke with us, but should resist us with all the force they could.

Here perceiving no trafficke to be had with them nor yet water for the refreshing of our men, we were driven to depart the twentieth day, and the 2 and twentieth we came to a place in the maine called Cumana, whither the Captaine going in his Pinnisse, spake with certaine Spaniards, of whom he demanded trafficke, but they made him answere, they were but souldiers newly come thither, and were not able to by one Negro: whereupon hee asked for a watring place, and they pointed him a place two leagues off, called Santa Fe, where we found marveilous goodly watering, and commodious for the taking in thereof: for that the fresh water came into the Sea, and so our shippes had aboord the shore twentie fathome water.

Wee kept our course along the coast, and came the third of April to a Towne called Burborata, where his ships came to an ancker, and hee himselfe went a shore to speake with the Spaniards, to whome hee declared himselfe to be an Englishman, and came thither to trade with them by the way of marchandize, and therefore required licence for the same. Unto whom they made answere, that they were forbidden by the king to trafique with any forren nation, upon penaltie to forfeit their goods, therefore they desired him not to molest them any further, but to depart as he came, for other comfort he might not looke for at their handes, because they were subjects and might not goe beyond the law. But hee replied that his necessitie was such, as he might not so do: for being in one of the Queens Armadas of England, and having many

souldiours in them, hee had neede both of some refreshing for
them, and of victuals, and of money also, without the which
hee coulde not depart, and with much other talke perswaded
them not to feare any dishonest part of his behalfe towards
them, for neither would hee commit any such thing to the dis-
honour of his prince, nor yet for his honest reputation and
estimation, unlesse hee were too rigorously dealt withall, which
hee hoped not to finde at their handes, in that it should as well
redound to their profite as his owne, and also hee thought they
might doe it without danger, because their princes were in
amitie one with another, and for our parts wee had free trafique
in Spain and Flanders, which are in his dominions, and therefore he knew no reason why he should not have the like in all
his dominions. To the which the Spaniards made answere, that
it lay not in them to give any licence, for that they had a governour to whom the government of those parts was committed,
but if they would stay tenne dayes, they would send to their
governour who was threescore leagues off, and would returne
answere within the space appointed, of his minde.

   In the meane time, they were contented hee should bring
his ships into harbour, and there they would deliver him any
victuals he would require. Whereupon the fourth day we went
in, where being one day and receiving all things according to
promise, the Captaine advised himselfe, that to remaine there
tenne dayes idle, spending victuals and mens wages, and perhaps in the ende receive no good answere from the governour,
it were meere follie, and therefore determined to make request
to have licence for the sale of certaine leane and sicke Negros
which hee had in his shippe like to die upon his hands if he
kept them ten dayes, having little or no refreshing for them,
whereas other men having them, they would bee recovered well
ynough. And this request hee was forced to make, because he
had not otherwise wherewith to pay for victuals and for necessaries which he should take: which request being put in writing
and presented, the officers and towne-dwellers assembled together, and finding his request so reasonable, granted him
licence for thirtie Negros, which afterwards they caused the
officers to view, to the intent they should graunt to nothing
but that were very reasonable, for feare of answering thereunto

afterwards. This being past, our Captaine, according to their licence, thought to have made sale, but the day past and none came to buy, who before made shewe that they had great neede of them, and therefore wist not what to surmise of them, whether they went about to prolong the time of the Governour his answere because they would keepe themselves blameless, or for any other pollicie hee knew not, and for that purpose sent them worde, marveiling what the matter was that none came to buy them. They answere, because they had granted licence onely to the poore to buy those Negros of small price, and their money was not so ready as other mens of more wealth. More than that, as soone as ever they sawe the shippes, they conveyed away their money by their wives that went into the mountaines for feare, and were not yet returned, and yet asked two dayes to seeke their wives and fetch their money. Notwithstanding, the next day divers of them came to cheapen, but could not agree of price, because they thought the price too high. Whereupon the Captaine perceiving they went about to bring downe the price and meant to buy, and would not confesse if hee had licence, that he might sell at any reasonable rate, as they were worth in other places, did send for the principals of the Towne, and made a shewe hee would depart, declaring himselfe to be very sory that he had so much troubled them, and also that he had sent for the governour to come downe, seeing nowe his pretence was to depart, whereat they marveiled much, and asked him what cause mooved him thereunto, seeing by their working he was in possibilitie to have his licence.

To the which he replied, that it was not onely a licence that he sought, but profit, which he perceived was not there to bee had, and therefore would seeke further, and withall shewed him his writings what he payed for his Negros, declaring also the great charge he was at in his shipping, and mens wages, and therefore to countervaile his charges, hee must sell his Negros for a greater price then they offered. So they doubting his departure, put him in comfort to sell better there then in any other place. And if it fell out that he had no licence that he should not loose his labour in tarying, for they would buy without licence. Whereupon, the Captaine being put in comfort, promised them to stay, so that hee might make sale of

his leane Negros, which they granted unto. And the next day
did sell some of them, who having bought and payed for them,
thinking to have had a discharge of the Customer, for the custome of the Negros being the Kings duetie, they gave it away
to the poore for Gods sake, and did refuse to give the discharge
in writing, and the poore not trusting their wordes, for feare,
least hereafter it might be demanded of them, did refraine
from buying any more, so that nothing else was done untill the
Governours comming downe, which was the fourteenth day,
and then the Captaine made petition, declaring that hee was
come thither on a shippe of the Queenes Majesties of England,
being bound to Guinie, and thither driven by winde and wather,
so that being come thither, hee had neede of sundry necessaries
for the reparation of the said Navie, and also great need of
money for the paiment of his Souldiours, unto whom hee had
promised paiment, and therefore although hee would, yet would
not depart without it, and for that purpose he requested licence
for the sale of certaine of his Negros, declaring that although
they were forbidden to traffique with strangers, yet for that
there was a great amitie betweene their princes, and that the
thing pertained to our Queenes highnesse, he thought hee
might doe their prince great service, and that it would bee
well taken at his hands, to doe it in this cause. The which alle-
gations with divers others put in request, were presented unto
the Governour, who sitting in counsell for that matter, granted
unto his request for licence. But yet there fell out another thing
which was the abating of the kings Custome, being upon every
slave 30. duckets, which would not be granted unto.

Whereupon the Captaine perceiving that they would neither
come neere his price hee looked for by a great deale, nor yet
would abate the Kings Custome of that they offered so that
either he must be a great looser by his wares, or els compell
the officers to abate the same kings Custome which was too
unreasonable, for to a higher price hee coulde not bring the
buyers: Therefore the sixteenth of April hee prepared one
hundred men well armed with bowes, arrowes, harquebuzes
and pikes, with the which hee marched to the towne-wards,
and being perceived by the Governour, he straight with all

expedition sent messengers to knowe his request, desiring him to march no further forward until he had answere againe, which incontinent he should have. So our Captaine declaring how unreasonable a thing the Kings Custome was, requested to have the same abated, and to pay seven and a halfe per centum, which is the ordinarie Custome for wares through his dominions there, and unto this if they would not graunt, hee would displease them. And this word being caried to the Governour, answere was returned that all things should bee to his content, and thereupon hee determined to depart, but the souldiers and Mariners finding so little credit in their promises, demanded gages for the performance of the premisses, or els they would not depart. And thus they being constrained to send gages, wee departed, beginning our traffique, and ending the same without disturbance.

THE CODIFICATION OF NEGRO INFERIORITY

The severity of the slave codes varied from colony to colony. Based on the assumption that blacks were inferior, it became law that slaves were to be regarded as chattels rather than as human beings. Those slaves who violated the codes were tried either by regular courts, special tribunals, or by their masters. Although trials did take place, due process of law and the application of justice were conspicuously absent.

The codes presented in this volume eventually became the models for the legal control of slaves in the nineteenth century. Reproduced below are the laws of two colonies; they range from Virginia's severe law which legislated the castration of fugitive slaves, to New York's more lenient codes.

Sources: [2] *The Statutes at Large Being a Collection of All the Laws of Virginia,* William W. Hening, ed., 13 vols. (Richmond and New York, 1809–23), II, pp. 170, 260, 270, III, pp. 86–88, 43, 54; [3] *The Colonial Laws of New York from the Year 1664 to the Revolution,* 5 vols. (Albany, 1894–96), I, pp. 597–598, II, pp. 684–685.

The Slave Code of Virginia

ACT XII (1662)

Negro womens children to serve according to the condition of the mother.

WHEREAS, some doubts have arrisen whether children got by any Englishman upon a negro woman, should be slave or free, *Be it therefore enacted,* that all children borne in this country shalbe held bond or free only according to the condition of the mother, *And* that if any christian shall committ fornication with a negro man or woman, hee or shee soe offending shall pay double the fines imposed by the former act.

An act about the casuall killing of slaves.

WHEREAS, the only law in force for the punishment of refractory servants (*a*)resisting their master, mistris or overseer cannot be inflicted upon negroes, nor the obstinacy of many of them by other than violent meanes supprest, *Be it enacted,* if any slave resist his master (or other by his masters order correcting him) and by the extremity of the correction should chance to die, that his death shall not be accompted felony, but the master (or that other person appointed by the master to punish him) be acquit from molestation, since it cannot be presumed that prepensed malice (which alone makes murther felony) should induce any man to destroy his owne estate.

ACT XVI (1691)

An act for suppressing outlying Slaves.

WHEREAS many times negroes, mulattoes, and other slaves unlawfully absent themselves from their masters and mistresses service, and lie hid and lurk in obscure places killing hoggs and committing other injuries to the inhabitants of this dominion, for remedy whereof for the future, *Be it enacted,* that in all such cases upon intelligence of any such negroes, mulattoes or other slaves lying out, two of their majesties justices of the peace of that country, whereof one to be of the quorum, where such negroes, mulattoes or other slaves shall be, shall be impowered and commanded, and are hereby impowered and commanded to issue out their warrants directed to the sherrife of the same county to apprehend such negroes, mulattoes, and other slaves, which said sherriffe is hereby likewise required upon all such occasions to raise such and soe many forces from time to time as he shall think convenient and necessary for the effectual apprehending such negroes, mulattoes and other slaves, and in case any negroes, mulattoes or other slave or slaves lying out as aforesaid shall resist, runaway, or refuse to deliver and surrender him or themselves to any person or persons that shall be by lawfull authority employed to apprehend and take such negroes, mulattoes or other slaves that in such cases it shall and may be lawfull for such person and persons to kill and distroy such negroes, mulattoes, and other slave or slaves by gunn or any otherwise whatsoever.

Provided that where any negroe or mulattoe slave or slaves shall be killed in pursuance of this act, the owner or owners of such negro or mulatto slave shall be paid for such negro or mulatto slave four thousand pounds of tobacco by the publique. And for prevention of that abominable mixture and spurious issue which hereafter may encrease in this dominion, as well by negroes, mulattoes, and Indians intermarrying with English, or other white women, as by their unlawfull accompanying with one another, *Be it enacted,* that for the time to come, whatsoever English or other white man or woman being free shall intermarry with a negro, mulatto, or Indian man or woman bond or free shall within three months after such marriage be banished and removed from this dominion forever, and that the justices of each respective countie within this dominion make it their particular care, that this act be put in effectuall execution. *And be it further enacted,* that if any English woman being free shall have a bastard child by any negro or mulatto, she pay the sume of fifteen pounds sterling, within one moneth after such bastard child shall be born, to the Church wardens of the parish where she shall be delivered of such child, and in default of such payment she shall be taken into the possession of the said Church wardens and dis-

posed of for five yeares, and the said fine of fifteen pounds,
or whatever the woman shall be disposed of for, shall be paid,
one third part to their majesties for and towards the support
of the government and the contingent charges thereof, and
one other third part to the use of the parish where the offence
is committed, and the other third part to the informer, and
that such bastard child be bound out as a servant by the said
Church wardens untill he or she shall attaine the age of thirty
yeares, and in case such English woman that shall have such
bastard child be a servant, she shall be sold by the said Church
wardens, (after her time is expired that she ought by law to
serve her master) for five yeares, and the money she shall be
sold for divided as is before appointed, and the child to serve
as aforesaid.

And forasmuch as great inconveniences may happen to this
country by the setting of negroes and mulattoes free, by their
either entertaining negro slaves from their masters service, or
receiving stolen goods, or being grown old bringing a charge
upon the country; for prevention thereof, *Be it enacted,* That
no negro or mulatto be after the end of this present session
of assembly set free by any person or persons whatsoever, unless such person or persons, their heires, executors or adminis-
trators pay for the transportation of such negro or negroes out
of the countrey within six moneths after such setting them free,
upon penalty of paying of tenn pounds sterling to the Church
wardens of the parish where such person shall dwell with which
money, or so much thereof as shall be necessary, the said
Church wardens are to cause the said negro or mulatto to be
transported out of the countrey, and the remainder of the said
money to imploy to the use of the poor of the parish.

An Act Concerning Servants and Slaves (1705)

XIX. And for a further prevention of that abominable mixture and spurious issue, which hereafter may increase in this
her majesty's colony and dominion, as well by English, and
other white men and women intermarrying with negros or
mulattos, as by their unlawful coition with them, *Be it enacted,*
That whatsoever English, or other white man or woman, being
free, shall intermarry with a negro or mulatto man or woman,

bond or free, shall, by judgment of the county court, be committed to prison, and there remain, during the space of six months, without bail or mainprize; and shall forfeit and pay ten pounds current money of Virginia, to the use of the parish, as aforesaid.

XX. *And be it further enacted,* That no minister of the church of England, or other minister, or person whatsoever, within this colony and dominion, shall hereafter wittingly presume to marry a white man with a negro or mulatto woman; or to marry a white woman with a negro or mulatto man, upon pain of forfeiting and paying, for every such marriage the sum of ten thousand pounds of tobacco; one half to our sovereign lady the Queen, her heirs and successors, for and towards the support of the government, and the contingent charges thereof; and the other half to the informer; To be recovered, with costs, by action of debt, bill, plaint, or information, in any court of record within this her majesty's colony and dominion, wherein no essoin, protection, or wager of law, shall be allowed.

XXXVII. And whereas, many times, slaves run away and lie out, hid and lurking in swamps, woods, and other obscure places, killing hogs, and committing other injuries to the inhabitants of this her majesty's colony and dominion. *Be it therefore enacted,* That in all such cases, upon intelligence given of any slaves lying out, as aforesaid, any two justices of the peace of the county wherein such slave is supposed to lurk or do mischief, shallbe and are impowered and required to issue proclamation against all such slaves, reciting their names, and owners names, if they are known, and thereby requiring them, and every of them, forthwith to surrender themselves; and also impowering the sheriff of the said county, to take such power with him, as he shall think fit and necessary, for the effectual apprehending such out-lying slave or slaves, and go in search of them: Which proclamation shall be published on a Sabbath day, at the door of every church and chapel, in said county, by the parish clerk, or reader, of the church, immediately after divine worship: And in case any slave, against whom proclamation hath been thus issued, and once published at any church or chapel, as aforesaid, stay out, and do not immediately return home, it shall be lawful for any person or persons

whatsoever, to kill and destroy such slaves by such ways and
means as he, she, or they shall think fit, without accusation or
impeachment of any crime for the same: And if any slave, that
hath run away and lain out as aforesaid, shall be apprehended
by the sheriff, or any other person, upon the application of
the owner of the said slave, it shall and may be lawful for the
county court, to order such punishment to the said slave, either
by dismembering, or any other way, not touching his life, as
they in their discretion shall think fit, for the reclaiming any
such incorrigible slave, and terrifying others from the like
practices.

The Slave Code of New York

*An Act to Incourage the Baptizing of Negro, Indian and
Mulatto Slaves* (1706)

WHEREAS . . . Inhabitants of this Colony now are and have
been willing that such Negro, Indian and Mulatto slaves who
belong to them and desire the same, should be Baptized, but
are deterr'd and hindered therefrom by reason of a Groundless
opinion that hath spread itself in the Colony, that by the Baptizing of such Negro, Indian or Mulatto slave they would
become free and ought to be sett at liberty. Inorder therefore
to put an end to all such Doubts and Scruples as have or hereafter at any time may arise about the same. Be it enacted . . .
that the Baptizing of any Negro, Indian or Mulatto slave shall
not be any Cause or reason for the setting them or any of them
at Liberty.

And be it declar'd and Enacted . . . that all and every
Negro, Indian and Mestee Bastard Child and Children who is,
are, and shalbe born of any Negro, Indian, Mulatto or Mestee,
shall follow ye State and Condition of the Mother and be
esteemed . . . and adjudged a Slave and Slaves to all intents
and purposes whatsoever.

. . . And be it declared that no slave whatsoever in this
Colony shall att any time be admitted as a Witness for, or

against, any Freeman, in any Case matter or Cause, Civill or Criminal whatsoever.

An Act for the more Effectual Preventing and Punishing and Conspiracy and Insurrection of Negro and other Slaves (1730)

And be it Enacted no Slave or Slaves shall be allowed as Evidence or Evidences in any Matter Cause or thing whatsoever excepting in Cases of Plotting or Confederacy among themselves, either to run away Kill or distroy their Master Mistress or any other Person, or burning of houses, Barns, barracks or Stacks of hay or of Corne or the Killing of their Master or Mistresses Cattle or Horses and that only against one another, in which Case the evidence of one Slave Shall be allowed good against an other Slave.

And be it Enacted that all and every Negro, Indian or other Slave or Slaves who after the Publication of this act Shall Murther or other wise Kill unless by misadventure or in the Execution of Justice, or Conspire or attempt the death of any of his Majesties Leige people not being Slaves or shall attempt or committ any rape on any of the said Subjects or Shall willfully burn any Dwelling House barne Stable out House Stacks of Corn or hay or Shall willfully mutilate mayhem or Dismember any of the said Subjects not being Slaves as aforesaid or shall willfully murder any negro, Indian or Mulatto Slave within this Colony and shall thereof be Convicted shall suffer the pains of death in Such manner and with Such Circumstances as the Aggravation or Enormity of their Crimes, in the Judgment of the Justices of those Courts.

A Rebuttal to *The Selling of Joseph*

Judge Samuel Sewall's tract, The Selling of Joseph: A Memorial *(1700) was the first New England anti-slavery appeal*

Source: [4] John Saffin, *A Brief and Candid Answer to a Late Printed Sheet, Entitled The Selling of Joseph* (Boston, 1701), reprinted from George H. Moore, *Notes on the History of Slavery in Massachusetts* (Boston, 1866), pp. 251–256.

*of serious consequence. The Memorial, written in the form of
a Puritan sermon, affirmed that all men had an "equal Right
unto liberty, and all other outward Comforts of life." Although
his appeal demanded the abolition of slavery, Sewall rejected
any possibility of the Negro's acceptance into New England
society because of the "disparity in their Conditions, Colour,
and Hair." He asserted, "the Negro could never embody with
us, and grow up in orderly Families, to the Peopling of the
land."*

*Samuel Sewall's tract was not without its critics. Many New
Englanders, such as John Saffin, supported the theory of the
curse of Ham, for which bondage was a way of expiation.*

*In the first defense of slavery in America, Saffin rejected
the plea made in* The Selling of Joseph *and in a point-by-point
analysis refuted the totality of the Sewall argument. He concluded, that by the law of "Scripture and Reason," it was in
accordance with God to "keep Bond men, and use them in
[his] service."*

THAT Honourable and Learned Gentleman, The Author of a
Sheet, Entituled, *The Selling of Joseph*, A Memorial, seems
from thence to draw this conclusion, that because the Sons of
Jacob did very ill in Selling their Brother *Joseph* to the *Ish-
maelites*, who were Heathens, therefor it is utterly unlawful to
Buy and Sell Negroes, though among Christians; which Conclusion I presume is not well drawn from the Premises, nor is
the case parallel; for it was unlawful for the *Israelites* to Sell
their Brethren upon any account, or pretence whatsoever during life. But it was not unlawful for the Seed of *Abraham* to
have Bond men, and Bond women either born in their House,
or bought with their Money.

To speak a little to the Gentlemans first Assertion: *That
none ought to part with their Liberty themselves or deprive
others of it but upon mature consideration;* a prudent exception, in which he grants, that upon some consideration a man
may be deprived of his Liberty. And then presently in his next
Position or Assertion he denies it, *viz: It is most certain, that
all men as they are the Sons of Adam are Coheirs, and have
equal right to Liberty, and all other Comforts of Life. The*

Earth hath he given to the Children of Men. True, but what is all this to the purpose, to prove that all men have equal right to Liberty, and all outward comforts of this life; which Position seems to invert the Order that God hath set in the World, who hath Ordained different degrees and orders of men, some to be High and Honourable, some to be Low and Despicable; some to be Monarchs, Kings, Princes, and Governours, Masters and Commanders, others to be Subjects, and to be Commanded; Servants of sundry sorts and degrees, bound to obey; yea, some to be born Slaves, and so to remain during their lives as hath been proved. Otherwise there would be a meer parity among men, contrary to that of the Apostle . . . where he sets forth (by way of comparison) the different sorts and offices of the Members of the Body, indigitating that they are all of use, but not equal, and of like dignity. So God hath set different Orders and Degrees of Men in the World, both in Church and Common weal. Now, if this Position of parity should be true, it would then follow that the ordinary Course of Divine Providence of God in the World should be wrong, and unjust (which we must not dare to think, much less to affirm) and all the sacred Rules, Precepts and Commands of the Almighty which he hath given the Son of Men to observe and keep in their respective Places, Orders and Degrees, would be to no purpose; which unaccountably derogate from the Divine Wisdom of the most High, who had made nothing in vain, but hath Holy Ends in all his Dispensations to the Children of men.

In the next place, this worthy Gentleman makes a large Discourse concerning the Utility and Conveniency to keep the one, and inconveniency of the other; respecting white and black Servants, which conduceth most to the welfare and benefit of this Province: which he concludes to be white men, who are in many respects to be preferred before Blacks; who doubts that? doth it therefore follow, that it is altogether unlawful for Christians to buy and keep Negro Servants (for this is the Thesis) but that those that have them ought in Conscience to set them free, and so lose all the money they cost (for we must not live in any known sin) this seems to be his opinion; but it is a Question whether it ever was the Gentleman's practice?

But if he could perswade the General Assembly to make an
Act, That all that have Negroes, and do set them free, shall
be Reimbursed out of the Publick Treasury, and that there
shall be no more Negroes brought into the Country; 'tis probable there would be more of his opinion; yet he would find it
a hard task to bring the Country to consent thereto; for then
the Negroes must be all sent out of the Country, or else remedy
would be worse than the Disease; and it is to be feared that
those Negroes that are free, if there be not some strict course
taken with them by Authority, they will be a plague to this
Country.

Again, If it should be unlawful to deprive them that are
lawful Captives, or Bondmen of their Liberty for Life being
Heathens; it seems to be more unlawful to deprive our Brethren, of our own or other Christian Nations of the Liberty,
(though but for a time) by binding them to Serve some Seven,
Ten, Fifteen, and some Twenty Years, which oft times proves
for their whole Life, as many have been; which in effect is the
same in Nature, though different in the time, yet this was allo'd
among the *Jews* by the Law of God; and is the constant practice of our own and other Christian Nations in the World: the
which our Author by his Dogmatical Assertions doth condemn
as Irreligious; which is Diametrically contrary to the Rules and
Precepts which God Hath given the diversity of men to observe
in their respective Stations, Callings, and Conditions of Life,
as hath been observed.

And to illustrate his Assertion our Author brings in by way
of Comparison the Law of God against man Stealing, on pain
of Death: Intimating thereby, that Buying and Selling of Negro's is a breach of that Law, and so deserves Death: A severe
Sentence: But herein he begs the Question with a *Caveat
Emptor.* For, in that very Chapter there is a Dispensation to
the People of *Israel,* to have Bond men, Women and Children,
even of their own Nation in some case; and Rules given therein
to be observed concerning them. Though *Israelites* were forbidden (ordinarily) to make Bond men and Women of their
own Nation, but of Strangers they might: the words run thus.
Both thy Bond men, and thy Bond maids which thou should

have shall be of the Heathen, that are round about you: of them shall you Buy Bond men and Bond maids, &c. Whether we be Bond or Free, which shows that in the times of the New Testament, there were Bond men also, &c.

In sine, The sum of this long Haurange, is no other, than to compare the Buying and Selling of Negro's unto the Stealing of Men, and the Selling of *Joseph* by his Brethren, which bears no proportion therewith, nor is there any congruiety therein, as appears by the foregoing Texts. Our Author doth further proceed to answer some Objections of his own framing, which he supposes some might raise.

"Object 1. *That these Blackamores are of the Posterity of Cham, and therefore under the Curse of Slavery.* Which the Gentlemen seems to deny, saying *they were the Seed of Canaan that were Cursed, &c.*

"Ans. Whether they were so or not, we shall not dispute: this may suffice that not only the seed of *Cham or Canaan,* but any lawful captives of other Heathen Nations may be made Bond men as hath been proved.

"Obj. 2. *That the Negroes are brought out of Pagan Country; places where the Gospel is not Preached.* To which he Replies, *that must not doe Evil that Good may come out of it.*

"Ans. To which we answer, That it is no Evil thing to bring out of their own Heathenish Country, where they may have the knowledge of the True God, be Converted and Eternally saved.

"Obj. 3. *The* Affricans *have Wars one with another:* our Ships bring lawful Captives taken in those Wars.

"To which our Author answers Conjecturally, and Doubtfully, for ought we know, that which may or may not be: which is insignificant, proves nothing. He also compares the Negroes Wars, one Nation another, with the Wars between *Joseph* and his Brethren. But where doth he read of any such War? We read indeed of a Domestick Quarrel they had with him, they envyed and hated *Joseph;* but by what is Recorded, he was meerly passive and meek as a Lamb. This Gentlemen further adds, *That there is not any War but is unjust on one side, &c.* Be it so, what doth that signify: We read of lawful Captives

taken in the Wars, and lawful to be Bought and Sold without
contracting the guilt of the *Agressors:* for which we have the
example of *Abraham* before quoted; but if we must stay while
both parties warring are in the right, there would be no lawful
Captives at all to be Bought; which seems to be ridiculous to
imagine, and contrary to the tenour of Scripture, and all Humane Histories on that subject.

"Obj. 4. *Abraham had Servants bought with his Money and
in his House.* To which our worthy Author answers, *until the
Circumstances of Abraham's purchase be recorded, no argument can be drawn from it.*

"Ans. To which we Reply, this is also Dogmatical, and
proves nothing. He farther adds, *In the mean time Charity
Obliges us to conclude, that he knew it was lawful and good.*
Here the gentleman yields the case; for if we are in Charity
bound to believe *Abrahams* practice, in buying and keeping
Slaves in his house to be lawful and good: then it follows, that
our Imitation of him in this his Moral Action, is as warrantable
as that of his Faith; *who is the Father of all them that believe.*

"In the close of all, Our Author Quotes two more places
of Scripture. To prove that the people of Israel were strictly
forbidden the Buying and Selling one another for *Slaves:* who
questions that? and what is that to the case in hand? What a
strange piece of Logick is this? Tis unlawful for Christians
to Buy and Sell one another for slaves. *Ergo,* It is unlawful to
Buy and Sell Negroes that are lawful Captiv'd Heathens.

"And after a Serious Exhortation to us all to Love one
another according to the Command of Christ. This worthy
Gentleman concludes with this Assertion, *That these Ethiope-
ans as Black as they are, seeing they are the Sons and Daughters
of the first Adam; the Brethren and Sisters of the Second Adam,
and the Offspring of God; we ought to treat them with a respect
agreeable.*

"Ans. We grant it for a certain and undeniable verity. That
all Mankind are the Sons and Daughters of *Adam,* and the
Creatures of God: But it doth not therefore follow that we
are bound to love and respect all men alike; this under favour
we must take leave to deny; we ought in charity, if we see

our Neighbour in want, to relieve them in a regular way, but we are not bound to give them so much of our Estates, as to make them equal with our selves, because they are our Brethren, the Sons of Adam, no, not our own natural kinsmen: We are exhorted *to do good unto all, but especially to them who are of the Household of Faith.* And we are to love, honour and respect all men according to the gift of God that is in them: I may love my Servant well, but my Son better; Charity begins at home, it would be a violation of common prudence, and a breach of good manners, to treat a Prince like a Peasant. And this worthy Gentleman would deem himself much neglected, if we should show him no more Defference than to an ordinary Porter: And therefore these florid expressions, the Sons and Daughters of the First *Adam,* the Brethren and Sisters of the Second *Adam,* and the Offspring of God, seem to be misapplied to import and insinuate, that we ought to tender Pagan Negroes with all love, kindness, and equal respect as to the best of men."

By all which it doth evidently appear both by Scripture and Reason, the practice of the People of God in all Ages, both before and after the giving of the Law, and in the times of the Gospel, that there were Bond men, Women and Children commonly kept by holy and good men, and improved in Service; and therefore by the Command of God, and their venerable Example, we may keep Bond men, and use them in our Service still; yet with all candour, moderation and Christian prudence, according to their state and condition consonant to the Word of God.

The Negroes Character
Cowardly and crewl are those Blacks Innate,
Prone to Revenge, Imp of inveterate hate.
He that exasperates them, soon espies
Mischief and Murder in their very eyes.
Libidinous, Deceitful, False and Rude,
The Spume Issue of Ingratitude.
The Premises consider'd, all may tell,
How near good Joseph they are parallel.

COLONIAL HOSTILITY TO THE PRESENCE OF BLACKS

Although Africans were a primary source of labor, they were by no means a welcome group in all parts of colonial America. Numerous individuals protested the presence of the black man in white society.

The following documents are indicative of colonial racial hostility. The first selection, Document 5, is a letter (dated July 12, 1736) written by William Byrd, a Virginia official, to John Perceval, a co-founder of Georgia. The letter protests the African slave trade and reveals Byrd's fear of the consequences of the sharp increase in Virginia's black population.

The second selection, Document 6, is a presentation of grievances by the people of Charleston, South Carolina. This anti-black petition demands an end to alleged black defiance of the South Carolina Negro Acts. The citizens who drew up the list of grievances went so far as to protest the fact that blacks were dressing "quite gay and beyond their condition."

Letter written by William Byrd

. . . These foul Traders import so many negro's hither, that I fear this Colony will sometime or other be confounded by the name of New Guinea. I am sensible of many bad consequences of multiplying these Ethiopians amongst us. They blow up the pride, & ruin the Industry of our White People, who Seeing a Rank of poor Creatures below them, detest work for fear it should make them look like Slaves. Then that poverty

Sources: [5] *Virginia Magazine of History and Biography,* XXXVI (July, 1928), pp. 220–221; [6] Charleston South Carolina *Gazette,* November 5, 1744.

which will ever attend upon Idleness, disposed them, as much
to pilfer as it dos the Portuguise, who account it much more
like gentleman to steal, than to dirty their hands with Labour
of any kind. Another unhappy Effect of many Negroes is, the
necessity of being severe. Numbers make them insolent & then
foul Means must do what fair will not. We have however nothing like the Inhumanity here, that is practiced in the Islands
& God forbid we ever shou'd. But these base Tempers require
to be rid with a tort rein, or they will be apt to throw their
Rider. Yet even this is terrible to a good natured Man, who
must submit to be either a Fool or a Fury. And this will be
more our unhappy case, the more the Negroes are increast
amongst us. But these private mischeifs are nothing, if compared to the publick danger. We have already at least 10,000
men of these descendants of Ham, fit to bear Arms, & these
numbers increase every day, as well by birth, as by Importation. And in case there should arise a Man of desperate courage
amongst us, exasperated by a desperate fortune, he might with
more advantage than Cataline kindle a Servile War. Such a
man might be dreadfully mischeivous before any opposition
could be formed against him, & tinge our Rivers as wide as
they are with blood, besides the Calamityes which wou'd be
brought upon us by such an attempt, it wou'd cost our Mother
Country many a fair Million to make us as profitable, as we
are at present. It were therefore, worth the consideration, of
a British Parliament, My Lord to put an end, to this unchristian Traffick, of makeing Merchandise of our Fellow Creatures.
At Least, the farther importation of them, into our Colonys,
should be prohibited, lest they prove as troublesome, & dangerous every where, as they have been lately in Jamaica, where
besides a vast expence of money, they have cost the lives of
many of his Majesty's Subjects. We have mountains in Virginia
too, to which they may retire, as Safely, & do as much mischief,
as they do in Jamaica. All these matters, duly considered, I
wonder the Legislature will indulge a few ravenous Traders,
to the danger of the Publick safety, & such Traders as would
freely sell their Fathers, their Elder Brothers, & even the Wives
of their bosomes if they could black their Faces & get anything
for them.

An anti-black petition by the people
of Charleston, South Carolina

. . . We present, as a Greivance, Negroes being allowed to
go from Town to Country, under Pretence of picking Myrtle
berries, & who at the same time carry Rum and other Goods,
to trade with Negroes in the Country, by which they are debauched, and encouraged to Steal and robb their Masters of
their Corn, Poultry and other Provisions.

We present, as a Grievance, the great Insolence of the Negroes in Charles-Towne, by Gaming in the Streets and caballing
in great Numbers through most parts of the Town, especially
on the Sabbath Day.

We present, as a Grievance, that many Negroes in Charles-
Towne, (in Defiance of the 31st Paragraph of the Negro Act)
do openly buy and sell sundry sorts of Wares. Also, that many
Retailers of Strong Liquors, (in Defiance of the 32d paragraph) do sell Rum to Negroes. Also, that Negro Men do hire
themselves to work, without a Ticket from their respective
Masters and Mistresses, (in Defiance of the 33rd Paragraph).
AND WHEREAS the 40th Paragraph restrains Negroes to
waring Apparel of a low Price, it is apparent, that Negro
Women in particular do not restrain themselves in their Cloathing as the Law requires, but dress in Apparel quite gay and
beyond their Condition, to purchase which they must steal
from their Masters and Mistresses, or gain them by other practices equally vicious.

PART 2

The Pursuit of Racism in Revolutionary America, 1750-1800

INTRODUCTION

To perceptive men dedicated to freedom, the period after 1763 held great promise. It was an era of growing self-awareness on the part of Americans. Recently the colonists had contributed to the successful culmination of the French and Indian War, and thus, many began to think of themselves as Americans rather than as Englishmen. This new self-consciousness caused Americans to be introspective regarding their institutions, particularly that of slavery. The early Quaker abolitionist movement helped to make Americans aware of their prejudices toward Negroes and the uniqueness of American bondage.

The cause of freedom was also aided by the pre-Revolutionary War ideas of the natural rightists and environmentalists. The natural rights theory raised questions relative to the God-given rights of blacks. In addition, if, as the environmentalists held, differences among men were due mainly to their surroundings and could be changed, then it was logical to assume that the emancipation of blacks and their adjustment to American society was possible.

The American Revolution itself could have been the greatest opportunity for the anti-slavery movement. For one thing, many blacks participated in the fight. According to John Adams the "Boston Massacre," often considered the real beginning of the rebellion, had been precipitated by a "motley rabble" including "Negroes and mulattoes." Peter Salem, one of the heroes of the Battle of Bunker Hill, was probably one of a number of slaves who had been freed shortly before the battle. The order of Lord Dunmore, Virginia's Governor, offering freedom to slaves who took up arms with the British, induced General Washington to modify an earlier policy which had excluded Negroes from enlistment. The revised policy, approved by Congress, permitted the enlistment of free Negroes. Eventually most states allowed both slaves and free blacks to join in the Revolution. It has been estimated that of the 300,000 soldiers in the Continental forces, approximately 5,000 were blacks.

The black soldiers' hope for freedom also was encouraged by the ideas at the root of the Revolution. The theories of natural rights and environmentalism became the philosophical heart of the Declaration of Independence. To James Otis, the rebellion was clearly a struggle for the freedom of black as well as white Americans. During and after the war, most states terminated their slave trade. Manumission was promoted by the writings of such leading publicists and theologians as Benjamin Franklin, Benjamin Rush, Samuel Hopkins, and Ezra Stiles; and the ideology of the Revolution proliferated the number of anti-slavery societies. In 1780, Pennsylvania officially provided for the gradual abolition of slavery. And finally, one northern state after another legislated either immediate or gradual emancipation, and even two southern states made it possible for slave-owners to free their blacks. Congress took an historic, giant step forward in support of human freedom when it enacted the Northwest Ordinance of 1787, which prohibited slavery from a vast territory.

Despite the encouragement that the American Revolution had given the anti-slavery cause, and the splendid chance for freedom that the Revolution afforded, the complete emancipation of blacks at this time in American history was finally a lost cause. In fighting British "enslavement," colonials operated on different levels. To some, the struggle for freedom was a fight for all men, black as well as white. To others, however, the Revolution had been fought exclusively against the British attempt to enslave freeborn Englishmen.

Moreover, in the interests of national unity, Americans felt obliged to compromise some of their principles. During the debate on the Declaration of Independence, the anti-slavery delegates to the Continental Congress had been induced to accept the southern demand that Jefferson's strongly worded statement relative to the slave trade be removed. At the Constitutional Convention, unity again demanded the adoption of the three-fifths compromise which, in effect, declared the Negro a slave who was but three-fifths of a man. Furthermore, the Constitution legally extended the slave trade for twenty years; and Roger Sherman's plea to exclude the fugitive slave provision of Article IV, Section 2, from the document, found no support even among his New England colleagues.

Another factor that helped to produce the "conservative reaction" of the post-Revolutionary period was related to the economics of slavery. The rapidly improving technology of the English cotton mills demanded huge increases in the production of raw cotton. Eli Whitney's cotton gin helped to meet the needs of English mills by making possible the use of vast areas of the South where the short-staple variety of cotton could be grown. Whitney's invention enhanced the importance of slavery to the South. As one authority has ironically noted: the cotton gin symbolized the nature of the new economy which was both national and sectional; a New Englander provided the South with its technological needs while New England ships helped to keep it supplied with slaves. The pursuit of economic gain and political unity shifted the emphasis of the Lockean appeal away from the rights of life and liberty to the protection and promotion of property rights.

The anti-slavery movement was hindered by other developments as well. The prominence of humanitarianism with its emphasis upon the elimination of the inhuman aspects of slavery served to change the attitude of many manumissionists from one of militancy to paternalism. The excesses of the Santo Domingo uprising against French rule and the subsequent series of slave rebellions in the United States had a traumatic effect upon many Americans to the extent that they felt that slavery no longer was a fit subject for discussion. If the American Revolution was not a true social revolution for most Americans, it was less so for blacks. In its first major opportunity to grant justice to Negroes, this nation was found wanting.

Nativism also had roots deeply imbedded in the American past. In colonial times it was primarily in the form of anti-Catholicism or anti-papal sentiment. The thirteen colonies were settled by the grandchildren of Englishmen who had lived through the Reformation and the bloody seventeenth-century religious wars. The English Puritan Revolution added fuel to the fires of religious hatred which existed both in the mother country and in the colonies.

But nativism contained an additional meaning: distrust of the foreigner and alien institutions. The anti-foreign aspect of nativism began to loom large in the views of the founding fathers with regard to the "importation of foreigners."

JUSTICE DENIED: THE NEGRO FROM THE REVOLUTION TO THE CONSTITUTION

Thomas Jefferson and Negro Inferiority

One of the most common myths in American history has been the egalitarian ideas of Thomas Jefferson. An examination of Jefferson's own writings has revealed that the author of the Declaration of Independence did not believe that "all men are created equal." In an obvious contradiction to his own words in the Declaration, Jefferson owned more than 180 slaves at the time of his death. He asserted that "the blacks, whether originally a distinct race, or made distinct by time and circumstances [slavery], are inferior to the whites in the endowments both of body and mind." This belief led Jefferson to conclude that "when freed, he [the slave] is to be removed beyond the reach of [racial] mixture."

Jefferson's racial ideology appeared in several of his writings, and most clearly in his Notes on the State of Virginia *(1781).*

Source: [1] Thomas Jefferson, *Notes on the State of Virginia,* 2nd ed. (London, 1787), pp. 228–240.

. . . To emancipate all slaves born after passing the act. The bill reported by the revisors does not itself contain this proposition; but an amendment containing it was prepared, to be offered to the legislature whenever the bill should be taken up, and further directing, that they should continue with their parents to a certain age, then be brought up, at the public expence, to tillage, arts or sciences, according to their geniusses, till the females should be eighteen, and the males twenty-one years of age, when they should be colonized to such place as the circumstances of the time should render most proper, sending them out with arms, implements of household and of the handicraft arts, seeds, pairs of the useful domestic animals, etc., to declare them a free and independent people, and extend to them our alliance and protection, till they shall have acquired strength; and to send vessels at the same time to other parts of the world for an equal number of white inhabitants; to induce whom to migrate hither, proper encouragements were to be proposed. It will probably be asked, Why not retain and incorporate the blacks into the state, and thus save the expence of supplying, by importation of white settlers, the vacancies they will leave? Deep rooted prejudices entertained by the whites; ten thousand recollections, by the blacks, of the injuries they have sustained; new provocations; the real distinctions which nature has made; and many other circumstances, will divide us into parties; and produce convulsions which will probably never end but in the extermination of the one or the other race—To these objections; which are political, may be added others, which are physical and moral. The first difference which strikes us is that of colour. Whether the black of the negro resides in the reticular membrane between the skin and scarf-skin, or in the scarf-skin itself; whether it proceeds from the colour of the blood, the colour of the bile, or from that of some other secretion, the difference is fixed in nature, and is as real as if its seat and cause were better known to us. And is this difference of no importance? Is it not the foundation of a greater or less share of beauty in the two races? Are not the fine mixture of red and white, the expressions of every passion by greater or less suffusions of colour in the one, preferable to that eternal monotony, which reigns in the coun-

tenances, that imoveable veil of black which covers all the
emotions of the other race? Add to these, flowing hair, a more
elegant symmetry of form, their own judgment in favour of the
whites, declared by their preference of them, as uniformly as
is the preference of the Oranootan for the black women over
those of his own species. The circumstances of superior beauty
is thought worthy attention in the propagation of our horses,
dogs, and other domestic animals; why not in that of man?
Besides, those of colour, figure, and hair, there are other physical distinctions proving a difference of race. They have less
hair on the face and body. They secrete less by the kidnies and
more by the glands of the skin, which gives them a very strong
and disagreeable odour. This greater degree of transpiration
renders them more tolerant of heat, and less so of cold, than
the whites. Perhaps too a difference of structure in the pul-
monary apparatus, which a late ingenious experimentalist has
discovered to be the principal regulator of animal heat, may
have disabled them from extricating, in the act of inspiration,
so much of that fluid from the outer air, or obliged them in
expiration, to part with more of it. They seem to require less
sleep. A black, after hard labour through the day, will be induced by the slightest amusements to sit up till midnight, or
later, though knowing he must be out with the first dawn of
the morning. They are at least as brave, and more adventure-
some. But this may perhaps proceed from a want of forethought, which prevents their seeing a danger till it be present.
When present, they do not go through it with more coolness or
steadiness than the whites. They are more ardent after their
female: but love seems with them to be more an eager desire,
than a tender delicate mixture of sentiment and sensation. Their
griefs are transient. Those numberless afflictions, which render
it doubtful whether heaven has given life to us in mercy or in
wrath, are less felt, and sooner forgotten with them. In general,
their existence appears to participate more of sensation than
reflection. To this must be ascribed their disposition to sleep
when abstracted from their diversions, and unemployed in labour. An animal whose body is at rest, and who does not
reflect, must be disposed to sleep of course. Comparing them
by their faculties of memory, reason, and imagination, it ap-

pears to me, that in memory they are equal to the whites; in reason much inferior, as I think one could scarcely be found capable of tracing and comprehending the investigations of Euclid; and that in imagination they are dull, tasteless, and anomalous. It would be unfair to follow them to Africa for that investigation. We will consider them here, on the same stage with the whites, and where the facts are not apocryphal on which a judgment is to be formed. It will be right to make great allowances for the difference of condition, of education, of conversation, of the sphere in which they move. Many millions of them have been brought to, and born in America. Most of them indeed have been confined to tillage, to their own homes, and their own society: yet many have been so situated, that they might have availed themselves of the conversation of their masters; many have been brought up in the handicraft arts, and from that circumstance have always been associated with the whites. Some have been liberally educated, and all have lived in countries where the arts and sciences are cultivated to a considerable degree, and have had before their eyes samplers of the best works from abroad. The Indians, with no advantages of this kind, will often carve figures on their pipes not destitute of design and merit. They will crayon out an animal, a plant, or a country, first to prove the existence of a germ in their minds which only wants cultivation. They astonish you with strokes of the most sublime oratory; such as prove their reason and sentiment strong, their imagination glowing and elevated. But never yet could I find that a black had uttered a thought above the level of plain narration; never see even an elementary trait of painting or sculpture. In music they are more generally gifted than the whites with accurate ears for tune and time, and they have been found capable of imagining a small catch. Whether they will be equal in the composition of a more extensive run of melody, or of complicated harmony, is yet to be proved. Misery is often the parent of the most affecting touches in poetry. Among the blacks is misery enough, God knows, but no poetry. Love is the peculiar cestrum of the poet. Their love is ardent, but it kindles the senses only, not the imagination. Religion indeed has produced a Phyllis Wheatly; but it could not produce a poet. The compositions published under her name are below the dignity of criticism. The heroes of the Duncaid are to her, as Hercules to the author of that poem. Ignatius Sancho has approached nearer to merit in composition; yet his letters do more honour to the heart than the head. They breathe the purest effusions of friendship and general philanthropy, and show how great a degree of the latter may be compounded with strong religious zeal. He is often happy in the turn of his compliments, and his style is easy and familiar, except when he affects a Shandean fabrication of words. But his imagination is wild and extravagant, escapes incessantly from every restraint of reason and taste, and, in the course of its vagaries, leaves a tract of thought as incoherent and eccentric, as is the course of a meteor through the sky. His subjects should often have led him to a process of sober reasoning; yet we find him always substituting sentiment for demonstration. Upon the whole, though, we admit him to the first place among those of his own colour who have presented themselves to the public judgment, yet when we compare him with the writers of the race among whom he lived, and particularly with the epistolary class, in which he has taken his own stand, we are compelled to entroll him at the bottom of the column. This criticism supposes the letters published under his name to be genuine, and to have received amendment from no other hand; points which would not be of easy investigation. The improvement of the blacks in body and mind, in the first instance of their mixture with the whites, has been observed by every one, and proves that their inferiority is not the effect merely of their condition of life. We know that among the Romans, about the Augustan age especially, the condition of their slaves was much more deplorable than that of the blacks on the continent of America. The two sexes were confined to separate apartments, because to raise a child cost the master more than to buy one. Cato, for a very restricted indulgence to his slaves in this particular, took from them a certain price. But in this country the slaves multiply as fast as the free inhabitants. Their situation and manners place the commerce between the two sexes almost without restraint. The same Cato, on a principle of economy, always sold his sick and superannuated slaves. He gives it as a standing precept to a master visiting his farm; to sell his old oxen, old waggons, old tools, old and diseased servants, and every thing else become useless. . . . The American slaves cannot enumerate this among the injuries and insults they receive. It was the common practice to expose in the island of Esculapius, in the Tyber, diseased slaves, whose cure was like to become tedious. The Emperor Claudius, by an edict, gave freedom to such of them as should recover, and first declared, that if any person chose to kill rather than to expose them, it should be deemed homicide. The exposing them is a crime of which no instance has existed with us, and were it to be followed by death, it would be punished capitally. We are told of a certain Vedius Pollio, who, in the presence of Augustus, would have given a slave as food to his fish, for having broken a glass. With the Romans, the regular method of taking the evidence of their slaves was under torture. Here it has been thought better never to resort to their evidence. When a master was murdered, all his slaves, in the same house, or within hearing, were condemned to death. Here punishment falls on the guilty only, and as precise proof is required against him as against a freeman. Yet notwithstanding these and other discouraging circumstances among the Romans, their slaves were often their rarest artists. They excelled too in science, insomuch as to be usually employed as tutors to their master's children. Epictetus, Terence, and Phaedrus, were slaves. But they were of the race of whites. It is not their condition then, but nature, which has produced the distinction.—Whether further observation will or will not verify the conjecture, that nature has been less bountiful to them in the endowments of the head, I believe that in those of the heart she will be found to have done them justice. That disposition to theft with which they have been branded, must be ascribed to their situation, and not to any depravity of the moral sense. The man, in whose favour no laws of property exist, probably feels himself less bound to respect those made in favour of others. When arguing for ourselves, we lay it down as a fundamental, that laws, to be just, must give a reciprocation of right: that, without this, they are mere arbitrary rules of conduct, founded in force, and not in conscience; and it is a problem which I give to the master to solve, whether the religious precepts against the violation of property were not framed for him as well as his slave? And whether the slave may not as justifiably take a little from one, who has taken all from him, as he may slay one who would slay him? That a change in the relations in which a man is placed should change his ideas of moral right and wrong, is neither new, nor peculiar to the colour of the blacks, Homer tells us it was so 2600 years ago.

Jove fix'd it certain, that whatever day
Makes man a slave, takes half his worth away.

But the slaves of which Homer speaks were whites. Notwithstanding these considerations which must weaken their respect for the laws of property, we find among them numerous instances of the most rigid integrity, and as many as among their better instructed masters, of benevolence, gratitude, and unshaken fidelity. The opinion, that they are inferior in the faculties of reason and imagination must be hazarded with great diffidence. To justify a general conclusion, requires many observations, even where the subject may be submitted to the Anatomical knife, to Optical glasses, to analysis by fire, or by solvents. How much more then where it is a faculty, not a substance, we are examining; where it eludes the research of all the senses; where the conditions of its existence are various and variously combined; where the effects of those which are present or absent bid defiance to calculation, let me add too, as a circumstance of great tenderness, where our conclusions would degrade a whole race of men from the rank in the scale of beings which their Creator may perhaps have given them. To our reproach it must be said, that though for a century and a half we have had under our eyes the races of black and of red men, they have never yet been viewed by us as subjects of natural history. I advance it therefore as a suspicion only, that the blacks, whether originally a distinct race, or made distinct by time and circumstances, are inferior to the whites in the endowments both of body and mind. It is not against experience to suppose, that different species of the same genus, or varieties of the same species, may possess different qualifications. Will not a lover of natural history then, one who views the gradations in all the races of animals with the eye of philosophy, excuse an effort to keep those in the department of man as distinct as nature has formed them? This unfortunate difference of colour, and perhaps of faculty, is a powerful obstacle to the emancipation of these people. Many of their advocates, while they wish to vindicate the liberty of human nature, are anxious also to preserve its dignity and beauty. Some of these, embarrassed by the Question 'What further is to be done with them?' join themselves in opposition with those who are actuated by sordid avarice only. Among the Romans emancipation required but one effort. The slave, when made free, might mix with, without staining the blood of his master. But with us a second is necessary, unknown to history. When freed, he is to be removed beyond the reach of mixture.

The Black Man and the Brute Creation

Edward Long, the British author of the History *of Jamaica (1774) and a contributor to America's scientific racism, concluded that Caucasians and Negroes were formed from the "same genus, but were of a different species." Long reflected on the nature of blacks and their dissimilarity to the rest of mankind; he suggested that in the gradation of beings, the Negro was to be placed somewhere between the white man and the orangutan. Furthermore, he alleged that "If such has been the intention of the Almighty, we are then, perhaps, to regard the Oran-outang as—'the lag of human kind, nearest to brutes, by God design'd.' "*

The Negro, he claimed, would one day rise "progressively in the scale of intellect," and develop "above the Oran-outang and to hold some degree of distinction" since he would eventually "form the centre of connection between the two extremes,

Source: [2] Edward Long, "Observation on the Gradation in the Scale of Being between the Human and Brute Creation. Including some Curious Particulars respecting Negroes," *Columbian Magazine*, II (1788), pp. 14–15, 70–75.

[Caucasian and black]." This process would produce "three ranks of men, dependent on each other, and rising in a proper climax of subordination, in which the whites would hold the highest place."

The particulars wherein Negroes differ most essentially from the whites are, first, in respect to their bodies, viz. the dark membrane which communicates that black colour to their skins, which does not alter by transportion into other climates, and which they never lose, except by such diseases, or casualties, as destroy the texture of it; for example, the leprosy, and accidents of burning and scalding. Negroes have been introduced into the North American colonies near 150 years. The winters, especially at New York, and New England, are more severe than in Europe. Yet the blacks born here, to the third and fourth generation, are not at all different in colour from those Negroes who are brought directly from Africa; whence it may be concluded very properly, that Negroes, or their posterity do not change colour, though they continue ever so long in a cold climate.

Secondly, A covering of wool, like the bestial fleece, instead of hair.

Thirdly, The roundness of their eyes, the figure of their ears, tumid nostrils, flat noses, invariable thick lips, and general large size of the female nipples, as if adapted by nature to the peculiar conformation of their children's mouths.

Fourthly, The black colour of the lice which infest their bodies. This pecular circumstance I do not remember to have seen noticed by any naturalist; they resemble the white lice in shape, but in general are of larger size. It is known, that there is a very great variety of these insects; and some say, that almost all animals have their peculiar sort.

Fifthly, Their bestial or faetid smell, which they all have in a greator or less degree, the Congo's, Arada's, Quaqua's, and Angola's particularly the latter, who are likewise the most stupid of the Negroe race, are the most offensive; and those of Senegal (who are distinguished from the other herds by greater accuteness of understanding and mildness of disposition) have the least of this noxious odour.

This scent in some of them is so excessively strong, especially when their bodies are warmed either by exercise or anger, that it continues in places where they have been near a quarter of an hour.

I shall next consider their disparity, in regard to the faculties of the mind. Under this head we are to observe, that they remain at this time in the same rude situation in which they were found two thousand years ago.

In general, they are void of genius, and seem almost incapable of making any progress in civility or science. They have no plan or system of morality among them. Their barbarity to their children debase their nature even below that of brutes. They have no moral sensations; no taste but for women; gormandizing, and drinking to excess; no wish but to be idle. Their children, from their tenderest years, are suffered to deliver themselves up to all that nature suggests to them. Their houses are miserable cabbins. They conceive no pleasure from the most beautiful parts of their country, preferring the more sterile. Their roads, as they call them, are mere sheep-paths, twice as long as they need be, and almost impassible. Their country in most parts is one continued wilderness, beset with briars and thorns. They use neither carriages, nor beasts of burden. They are represented by all authors as the vilest of the human kind, to which they have little more pretension of resemblence than what arises from their exterior form.

In so vast a continent as that of Africa, and in so great a variety of climates and provinces, we might expect to find a proportionable diversity among the inhabitants, in regard to their qualifications of body and mind; strength, agility, industry, and dexterity, on the one hand; ingenuity, learning, arts, and sciences, on the other. But, on the contrary, a general uniformity runs through all these various regions of people; so that, if any difference be found, it is only in degrees of the same qualities; and, what is more strange, those of the worst kind; it being a common known proverb, That all people on the globe have some good as well as ill qualities, except the Africans. Whatever great personages this country might anciently have produced, and concerning whom we have no information, they are now everywhere degenerated into a brutish, ignorant, idle, crafty, treacherous, bloody, thievish, mistrustful and superstitious people, even in those states where we might expect to find them more polished, humane, docile, and industrious. It is doubtful whether we ought to ascribe any superior qualities to the more ancient Africans; for we find them represented by the Greek and Roman authors under the most odious and despicable character; as proud, lazy, deceitful, thievish, addicted to all kinds of lust, and ready to promote them in others, incestuous, savage, cruel, and vindictive, devourers of human flesh, and quaffers of human blood, inconstant, base, and cowardly, devoted to all sorts of superstition; and, in short to every vice that came in their way, or within their reach.

For the honour of human nature it were to be withheld, that these descriptions could with justice be accused of exaggeration; but, in respect to the modern Africans, we find the charge corroborated, and supported by a consistent testimony of so many men of different nations, who have visited the coast, that it is difficult to believe they have all been guilty of misrepresenting these people; more especially, as they tally exactly with the characters of the Africans that are brought into our plantations.

We have seen the bodies of the Oran-outang race hitherto in miniature only, which conveys very little further information of their intellect than might be gained from the view of a picture, or a statue. . . .

But if we admit with Mr. Buffon, that with all this analogy of organization, the Oran-outang's brain is a senseless *icon* of the human; that it is mere matter, unanimated with a thinking principle, in any, or at least in a very minute and imperfect degree, we must then infer the strongest conclusion to establish our belief of a natural diversity of the human intellect, in general, *aborigine;* an Oran-outang, in this case, is a human being, *quoad* his form and organs; but of an inferior species, *quoad* his intellect; he has in form a much near resemblance to the Negroe race, than the latter bear to White men; the supposition then is well founded, that the brain, and intellectual organs, so far as they are dependent upon mere matter, though similar in texture and modification to those of other men, may in some of the Negroe race be so constituted, as *not to result to the same effects;* for we cannot but allow, that the Deity might, if it was his pleasure, diversify his works in this manner, and either withhold the superior principle entirely, or in part only, or infuse it into the different classes and races of human creatures, in such portions as to form the same gradual climax towards perfection in this human system, which is so evidently designed in every other.

If such has been the intention of the Almighty, we are then, perhaps, to regard the Oran-outang as,

> "—the lag of human kind,
> "Nearest to brutes, by God design'd."

The Negroe race (consisting of varieties) will then appear rising progressively in the scale of intellect, the further they mount above the Oran-outang and brute creation. The system of man will seem more consistent, and the measure of it more complete and analagous to the harmony and order that are visible in every other line of the world's stupendous fabric. Nor is this conclusion degrading to human nature, while it tends to exalt our idea of the infinite perfections of the Deity; for how vast is the distance between inert matter, and matter endued with thought and reason! The series and progression from a lump of dirt to a perfect human being is amazingly extensive; nor less so, perhaps, the interval between the latter and the most perfect angelic being, and between this being and the Deity himself. Let us shake off those clouds with which prejudice endeavours to invelope the understanding; and, exerting that freedom of thought which the Best of Beings has granted to us, let us take a noon tide view of the human *genus;* and shall we say, that it is totally different from, and less perfect than, every other system of animal beings? The species of every other *genus* have their certain mark and distinction, their varieties, and subordinate classes: and why should the race of mankind be singularly indiscriminate?

> "In the catalogue they go for men,
> "As hounds and greyhounds, mongrels,
>   spaniels, curs,

"Shocks, water-rugs, and demywolves,
    are 'clep'd.
"*All* by the *name of dogs;* the
    valued file
"Distinguishes the swift, the slow, the
    subtile,
"The housekeeper, the hunter, every one
"According to the gift which bounteous
    nature
"Hath in him clos'd; whereby he does
    receive
"Particular addition, from the bill
"That writes them all alike:—*And so*
    of men—"

says that faithful observer of nature, our immortal Shake-speare; and with him so far agrees that truly learned and sagacious naturalist, Mons. Buffon, who investigates the marks of variation among mankind in the following manner: "Men differ from white to black, from compound to simple, by the height of stature, size, activity, strength, and other bodily characteristics; and from the genius to the dolt, from the greatest to the least, *by the measure of intellect.*"

Benjamin Rush and Observations on the Color Black

Dr. Benjamin Rush was a leading physician and scientist of late eighteenth-century America. As an organizer and president of the Pennsylvania Society for Promoting the Abolition of Slavery, he contributed to numerous anti-slavery publications. Rush denied the charge of Negro inferiority and asserted that the Old Testament was the "strongest argument that [could] be used in favor of the original and natural equality of mankind." Nevertheless, in the cause of scientific research, he

Source: [3] *Transactions of the American Philosophical Society* (Philadelphia, 1799), Vol. IV, pp. 289–297.

unwittingly contributed to the ideology of Negro inferiority. In an address to the American Philosophical Society on July 14, 1792, he affirmed that the color black was caused by endemic leprosy. He drew three conclusions from his research and asked his audience: (1) to refute white supremacy based on color because its foundation was built on "ignorance and inhumanity"; (2) to recognize that intermarriage would "tend to infect" future generations with the same affliction as the blacks; and (3) that "science and humanity combine their efforts, and endeavor to discover a remedy for it [leprosy]."

Although Rush had no intention of promoting the idealogy of Negro inferiority, by implication his essay, Observations intended to Favour a Supposition that the Black Color (as it is called) of the Negroes is derived from the LEPROSY, *helped to advance the concept of the diseased and outcast Negro.*

Dr Smith* in his elegant and ingenious Essay upon the Variety of Color and Figure in the Human Species has derived it from four causes, viz. Climate, diet, state of society, and diseases. I admit the Doctor's facts, and reasonings as far as he has extended them, in the fullest manner. I shall only add to them a few observations which are intended to prove that the color and figure of that part of our fellow creatures who are known by the epithet of negroes, are derived from a modification of that disease, which is known by the name of Leprosy.

Many facts recorded by historians, as well as physicians show the influence of unwholesome diet in having produced the leprosy in the middle and northern parts of Europe in the 13th and 14th centuries. The same cause, combined with greater heat, more savage manners, and bilious fevers, probably produced this disease in the skin among the natives of Africa. But I will not rest the proofs of the color and figure of

* Samuel Stanhope Smith, professor of moral philosophy at the College of New Jersey (now Princeton University), denied the theory that espoused the separate creation of the races. In his *Essay on the causes of the Variety of Complexion and Figure in the Human Species* (1787), he attempted to "establish the unity" of all mankind. His central thesis suggested that man's apparent racial differences were solely the products of his climatic environment, surrounding society, mode of life, and disease symptoms. (Ed.)

the negroes being a leprosy simply upon its causes. Other circumstances make it much more probable. I shall briefly enumerate them.

1. The leprosy is accompanied in some instances with a
black color of the skin. Of this I have met with a satisfactory
proof in Dr Theiry's account of the disease of Asturia in Spain.
I shall insert a translation of his own words upon this subject.
"There are [says this excellent physician] above twenty hospitals for lepers in this province, and I have observed six
species of the disorder. One of them, viz. the second, is called
the *black albaras* of the Arabians. The skin becomes black,
thick and greasy. There are neither pustules, nor turbercles, nor
scales, nor anything out of the way on the skin. The body is
not in the least emaciated. The breathing is a little difficult, and
the countenance has some fierceness in it. They exhale per-
petually a peculiar and disagreeable smell, which I can compare to nothing but the smell of a mortified limb." This smell
mentioned by Dr Theiry continues with a small modification
in the native African to this day.

2. The leprosy is described in the Old Testament, and by
many ancient writers as imparting a preternatural whiteness to
the skin. Persons thus marked, have lately received the name
of *Albanos*. Solitary instances of this disease are often met with
it upon the Alps, but travellers tell us that it is one of the en-
demics of Java, Guinea and Panama where it is perpetuated
through many generations. Mr Hawkins in his travels into the
interior parts of Africa has described the persons afflicted with
this disease in the following words. "They go entirely naked;
their skin is white, but has not that animated appearance so
perceptible in Europeans. It has a dull deathlike whitish cast
that conveys an idea more of sickness, than of health. Their
hair is red, or ashes-coloured, yellowish wool, and their eyes
are uniformly white, in that part by which others are distinguished into the black, grey and blue eyes. They are set deep
in the head, and very commonly squint, for as their skin is deprived of the black mucous web, the distinguishing characteristic of these Africans, so their eyes are destitute of that black
matter resembling a pigment, so universally found in people of
all countries, and so useful in preventing the eye from being

injured in cases of exposure to strong light." This artless trav-
eller does not stop here. The idea of this peculiarity in the color
and features of these people being a disease, and even its specific nature did not escape him, hence he adds "These people
rendered unfortunate by the prejudices of their countrymen,
are born of black parents; they have all the features of other
inhabitants, but differ from them only in the above circumstances. The difference of color cannot arise from the intercourse of whites and blacks, for the whites are very rarely
among them, and the result of this union is well known to be
the yellow color, or mulatto. Many of the natives assert that
they are produced by the women being debauched in the woods
by the large baboon, ourang-outang, and by that species in particular called the guaga mooroos. No satisfactory discovery has
been made to account for such singular, but not unfrequent
phenomena in the species. It may perhaps be ascribed to
disease, and that of the *leprous* kind, with more reason than
to any other cause that has been yet assigned." Mr Bernardin
concurs with Mr Hawkins in ascribing this morbid whiteness
in the skins of the Africans wholly to the leprosy. However,
opposed it may be to their morbid blackness, it is in strict con-
formity to the operations of nature in other diseases. The same
state of malignant fever is often marked by opposite colors in
the stools, by an opposite temperature of the skin, and by opposite states of the alimentary canal.

The original connection of the black color of the negroes
with the leprosy is further suggested by the following fact
taken from Bougainvillé's voyage round the world. He tells
us that on an island in the Pacific Ocean which he visited, the
inhabitants were composed of negroes and mulattoes. They
had thick lips, woolly hair, and were sometimes of a yellowish
color. They were short, ugly, ill proportioned, and most of
them infected with the leprosy, a circumstance from which he
called the island they inhabit, the Isle of Lepers.

3. The leprosy sometimes appears with white and black
spots blended together in every part of the body. A picture of
a negro man in Virginia in whom this mixture of white and
black had taken place, has been happily preserved by Mr Peale
in his museum.

4. The leprosy induces a morbid insensibility in the nerves. In countries where the disease prevails, it is common to say that a person devoid of sensibility has no more feeling than a leper. This insensibility belongs in a peculiar manner to the negroes. Dr Moseley says, "they are void of sensibility to a sur-prizing degree. They sleep sound in every disease, nor does any mental disturbance ever keep them awake. They bear surgical operations much better than white people, and what would be a cause of insupportable pain to a white man, a negro would almost disregard. I have amputated the legs of many negroes, who have held the upper part of the limb themselves." This morbid insensibility in the negroes discovers itself further in the apathy with which they expose themselves to great heat, and the indifference with which they handle coals of fire.

5. Lepers are remarkable for having strong venereal de-sires. This is universal among the negroes, hence their uncom-mon fruitfulness when they are not depressed by slavery; but even slavery in its worst state does not always subdue the ve-nereal appetite, for after whole days, spent in hard labor in a hot sun in the West Indies, the black men often walk five or six miles to comply with a venereal assignation.

6. The big lip, and flat nose so universal among the negroes, are symptoms of the leprosy. I have more than once seen them in the Pennsylvania hospital.

7. The woolly heads of the negroes cannot be accounted for from climate, diet, state of society, or bilious diseases, for all those circumstances, when combined have not produced it in the natives of Asia and America who inhabit similar latitudes. Wool is peculiar to the negro. Here the proofs of similiarity in the symptoms of leprosy, and in the peculiarities of the negro body appear to fail, but there is a fact in the history of the leprosy which will probably throw some light upon this part of our subject. The Trichoma, or Plica Polonica of the Poles is a symptom of leprosy. This is evident not only from the causes which originally produced it, but from its symptoms as described in a late publication by F. L. DeLa Fontaine. From this fact it would seem that the leprosy had found its way to the covering of the head, and from the variety of its effects upon the skin, I see no difficulty in admitting that it may

as readily have produced wool upon the head of a negro, as matted hair upon the head of the Poles.

But how shall we account for the long duration of this color of the skin through so many generations and even ages?—I answer 1. That the leprosy is the most durable in its descent to posterity, and the most indestructable in its nature of any disease we are acquainted with. In Iceland Dr Van Troil tells us, it often disappears in the second and third, and appears in the fourth generation. 2dly, No more happens here than what happens to many nations who are distinguished by a peculiarity of figure, in any part of the body. Many of the inhabitants of the highlands of Scotland, have the same red hair, and the same high cheek bones which are ascribed to their ancestors by Tacitus after the invasion of Britain. Even the tumors in the throat in the Cretins who inhabit the Alps, are transmitted from father to son, through a long succession of generations. Madness, and consumption in like manner are hereditary in many families, both of which occupy parts of the body, much more liable to change in successive generations, than the skin.

Should it be objected to this theory that the leprosy is an infectious disorder, but that no infectious quality exists in the skin of the negro, I would reply to such objection by remarking in the first place, that the leprosy has in a great degree ceased to be infectious, more especially from contact, and secondly that there are instances in which something like an infectious quality has appeared in the skin of a negro. A white woman in North Carolina not only acquired a dark color, but several of the features of a negro, by marrying and living with a black husband. A similar instance of a change in the color and features of a woman in Buck's county in Pennsylvania has been observed and from a similar cause. In both these cases, the women bore children by their black husbands.

It is no objection to the theory I have attempted to establish, that the negroes are as healthy, and long lived as the white people. Local diseases of the skin seldom affect the general health of the body, or the duration of human life. Dr Theiry remarks that the itch, and even the leprosy, did not impair longevity in those people who lived near the sea-shore in the healthy climate of Galicia.

The facts and principles which I have delivered, lead to the following reflections.

1. That all the claims of superiority of the whites over the blacks, on account of their color, are founded alike in ignorance and inhumanity. If the color of the negroes be the effect of a disease, instead of inviting us to tyrannise over them, it should entitle them to a double portion of our humanity, for disease all over the world has always been the signal for immediate and universal compassion.

2. The facts and principles which have been delivered, should teach white people the necessity of keeping up that prejudice against such connections with them, as would tend to infect posterity with any portion of their disorder. This may be done upon the ground I have mentioned without offering violence to humanity, or calling in question the sameness of descent, or natural equality of mankind.

3. Is the color of the negroes a disease? Then let science and humanity combine their efforts, and endeavour to discover a remedy for it. Nature has lately unfurled a banner upon this subject. She has begun spontaneous cures of this disease in several black people in this country. In a certain Henry Moss who lately travelled through this city, and was exhibited as a show for money, the cure was nearly complete. The change from black to a natural white flesh color began about five years ago at the ends of his fingers, and has extended gradually over the greatest part of his body. The wool which formerly perforated the cuticle has been changed into hair. No change in the diet, drinks, dress, employments, or situations of this man had taken place previously to this change in his skin. But this fact does not militate against artificial attempts to dislodge the color in negroes, any more than the spontaneous cures of many other diseases militate against the use of medicine in the practice of physic. To direct our experiments upon this subject I shall throw out the following facts.

1. In Henry Moss the color was first discharged from the skin in those places, on which there was most pressure from cloathing, and most attrition from labor, as on the trunk of his body, and on his fingers. The destruction of the black color was probably occasioned by the absorption of the coloring

matter of the rete mucosum, or perhaps of the rete mucosum itself, for pressure and friction it is well known aid the absorbing action of the lymphatics in every part of the body. It is from the latter cause, that the palms of the hands of negro women who spend their lives at a washing tub, are generally as fair as the palms of the hands in labouring white people.

2. Depletion, whether by bleeding, purging, or abstinence has been often observed to lessen the black color in negroes. The effects of the above remedies in curing the common leprosy, satisfy me that they might be used with advantage in that state of leprosy which I conceive to exist in the skin of negroes.

3. A similar change in the color of the negroes, though of a more temporary nature, has often been observed in them from the influence of fear.

4. Dr Beddoes tells us that he has discharged the color in the black wool of a negro by infusing it in the oxygenated muriatic acid, and lessened it by the same means in the hand of a negro man. The land-cloud of Africa called by the Portuguese Ferrino Mr Hawkins tells us has a peculiar action upon the negroes in changing the black color of their skins to a dusky grey. Its action is accompanied, he says, with an itching and prickling sensation upon every part of the body which increases with the length of exposure to it so as to be almost intolerable. It is probably air of the carbonic kind, for it uniformly extinguishes fire.

5. A citizen of Philadelphia upon whose veracity I have perfect reliance, assured me that he had once seen the skin of one side of the cheek inclining to the chin, and of part of the hand in a negro boy, changed to a white color by the juice of unripe peaches (of which he ate a large quantity every year) falling, and resting frequently upon those parts of his body.

To encourage attempts to cure this disease of the skin in negroes, let us recollect that by succeeding in them, we shall produce a large portion of happiness in the world. We shall in the first place destroy one of the arguments infavor of enslaving the negroes, for their color has been supposed by the ignorant to mark them as objects of divine judgments, and by the learned to qualify them for labor in hot, and unwholesome climates.

Secondly, We shall add greatly to *their* happiness, for however well they appear to be satisfied with their color, there are many proofs of their preferring that of the white people.

Thirdly, We shall render the belief of the whole human race being descended from one pair, easy, and universal, and thereby not only add weight to the Christian revelation, but remove a material obstacle to the exercise of that universal benevolence which is inculcated by it.

THE INCEPTION OF THE AMERICAN NATIVIST MOVEMENT

The Massachusetts General Court Banishes All "Jesuits" (1636)

Nativism and anti-Catholic sentiment appeared quite early in the Plymouth and Massachusetts Bay colonies. In 1636, the General Court of Plymouth decreed that no person was to be admitted to the colony without the permission of the Governor. Shortly after, the General Court also proclaimed that the needs of native-born persons for land were to be given priority over those who "either come from England or elsewhere."

"Massachusetts Bay was a center of No-Popery sentiment second only to Maryland." The Bay colony's anti-Catholicism resulted from Puritanism's general intolerance of all dissent. In 1647, the Massachusetts General Court banished all Jesuits or other officials of the Catholic Church and warned that if they should return, they would be executed.

This Court, taking into consideration the great wars & combustions which are this day in Europe, & that the same are observed to be chiefly raised & fomented by the secret practices of those of the Jesuiticall order, for the prevention of like evils

Source: [4] *Records of the Governor and Company of Massachusetts, 1644–1657*, Nathaniel B. Shurtleff, ed. (Boston, 1854), III, p. 112.

amongst o'selves, its ordered, by the authoritie of this Court, that no Jesuit or eclesiaticall person ordained by ye authoritie of the pope shall henceforth come within our jurisdiction; & if any person shall give any cause of suspicion that he is one of such societie, he shall be brought before some of the magistrates, & if he cannot free himself of such suspicion, he shall be comitted or bound out to the next Court of Assistants, to be tried & proceeded with by banishment or otherwise, as the Court shall see cause; & if any such person so banished shall be taken the 2d time within this jurisdiction, he shall, upon lawful trial & conviction, be put to death; provided this law shall not extend to any such Jesuit as shall be cast upon our shores by shipwreck or other accident, so as he continues no longer than he may have opportunitie of passage for his departure, nor to any such as shall come in company with any messenger sent hither upon public occasions, or any merchant or master of any ship belonging to any place not in enmitie with the state of England or o'selves, so as they depart again with the same messenger merchant, or . . . behave themselves inoffencively during their abode here.

Benjamin Franklin's Opposition to Immigration

The Restrictionists, or critics of a free immigration policy, have generally been associated with the late nineteenth and early twentieth centuries. At least two of the Restrictionists' arguments were anticipated by three of the country's most illustrious founding fathers: Benjamin Franklin, Thomas Jefferson and Alexander Hamilton. These men argued that immigration, as compared with the people's natural ability to multiply, was a negligible factor in the country's population growth. Moreover, these early leaders maintained that immigration introduced elements that would threaten the country's basic institutions.

Source: [5] *The Works of Benjamin Franklin,* Jared Sparks, ed. (Boston, 1836), II, pp. 318–321.

In his Notes on Virginia, *written in 1781, Jefferson used the
statistics of Virginia's population growth to show that the
increase in the province's inhabitants was due to "natural
propagation" rather than the "importation of foreigners." In
addition, he held that a population increase resulting from natural causes, rather than immigration, would produce a "more
homogeneous, more peaceable, more durable government."
Similarly, in 1751, Benjamin Franklin had doubted the necessity "to bring in foreigners to fill any occasional vacancy" and
asked, "Why should Pennsylvania, founded by the English, become a colony of aliens, who will shortly be so numerous as to
Germanize us instead of Anglifying them?" Even more emphatic was Franklin's opposition to black immigration.*

. . . The importation of Foreigners into a country, that has as
many inhabitants as the present employments and provisions
for subsistence will bear, will be in the end no increase of
people, unless the new comers have more industry and frugality
than the natives, and then they will provide more subsistence,
and increase in the country; but they will gradually eat the natives out. Nor is it necessary to bring in foreigners to fill up any
occasional vacancy in a country; for such vacancy (if the laws
are good), will soon be filled by natural generation. Who can
now find the vacancy made in Sweden, France or other warlike nations, by the plague of heroism, forty years ago; in
France, by the expulsion of the Protestants; in England, by the
settlement of her colonies; or in Guinea, by one hundred years'
exportation of slaves, that has blackened half America? The
thinness of inhabitants in Spain is owing to national pride and
idleness, and other causes, rather than to the expulsion of the
Moors, or to the making of new settlements.

There is, in short, no bound to the prolific nature of plants
or animals, but what is made by their crowding and interfering
with each other's means of subsistence. Was the face of the
earth vacant of other plants, it might be gradually sowed and
overspread with one kind only, as, for instance, with fennel;
and, were it empty of other inhabitants, it might in a few ages
be replenished from one nation only, as, for instance, with Englishmen. Thus, there are supposed to be now upwards of one

million English souls in North America, (though it is thought scarce eighty thousand has been brought over sea,) and yet perhaps there is not one the fewer in Britain, but rather many more, on account of the employment the colonies afford to manufacturers at home. This million doubling, suppose but once in twenty-five years, will, in another century, be more than the people of England, and the greatest number of Englishmen will be on this side of the water. What an accession of power to the British empire by sea as well as land! What increase of trade and navigation! What numbers of ships and seamen! We have been here but little more than one hundred years, and yet the force of our privateers in the late war, united, was greater, both in men and guns, than that of the whole British navy in Queen Elizabeth's time. How important an affair then to Britain is the present treaty for settling the bounds between her colonies and the French, and how careful should she be to secure room enough, since on the room depends so much the increase of her people.

In fine, a nation well regulated is like a polypus; take away a limb, its place is soon supplied; cut it in two, and each deficient part shall speedily grow out of the part remaining. Thus, if you have room and subsistence enough, as you may, by dividing, make ten polypuses out of one, you may of one make ten nations, equally populous and powerful; or rather increase a nation ten fold in numbers and strength.

And since detachments of English from Britain, sent to America, will have their places at home so soon supplied and increase so largely here; why should the Palatine boors be suffered to swarm into our settlements, and, by herding together, establish their language and manners, to the exclusion of ours? Why should Pennsylvania, founded by the English, become a colony of aliens, who will shortly be so numerous as to Germanize us instead of our Anglifying them, and will never adopt our language or customs any more than they can acquire our complexion?

Which leads me to add one remark, that the number of purely white people in the world is proportionably very small. All Africa is black or tawny, Asia chiefly tawny; America (exclusive of the newcomers) wholly so. And in Europe, the Span-

iards, Italians, French, Russians, and Swedes, are generally of
what we call a swarthy complexion; as are the Germans, also,
the Saxons only excepted, who, with the English, make the
principal body of white people on the face of the earth. I could
wish their numbers were increased. And while we are, as I may
call it, scouring our planet, by clearing America of woods, and
so making this side of our globe reflect a brighter light to
the eyes of the inhabitants in Mars or Venus, why should we,
in the sight of superior beings, darken its people? Why increase
the sons of Africa, by planting them in America, where we have
so fair an opportunity, by excluding all blacks and tawnys, of
increasing the lovely white and red? But perhaps I am partial
to the complexion of my country, for such kind of partiality is
natural to mankind.

Hamilton Uses Jefferson's Arguments in Opposing a Liberal Immigration Policy

*In December, 1801, in his first annual message to Congress,
President Jefferson asked for a "revision of the laws on the
subject of naturalization," which had been legislated during
the administration of John Adams. Fearing that the denial of
citizenship to newcomers for fourteen years would discourage
immigration to America, Jefferson asked, "Shall oppressed humanity find no asylum on this globe?" But Alexander Hamilton
ridiculed Jefferson's naturalization and immigration demands
by quoting extensively from the Virginian's earlier views on
the subject. With relish, Hamilton noted that in the* Notes on
Virginia *"the man of the people" had warned that immigrants
would destroy "the freest principles of the English Constitution" then enjoyed by all provincials. Moreover, he asserted
that the downfalls of past civilizations had resulted primarily
from the heavy infusion of foreigners. Hamilton's politics also
compelled him to observe that France's existing despotism in*

Source: [6] *The Works of Alexander Hamilton*, Henry Cabot Lodge, ed.
(New York, 1886), III, pp. 236–241.

1801 was the work of a foreigner (Napoleon Bonaparte), and that the attack on freedom of thought in the United States was attributable to another foreigner (Albert Gallatin, Jefferson's Secretary of the Treasury, who was Swiss-born).

January 7, 1802

The next most exceptionable feature in the message, is the proposal to abolish all restriction on naturalization, arising from a previous residence. In this the President is not more at variance with the concurrent maxims of all commentators on popular governments, than he is with himself. The Notes on Virginia are in direct contradiction to the message, and furnish us with strong reasons against the policy now recommended. The passage alluded to is here presented. Speaking of the *population* of America, Mr Jefferson says: "Here I will beg leave to propose a doubt. The present desire of America, is to produce rapid population, by as great *importations of foreigners* as possible. *But is this founded in good policy?"* "Are there no inconveniences to be thrown into the scale, against the advantage expected from a multiplication of numbers, by the *importation of foreigners?* It is for the happiness of those united in society, to harmonize as much as possible, in matters which they must of necessity transact together. Civil government being the sole object of forming societies, its administration must be conducted by common consent. Every species of government has its specific principles. Ours, perhaps, are more peculiar than those of any other in the universe. *It is a composition of the freest principles of the English Constitution,* with others, derived from natural right and reason. To these, nothing can be more opposed than the maxims of absolute monarchies. Yet from such, we are to expect the *greatest number of emigrants. They will bring with them the principles of the governments they leave, imbibed in their early youth; or if able to throw them off, it will be in exchange for the unbounded licentiousness, passing as is usual, from one extreme to another. It would be a miracle were they to stop precisely at the point of temperate liberty. Their principles with their language, they will transmit to their children.* In proportion to their numbers, *they will share with us in the legislation.* They will infuse *into it their spirit, warp and bias its direction, and render it heterogenous, incoherent, distracted mass.* I may appeal to experience, during the present contest, for a verification of these conjectures; but if they be not certain in event, are they not possible, are they not probable? *Is it not safer to wait with patience for the attainment of any degree of population desired or expected?* May not our government be more homogeneous, *more peaceable, more durable?* Suppose twenty millions of republican Americans, thrown all of a sudden into France, what would be the condition of that kingdom? If it would be more turbulent, less happy, less strong, we may believe that the addition of half a million of foreigners, to our present numbers, would produce a similar effect here." Thus wrote Mr Jefferson in 1781—Behold the reverse of the medal. The message of the President contains the following sentiments: "A denial of citizenship under a residence of fourteen years, is a denial to a great proportion of those who ask it, and controls a policy pursued from their first settlement, by many of these States, and *still believed of consequence to their prosperity.* And shall we refuse to the unhappy fugitives from distress, *that hospitality which the savages of the wilderness extended to our fathers arriving in this land?* Shall oppressed humanity find no asylum on this globe? Might not the general character and capabilities of a citizen, be safely communicated to *every one* manifesting a bona-fide purpose of embarking his life and fortune permanently with us?"

But if gratitude can be allowed to form an excuse for inconsistency in a public character—in the *man of the people*—a strong plea of this sort may be urged in behalf of our President. It *is certain,* that had the late election been decided entirely by native citizens, had foreign auxiliaries been rejected on both sides the man who ostentatiously vaunts that the *doors of public honor and confidence have been burst open to him,* would not now have been at the head of the American nation. Such a proof, then, of virtuous discernment in the *oppressed fugitives* had an imperious claim on him to a grateful return, and, without supposing any very uncommon share of *self-love,* would naturally be a strong reason for a revolution in his opinions.

The pathetic and plaintive exclamations by which the senti-ment is enforced might be liable to much criticism, if we are to consider it in any other light than as a flourish of rhetoric. It might be asked in return, Does the right to *asylum or hospital-ity* carry with it the right to *suffrage and sovereignty?* And what, indeed, was the courteous reception which was given to our forefathers by the savages of the wilderness? Why did these humane and philanthropic savages exercise the policy of in-corporating strangers among themselves on their first arrival in the country? When did they admit them into their huts, to make part of their families? and when did they distinguish them by making them their sachems? Our histories and tradi-tions have been more than apocryphal, if any thing like this kind and gentle treatment was really lavished by the much-belied savages upon our thankless forefathers. But the remark obtrudes itself. Had it all been true, prudence requires us to trace the history further and ask what has become of the nation of savages who exercised this policy, and who now occupies the territory which they then inhabited? Perhaps a lesson is here taught which ought not to be despised.

But we may venture to ask, What does the President really mean by insinuating that we treat aliens coming to this country with inhospitality? Do we not permit them quietly to land on our shores? Do we not protect them, equally with our own citizens, in their persons and reputation, in the acquisition and enjoyment of property? Are not our courts of justice open for them to seek redress of injuries? and are they not permitted peaceably to return to their own country whenever they please, and to carry with them all their effects? What, then, means this worse than idle declamation?

The impolicy of admitting foreigners to an immediate and unreserved participation in the right of suffrage, or in the sov-ereignty of a republic, is as much a received axiom as anything in the science of politics, and is verified by the experience of all ages. Among other instances, it is known that hardly any thing contributed more to the downfall of Rome than her precipitate communication of the privileges of citizenship to the inhabitants of Italy at large. And how terribly was Syracuse scourged by perpetual seditions, when, after the overthrow of the tyrants, a great number of foreigners were suddenly admitted to the rights of citizenship? Not only does ancient, but modern, and even domestic, story furnish evidence of what may be expected from the dispositions of foreigners when they get too early a footing in a country. Who wields the sceptre of France, and has erected a despotism on the ruins of her former government? *A foreigner.* Who rules the councils of our own ill-fated, unhappy country? and who stimulates persecution on the heads of its citizens for daring to maintain an opinion, and for daring to exercise the rights of suffrage? A foreigner! Where, then, is the virtuous pride that once distinguished Americans? where the indignant spirit, which, in defence of principle, hazarded a revolution to attain that independence now *insidiously* attacked?

PART 3
The Racism of Bondage, 1800-1860

INTRODUCTION

During the first half of the nineteenth century, the United States extended her borders to the Pacific coast. As the new nation grew, the world witnessed the successful development of the American experiment in the Western Hemisphere, and countries ruled by monarchies became increasingly exposed to America's revolutionary doctrines as expressed in the Declaration of Independence and the Constitution. Thus, the United States was able to vaunt its way of life as an alternative to, and a refuge from, the oppression of European governments.

While equality was an oft-proclaimed cornerstone of their new society, Americans nevertheless advanced the theory that it was their Anglo-Saxon superiority which enabled them to establish their new order. With their motivations cloaked in a self-righteousness of white supremacy and religious eminence, the professed "land of the free" advocated the expansion, by force if necessary, of its civilization, culture, religion, and system of government. Likewise, contrary to its purported ideology of equality, the nation enslaved millions of blacks, murdered and incarcerated its native Indians, embraced scientific racist theories, and sanctioned the anti-Catholic campaigns of the 1840's and 1850's.

In an attempt to apply the principles of 1776 to blacks, a number of humanitarians did express opposition to the practice of chattel slavery and racism. One representative of this rationale was Alexander McLeod, a New York City theologian. In his eloquently written *Negro Slavery Unjustifiable* (1802), he rejected the "inferiority of blacks to whites" and condemned slavery as a "practice . . . contrary to the general principles of the divine law." Although his struggle to re-ignite the anti-slavery movement of the Revolutionary era stirred the consciences of many, it soon became evident that, despite his efforts and those of others like him, the Negro would not yet share in the democratic processes of American society.

In spite of the fact that slavery was based on alleged racial inferiority, most attacks on the institution paradoxically confirmed the claim that whites were innately superior to Negroes. Moreover, many who demanded abolition stipulated that colonization be a condition of manumission. Thus, the American Colonization Society, whose aims epitomized the preponderance of racist anti-slavery thought, "condemned slavery as a sin," and concurrently pledged to deport all blacks, bond and free, to Africa.

With the subsequent failure of colonization as a "practical" solution to the race problem, the slaveholding states enacted legislation which made it almost impossible for a master to manumit his chattel. Recognizing that perpetual servitude would never be abolished voluntarily and requiring the institution as an integral part of their society, the slaveholders began to develop arguments, in addition to those based upon race, to justify slavery. The nation's non-slaveholding racists joined in the anti-Negro campaign, insisting that black subjugation was not inconsistent with America's democratic ideology.

In response to the deepening entrenchment of bondage, the abolitionists intensified their activities. To counter these assaults of the abolitionist societies, the defenders of the institution shifted from their pre-1830 assertion that slavery was a "necessary evil" to advocating, in the three decades prior to the Civil War, that it was a "positive good."

Accordingly, in 1837, Senator John C. Calhoun (D-S. Carolina) advanced the argument that the increase of the slave population was "conclusive proof of the general happiness of the race." In 1856, the "positive good" approach also impelled the religious zealot, Thornton Stringfellow, to preach that slavery was just, because it "was incorporated into the only National Constitution which ever emanated from God."

In addition to the "positive good" approach of Calhoun and Stringfellow, others in the antebellum South utilized the findings of nineteenth-century sociology, biology, and anthropology to justify their position. In their recourse to scientific research (the work done did not emanate solely from the South but was representative of the entire scientific community), the racists associated themselves with some of the nation's most reputable minds.

Though not expressly interested in providing the bigots with a basis for their belief in the inferiority of nonwhites, America's men of science knowingly contributed to the ideology of racist thought. In proclaiming that blacks, as well as Indians, did not possess the inborn intellectual and social capacities of whites, the scientific community became a conscious ally of hatred and oppression. Maintaining that blacks were the lowest order of beings, the scientists concluded that no environmental change could elevate their innately inferior status.

Moreover, with the advent of racist-oriented scientism, the southern slaveholders reasoned that they now had the rationale they needed to affirm that Negro slavery was wholly justifiable. Furthermore, it enabled the nation's non-slaveholding racial extremists to "marry themselves" to the "respectable" arguments which legitimized the inhuman treatment of nonwhites. Therefore, with the exhortation of pseudoscientific theories of racial inferiority, a powerful alliance developed between the advocates of white supremacy and the nation's scientific intellectuals.

In addition to their inquiries on the Negro, the scientific advocates of inequality probed the racial characteristics of the American Indian. They concluded that although the Indian belonged to a higher plane of being than the blacks, he was still subordinate to the whites. Some investigators even suggested that America's "noble savages" were nonhuman, and that all efforts to "civilize" them would be wasted. Consequently, the racism which fostered slavery among blacks also functioned to destroy the nation's original inhabitants.

Scientific beliefs and the general acknowledgment that the Indians were an obstacle to westward expansion propelled the government to intensify its efforts to eliminate them. Thus, with the inception of the westward movement, those who preached the superiority of American civilization promoted plans to remove the Indian to beyond the Mississippi River.

Indeed, in 1830 the United States Government actually passed a law which exiled all surviving eastern Indian tribes, more than twenty nations, to the Far West.

However, when removal plans failed, the Indian-haters were forced to seek new and more drastic methods to deal with the obstruction of the westward trek. Accordingly, in a heightened attempt to open the frontier to the teeming numbers of oppressed Europeans, the American Government, which in 1776 had declared that "all men are created equal," sanctioned a strategy for genocide.

With the subsequent murder of a substantial portion of its Indian population, the United States incarcerated the remainder of the tribes in semi-concentration camps commonly referred to as "reservations." Finally, with its "hostiles" decimated by bullets, disease, severe winters and imprisonment, the frontier was now safe enough for the secure propagation of the "white man's superior civilization."

The first six decades of the nineteenth century not only witnessed a rising tide of racism in the United States, but the period was also marked by the most bitter upsurge of nativism in American history. The major nativist themes prior to 1860 were anti-Catholicism and anti-foreignism. Anti-Catholic sentiment had had a long history dating from pre-Revolutionary America; and with the sudden, sharp increase in immigration in the 1820's it had a strong resurgence. Each succeeding decade from the 1820's to the 1850's witnessed greater numbers of Europeans migrating to the shores of the United States. Although most of the immigrants were Irish Catholics, numerous German Catholics were present in the influx of foreigners to America. Thus, the combination of Catholic and non-Catholic foreigners generated a native unrest in the country.

The flood of Catholic immigrants reaching our shores yearly led to a dramatic growth in the size and prestige of the Catholic Church in America. The rise of the Church, in turn, created resentment and fear among nativists, particularly those who were members of the Protestant clergy. This uneasiness led to a recurrence of religious revivalism and fundamentalism, and served to regenerate nativist emotionalism in Protestant ranks. In addition, the new source of labor competition created by the "foreign invader" came to be bitterly opposed by America's native workers.

The intellectual leadership for the nativist movements was provided by such publicists as James Richardson and the abolitionist, Lyman Beecher. Utilizing anti-Catholic organs such as the New York *Observer* and the *Protestant,* anti-Popery tracts found a ready market in the United States. This rash of anti-Catholic literature which appeared in the 1830's had as its favorite theme the alleged immorality of priests and nuns. The classic American version of the English anti-Catholic novel was Maria Monk's *Awful Disclosures,* which was described by the historian Ray Allen Billington in his book, *The Protestant Crusade,* as the "greatest of the nativistic propaganda works."

The Protestant attack upon two Catholic missionary societies in the 1830's brought nativism to a new peak of furor. Charges were made that the two societies were engaged in a plot, inspired by the Pope and kings of Europe, to seize the United States. It was at this time too that Samuel F. B. Morse took up his pen and became the leading nativist writer. His work, *A Foreign Conspiracy Against the Liberties of the United States,* which was widely reprinted, served to link, as he himself stated, "immigration and Catholicism . . . making both equally objectionable in American eyes."

In addition, state aid to parochial education and the issue of Bible-reading in public schools brought nativist feeling to a fever pitch in 1844. The efforts of Bishop Hughes of New York City to acquire his share of the school fund inspired Bishop Kendrick of Philadelphia to protest the fact that the Protestant Bible was read to Catholic children and that religious exercises were part of public school instruction. The embittered controversy that followed led to one of the bloodiest religious battles of the pre-Civil War period—the Philadelphia or Kensington Riots of 1844.

In the 1850's, immigration reached unprecedented levels. In 1854, over 427,000 immigrants, including more than 100,000 Irish, arrived on American shores. As a direct consequence, nativists began to emphasize the illiteracy, pauperism, criminality, and heavy drinking of the Irish. They appealed to the working classes by turning their attention to charges of unfair labor competition. Native workers became ideal recruits for the nativist labor organizations, such as the Order of United Americans, which flourished in the 1840's and 1850's. The new society was secret and highly patriotic, and it used elaborate handclasps and passwords.

The Know-Nothing Party had its inception in a secret society, started by Charles Allen in 1849, which was known as the Order of the Star Spangled Banner. It lingered for some years under the leadership of James W. Barker, a dry goods merchant. Adopting most of the secret rituals of the Order of United Americans, it played a part in several municipal elections in 1852. Its rapid rise was due to the unusually large influx of immigrants in the mid-1850's, the fragmentation of the existing major parties, and the keen competition between native and immigrant workers in certain job areas. Know-Nothingism achieved dramatic success in the 1854 and 1855 elections. It declined in the late 1850's as a result of the increased agitation over slavery, impending war, and the conversion of many nativists seeking respectability to the Republican Party.

BONDAGE FOREVER: SLAVERY DEFENDED

"What Shall Be Done with Free Negroes?"

George Fitzhugh, influential southern sociologist and social philosopher, was not only a leading advocate of slavery, but was opposed to most of the progressive legislation he witnessed in his lifetime. In his widely read book, Sociology for the South

Source: [1] George Fitzhugh, *What Shall Be Done With Free Negroes?* (Richmond, Va., 1851), pp. 1–6.

or the Failure of Free Society *(1854), he claimed that, due to slavery, white civilization in the American South had developed a unique and extremely high level of culture. Moreover, he affirmed that societies in which all were free were consequently "absurd and impractical."*

In a less known, but equally significant essay, What Shall Be Done With Free Negroes? *he suggested that the "problem" of the existence of free blacks be solved by subjecting them "to some modification of slavery." Fitzhugh asserted that if the free Negro was qualified for liberty, so too was the slave. And to settle the practical problem of the presence of the free black man, and to alleviate the conscience of the slaveholder, he concluded that it was not only "our right, but our duty to cherish and encourage that condition [slavery] of the negro race which works so well—[and] to abolish that which works badly [free blacks]."*

. . . In the United States the situation of the Free Blacks is becoming worse every day. The silly attempts of the abolitionists to put them on a footing of equality with the whites, has exasperated the laboring whites at the North, and excited odium and suspicion against them at the South. The natural antipathies of race have been fanned into such a degree of excitement that the free negro is bandied from pillar to post—from North to South and from South to North, till not a ray of hope is left him of a quiet, permanent residence any where, so long as he remains free. Illinois and California will not permit him to enter their dominions—Ohio places him under severe conditions, and is now moving to expel him altogether, and Virginia also proposes to send him back to Africa. Mobs in our Northern cities drive him from his home and hunt him like a wild beast. Two great movements, or rather one great and one very small movement, may be observed in constant and busy operation as to the negro race. The small movement is that of the fanatical abolitionists, who would free the whole race and put them on a social and political equality with the whites. The great movement is that proceeding from hostility of race, and proposes to get rid of the negroes altogether, not to free them. This movement is not confined to the North.

Thousands, we regret to say at the South, who think slavery a
blessing to the negro, believe the negro a curse to the country.
So far as the slaves are concerned, this opinion is fast changing.
Men begin to look more closely at what the slaveholders have
been doing since our Revolution, and find that they have been
exceeded in skill, enterprise and industry, by no people under
the sun. They have settled a vast territory from the Alleghany
to the La Platte—from the Rio Grande to the Ohio, contending all the while with the blood-thirsty savages and a climate
more to be dreaded than even those savages themselves—and
are already producing a greater agricultural surplus than any
people in the world. They see too, that the condition of the
white man is elevated and equalized, for the blacks perform
all menial duties and occupy the place of servants. The white
laborers of the North think the existence of negroes at the
North as free, or at the South as slaves, injurious to themselves.
They do not like the competition of human beings who have
all the physical powers of men, with the wants only of brutes
—Free Soilism pretty well represents and embodies this feeling. It is universal at the North, because the hostility to negroes
—the wish to get rid of their competition is universal there. It
excludes Free negroes from California as well as slaves, showing that the Wilmot Proviso is directed against the negro race
—not against slavery. This great movement which proposes to
get rid of negroes, rather than of slavery is gathering strength
every day, and so far as the Free negroes are concerned it must
soon sweep them away, for neither the feelings nor the interests of any part of the community, except of a few crazy abolitionists, can be enlisted in their behalf. The slaves have masters
to guard and protect them, and guard, protect and *hold* them
they will, cost what it may.

The Free negroes are no doubt an intolerable nuisance.
They blight the prosperity of every village and of every country
neighborhood where they settle. They are thieves from necessity, for nature has made them so improvident they cannot in
health provide for sickness—in youth for old age—nor in summer for winter. Nature formed them for a climate where all
their wants were supplied abundantly by her liberal hand at
every season. We knew their natures when we set them free.

Should we blame them or censure ourselves? We knew they were not fitted for Liberty, and yet confered Liberty on them. Our wiser ancestors made them slaves because as slaves they might be made civilized, useful and christian beings. We subject children till twenty-one years of age to the control of their parents, or appoint guardians for them. We subject wives to the dominion of their husbands—apprentices to their masters. We permit sailors and soldiers to sell their liberties for terms of years. We send criminals to jail and penitentiaries, and lunatics to hospitals. In all these cases, we take away the liberties of the whites, either for the benefit of the individuals or for the good of society. We act upon the principle that no one is entitled to liberty who will abuse it to the detriment of himself or of others. The *Law* curtails and restricts the freedom of the wisest and the best—the *straight jacket* and *manacles* of iron are applied to the weakest and most wicked. There is no perfect liberty with the whites, and every degree of slavery from law to straight jackets. The free blacks who most need the control of masters, guardians, curators or committees are left to the enjoyment of the largest liberty. *Law* alone is expected to control and regulate their conduct. We had as well publish laws to our herds and flocks. Men to be governed by mere law, must possess great intelligence and have acquired habits of self-control and self-denial. The whites from 15 to 21 years of age lack not intelligence, but habits of self-control to fit them for government by law alone. The arbitrary will of the parent or guardian must be super-added to the mandates of the law, to save them from the indiscretions into which their feelings and their passions would lead them. The free negroes as a class, have less intelligence and less self-control than the whites over 15 years of age. A good government graduates as nicely as is practicable each man's liberty to his capacity for its enjoyment —it is obliged however to establish general rules, and thus occasions many cases of individual hardship. The white male adults over twenty-one years of age are presumed to possess enough of virtue, intelligence and self-control, to be left with no other control than that of the law—yet of those we meet with thousands who from habitual drunkeness, from excessive improvidence and extravagance, or from strong criminal propensities, are wholly unfitted for the government of mere law, and stand in need of the will of a superior to control their conduct, and save them from ruining themselves, their friends and families. On the other hand, we find many instances of wisdom and prudence among whites under 21 years of age, whom the law nevertheless, subjects to the control of guardians and parents often less wise, less virtuous and less prudent than themselves. In subjecting the free blacks to the will of white masters, fewer instances of injustice of this kind would occur than now occur with the whites, because as a class, they are less fitted for self-government than the whites between the ages of 15 and 21. A free negro! Why, the very term seems an absurdity. 'Tis our daily boast and experience verifies it, that the Anglo-Saxons of America are the only people in the world fitted for freedom. The negroes' is not human freedom, but the wild and vicious license of the fox, the wolf or the hawk. He is from the necessity of his nature a very Ishmaelite, whose hand is against every man, and every man's hand is against him. It is as much the duty of government to take away liberty from those who abuse it, as to confer it on those who use it properly. It practices every day, as we have shown, on this principle in its treatment of the whites, and why should it hesitate to do so in regard to the blacks. It is the object and duty of government to protect men not merely from wrong and injustice from others, but from the consequences of their own vices, imprudence and improvidence. The humblest member of society no matter what the color of his skin has a right to this protection. The experience of all ages and of all countries shows that this protection to a weaker race like the negro, living among a superior race, can only be given by bestowing on him a master whose will shall be the law of his conduct, whose skill and foresight shall amass and provide for him in sickness and in old age, and whose power shall shield him from the consequences of his own improvidence. The vassalage and serfdom of Europe—the slavery of America and the peonage of Mexico, alike point to this as the natural and proper method of governing free negroes. The wisdom of the common law, and indeed of all ancient codes, distinctly teaches the same truth; for guardians, parents, husbands, committees, and various officers are but masters by another name. They are all intended to supply in more or less degree, that want of self-control which unfits large classes of the whites for self-government. But there is a peculiar necessity of some measure of this kind, with regard to the blacks, growing out of the antipathies of race. They are threatened with violent extermination. The fate of the Indians shows that they will be exterminated if they continue so useless and so troublesome. Had the Indian been useful as a slave he would have survived and become a civilized and christian being; but he was found as useless, as troublesome and as intractable as a beast of prey, and has shared the fate of a beast of prey. The negro in the condition of slavery is a happy, contented and useful being. 'Tis the state for which nature intended, and to which our ancestors quite as wise and virtuous as ourselves consigned him. We have fully and fairly tried the experiment of freeing him—we have witnessed its universal and deplorable failure, and it is now our right and our duty to listen to the voice of wisdom and experience, and reconsign him to the only condition for which he is suited.

There is another and an urgent reason why his very existence requires that he should be subjected to some modification of slavery. His lot is cast among the Anglo-Saxon race, and what people can stand free competition with that race. The Romans conquered England and the ancient Britons flourished and became civilized under their rule. The Saxon, Dane and Norman came, and nothing remains to tell of the existence of the Britons but the names of a few rivers. The Indian is exterminated from Maine to Georgia—the Indoos are perishing under British rule by millions—the Spaniard is hardly heard of in Florida, and Peonage alone can save the Mexican from annihilation. From the days of Hengist and Horsa to those of Houston the same adventurous, rapacious, exterminating spirit has characterized the race. Can the negro live with all his reckless improvidence under the shade of this Upas tree, whose deadly poison spares no other race? Is he fitted to compete with a people who, in the struggle of life, have outstripped and exterminated all other nations with whom they have come in contact? No. Throwing out of view, the signs of the times, pregnant with growing hate and hostility to the free negro, the experience of the past shows that his present condition is hopeless; but make him property and this same Anglo-Saxon will protect, guard and cherish him—for no people on earth love property more—will go to greater lengths, so far as danger is concerned to obtain it, or take better care of it after it is obtained.

We will not undertake to decide what degree or modification of servitude shall be adopted, but will suggest that peonage which is probably one of its mildest forms, might be instituted. To attain this, it is only necessary to repeal so much of the common law as prevents a man's parting with his personal liberty. Indeed, the common law, in the cases of soldiers and sailors, permits even white men to sell themselves and bind their person for a term of years. Grant the same privilege to the Free negro at all times, and we think there will be few of them left free in ten years to come. They cannot now, we know from experience, obtain much more than half the yearly hire of slaves, because the hirer has no security that they will remain till the end of the year. Their improvidence and their desire to obtain the protection of some white man, would drive them all into contracts of this kind. The nuisance would thus be abated and in its place we should acquire a class of strong and healthy laborers. If this plan did not work well, the State authorities should at the beginning of each year, hire all those out who owned not enough property to support themselves. Part of the hires might be paid over to them and the balance retained as a fund to support the infants, the aged and infirm here, or used as a means to send them all to Africa. If experience showed that nothing short of absolute slavery would meet the exigencies of the case, then give them a year's notice to quit the State, or be sold into unconditional slavery. This last alternative would still place them in a situation of much greater security and comfort than they now anywhere enjoy, or can ever probably enjoy in a state of unlimited freedom. We think it a more humane measure and a more politic one than to send them to Africa. If it be necessary, it must be right. Reducing men to slavery has been practiced throughout all time, and by men as good and as wise as ourselves. Practiced too, continually, upon men, much better, much wiser, and much more suited for freedom than the negroes. There is more of selfish-

ness, less of exalted, chivalrous disinterested virtue in this
utilitarian age, than in most of those with which we are acquainted, that have preceded it. We only

> Compound for sins *we* are inclined to,
> by damning those *we* have no mind to.

Liberty is the great hobby of this money-making age, and
the overruling argument in its favor is borrowed from the arithmetic. "Free labor is more productive than slave labor. It is
cheaper to hire the laborer when you want him and turn him
out to starve when you have done with him, than to buy a slave
and support him through all the seasons of the year, and
through all the periods of his life. Besides, the free man whose
very life depends on it, will work harder than the slave, who
is sure of a support, whether he works or not." Since the slave-
trade is abolished, which was a lucrative and favorite pursuit
of the Yankees and English, those gentry have from the above
interested calculations turned abolishionists. Our Southern
patriots at the time of the Revolution finding negroes expen-
sive and useless, became warm anti-slavery men. We, their
wiser sons, having learned to make cotton and sugar, find
slavery very useful and profitable, and think it a most excellent
institution. We of the South advocate slavery, no doubt, from
just as selfish motives, as induce the Yankees and English to
deprecate it. We have however, almost all human and divine
authority on one side of the argument. The Bible no where
condemns, and throughout recognises slavery. Slavery has been
so universal in the civilized world, and so little, if at all known
among savages, that its occasional absence of later years in
civilized nations, seems to indicate something wrong or rotten
in their condition. The starving state of the poor in all such
countries furnishes the solution of the difficulty and indicates
the character of the disease under which society is suffering.
They have become too poor to have slaves whom the law would
oblige them to support. We have never met with a Southern
man *of late years,* who did not think slavery a blessing to the
negro race. We have never heard a single white man maintain
that this race was qualified for freedom, nor with one who did
not complain of the free negroes as a nuisance. Now, how

strange and inconsistent in us to permit men to remain free whose freedom is a curse to themselves and a nuisance to society. How cruel and unwise in us not to extend this blessing of slavery to the free negroes, which works so well with the slaves. Humanity, self-interest, consistency, all require that we should enslave the free negro. We enslave the whites whenever the good of the individual or of society requires it in the many instances we have cited, and leave the free negro to roam at large in liberty as untrammelled and unconstrained as that of the beasts of the field or birds of the air. They are restrained neither by the conventionalities of society, the bonds of religion, the laws of morality, the chain of marriage, the authority of parents or guardians, nor by the power of a master. They who are least fitted for liberty are scarcely subjected to any government control whatever.

But if *they* be qualified for liberty, so are our slaves, and we are acting morally wrong in retaining in bondage, beings who would be better off as freemen. The slaves if set free, would be just what the free negroes now are, and if that be a desirable condition, one better for them, and for society than that they are now in, we ought to set about making free negroes of them. Both cases are before us—we have ample experience of the working of both. It is not only our right, but our duty to cherish and encourage that condition of the negro race which works well—to abolish that which works badly.

The free negroes corrupt our slaves and make them less contented with their situation. Their competition is injurious to our white laboring citizens. Their wants are so few and simple that when they do work, they will take lower wages than the white man can afford to receive; besides it is as well the policy as the duty of the State to elevate the condition of her citizens, not to send them in the labor market with negroes for competitors. Let the negro always occupy a situation subordinate to the white man. North and South, every deviation from this policy leads to violence, in which the blacks are the sufferers. The law cannot make negroes free if it would, because society will not tolerate it. The signs of the times North and South clearly show that the free negroes will be borne with no longer by society. If the subject be promptly attended to by State governments, some disposition of them may be made consistent with humanity. If legislative action be delayed, the people in their primary capacity, in vulgar parlance, mobs will take the case in hand. We heard but recently that the people in one of our counties had given them notice to quit. Quit! and go where? To be turned out and hunted like the bagged fox.

James Henry Hammond and the "Mud-Sill" of Society

In 1858, one of the central issues concerning the Congress of the United States was the admission of Kansas to the federal union. In opposition to its entering as a slave state, William H. Seward of New York delivered an anti-slavery speech before the United States Senate. The charges that Seward made, however, did not rest unanswered. On the following day, the South Carolina pro-slavery advocate, James Henry Hammond, rose to defend the institution. In the course of his speech, the slave-holding senator referred to the Negro as the "mud-sill" of society, who was destined to function as "a class to do the menial duties, [and] to perform the drudgery of life."

In his popular "mud-sill" speech, Hammond enlarged on several of the major pro-slavery concepts. He reemphasized the ideas of "King Cotton," northern "wage slavery," and Negro inferiority.

Although the viewpoints presented by Hammond were not originally his, the speech affords readers an opportunity to survey the pro-slavery rhetoric of the antebellum South.

. . . But if there were no other reason why we should never have a war, would any sane nation make war on cotton? Without firing a gun, without drawing a sword, when they make war on us we can bring the whole world to our feet. The South is perfectly competent to go on, one, two, or three years without planting a seed of cotton. I believe that if she was to plant but

Source: [2] *United States Congressional Globe,* 35th Cong. 1st Sess., pp. 961–962.

half her cotton, it would be an immense advantage to her. I
am not so sure but that after three years' cessation she would
come out stronger than ever she was before and better prepared
to enter afresh upon her great career of enterprise. What would
happen if no cotton was furnished for three years? I will not
stop to depict what every one can imagine, but this is certain:
old England would topple headlong and carry the whole civilized world with her. No, sir, you dare not make war on cotton.
No power on earth dares make war upon it. Cotton is king.
Until lately the Bank of England was king, but she tried to put
her screws as usual, the fall before last, upon the cotton crop,
and was utterly vanquished. The last power has been conquered. Who can doubt it that has looked at recent events?
When the abuse of credit had destroyed credit and annihilated
confidence, when thousands of the strongest commercial houses
in the world were coming down, and hundreds of millions of
dollars of supposed property evaporating in thin air, when you
came to a dead lock, and revolutions were threatened, what
brought you up? Fortunately for you it was the commencement
of the cotton season, and we have poured in upon you one
million six hundred thousand bales of cotton just at the crisis
to save you from sinking. That cotton, but for the bursting of
your speculative bubbles in the North, which produced the
whole of this convulsion, would have brought us $100,000,000.
We have sold it for $65,000,000, and saved you. Thirty-five
million dollars we, the slaveholders of the South, have put into
the charity box of your magnificent financiers, your cotton
lords, your merchant princes.

But, sir, the greatest strength of the South arises from the
harmony of her political and social institutions. This harmony
gives her a frame of society, the best in the world, and an
extent of political freedom, combined with entire security, such
as no other people ever enjoyed upon the face of the earth.
Society precedes government; creates it, and ought to control
it; but as far as we can look back in historic times we find the
case different; for government is no sooner created than it becomes too strong for society, and shapes and molds, as well as
controls it. In later centuries the progress of civilization and
of intelligence has made the divergence so great as to produce

civil wars and revolutions; and it is nothing now but the want of harmony between governments and societies which occasions all the uneasiness and trouble and terror that we see abroad. It was this that brought on the American Revolution. We threw off a Government not adapted to our social system, and made one for ourselves. The question is, how far have we succeeded? The South, so far as that is concerned, is satisfied, content, happy, harmonious, and prosperous.

In all social systems, there must be a class to do the mean duties, to perform the drudgery of life, that is, a class requiring but a low order of intellect and but little skill. Its requisites are vigor, docility and fidelity. Such a class you must have, or you would not have that other class which leads progress, refinement and civilization. It constitutes the very mud-sills of society and of political government; and you might as well attempt to build a house in the air, as to build either the one or the other, except on the mud-sills. Fortunately for the South, she found a race adapted to that purpose to her hand. A race inferior to herself, but eminently qualified in temper, in vigor, in docility, in capacity to stand the climate, to answer all her purposes. We use them for the purpose, and call them slaves. We are old-fashioned at the South yet; it is a word discarded now by ears polite; but I will not characterize that class at the North with that term; but you have it; it is there; it is everywhere; it is eternal.

The Senator from New York said yesterday that the whole world had abolished slavery. Ay, the name, but not the thing; and all the powers of the earth cannot abolish it. God only can do it when he repeals the *fiat*, "the poor ye always have with you"; for the man who lives by daily labor, and scarcely lives at that, and who has to put out his labor in the market and take the best he can get for it; in short, your whole class of manual laborers and operatives, as you call them, are slaves. The difference between us is, that our slaves are hired for life and well compensated; there is no starvation, no begging, no want of employment among our people, and not too much employment either. Yours are hired by the day, not cared for, and scantily compensated, which may be proved in the most deplorable manner, at any hour, in any street in any of your large towns. Why, sir, you meet more beggars in one day, in any single street of the city of New York, than you would meet in a lifetime in the whole South. Our slaves are black, of another inferior race. The *status* in which we have placed them is an elevation. They are elevated from the condition in which God first created them, by being made our slaves. None of that race on the whole face of the globe can be compared with the slaves of the South and they know it. They are happy, content, unaspiring, and utterly incapable, from intellectual degradation, ever to give us any trouble by their aspirations.

Your slaves are white, of your own race; you are brothers of one blood. They are your equals in natural endowment of intellect, and they feel galled by their degradation. Our slaves do not vote. We give them no political power. Yours do vote, and being the majority, they are the depositaries of all your political power. If they knew the tremendous secret, that the ballot-box is stronger than an army with bayonets, and could combine where would you be? Your society would be reconstructed, your government reconstructed, your property divided, not as they have mistakenly attempted to initiate such proceedings by meeting in parks, with arms in their hands, but by the quiet process of the ballot-box. You have been making war upon us to our very hearthstones. How would you like for us to send lecturers or agitators North, to teach these people this, to aid and assist in combining, and to lead them?

ANTI-SLAVERY RACISM EXPOSED!

From the official publication of the American Colonization Society

The American Colonization Society was established in 1817 for the express purpose of deporting both free Negroes and

Source: [3] "Amalgamation of Races," *The Colonizationist and Journal of Freedom* (June, 1833), pp. 102–106.

slaves to Africa. The Society's sole route to emancipation was through colonization. The initial impulse for colonization originated in the slave states, and by 1826 the various colonization societies numbered well over one hundred. By 1831, however, the movement had reached its peak, and it slowly declined in the ensuing years.

Although the motives for colonization had been thought to be humanitarian, some individuals, such as abolitionist William Lloyd Garrison, recognized that "in making the banishment of the slaves the condition of their emancipation, [it inflicted] upon them an aggravat[ed] wrong, perpetuated their thraldom, and disregard[ed] the claims of everlasting and immutable justice." Garrison further concluded that emancipation tied to colonization denied "the right of the slaves to enjoy freedom and happiness in this country," and that this denial tended "to rivet their fetters more firmly, [and] make them the victims of a relentless persecution."

In the article reprinted below from the official publication of the American Colonization Society, the writer makes it quite clear that racism was the prime motivation for eliminating all Negroes (both bond and free) from American soil.

. . . Let us look. Let us listen to the silent though powerful voice of nature, and ask ourselves if she does not forbid our union with the blacks. So far as human institutions have any thing to do with a moral and physical change like this, the laws of the land, of every State in the Union, forbid marriage between the two races which people it. If any such change is ever to be made, it can only be effected by reversing law, by outraging nature, by altering education and setting history at nought. The miseries which the country could have to undergo, during such momentous revolutions, should deter all men from prosecuting a theory which they cannot prove to be based upon moral certainty, and even such success as the wildest visionary can imagine, would never pay for the human blood and human suffering by which it can alone be effected. It is certain to my mind, that the change could only, if ever, be effected by violence, and this is proved by the course of some of the opponents of colonization in exasperating rather than conciliating in teaching the black to consider himself in a land of enemies, in which they are their only friends. When their principles become dominant, God protect the whites, for their safety will be beyond human power.

No augury can be drawn favorable to the ultimate success of amalgamation from the progress which it has hitherto made. The very cases of marriage between black and white persons, have been met with a general burst of indignation and horror wherever they have been reported, and we think that such a reception is ominous of the future.

'As coming events cast their shadows before,' it is reasonable to suppose that such a momentous change as this, would, if it is to be peaceably effected, be preceded by some signs of amelioration in the condition of the blacks. But even in this country, where liberty is the pole star of the patriot, and equality the alarm-cry of the demagogue, not a step has been taken towards such a change. The lot of the African is as hard now as ever, and it is even natural to suppose his condition will in time to come, be rendered worse rather than better, because the policy of the Southern States, dictated by their fears of the increase of the colored population, is continually imposing new restrictions and burdens upon it, so that in the slave-holding States, life itself is a tax upon the African, bond or free. The result of this policy is to drive the free blacks to the North; and the time will come, long before their condition is so ameliorated as to make their existence a blessing to the country, when we shall be obliged to put checks upon their immigration even for our own protection.

As for the present state of the free blacks, they neither possess present power nor the elements of future improvement. Our merchants, our farmers, our mechanics, our professional men, our instructors both of learning and religion, belong, with very few exceptions, to our own favored race. There is little inclination in the mass of the people of that race to extend a participation of their advantages to those whom they unjustly deem to be of an inferior caste, when they are in fact only to be justified in saying that they are of a different one.

Here then we leave this branch of the question, satisfied in our own mind, as we hope others may be, that this method of domesticating the blacks, and at the same time rendering them justice, can never be brought to a happy consummation.

Let us consider more briefly, whether the prospect of retaining them here as a separate people, with equal rights with ourselves, is a more hopeful one. Such a system has not been very strongly or very seriously urged; but it has a few supporters, whose names are a sufficient guaranty that the views which they advocate deserve consideration. It appears to us that a plan like this is a political chimera. It presents us at once with that monster which all nations, in all ages, have contended against, the *imperium in imperio,* the empire within an empire, the wheel within a wheel. Let us appeal again to history. We find that the existence of two equal or independent people on the same soil, has always been the cause of exterminating wars. Such were the cases already mentioned of the Spaniards and Moors, and the Americans and Europeans. Such has been the case in the East Indies, where the natives have urged an incessant partisan warfare upon the Europeans, and from whence every ship brings an account of a massacre. But, to confine ourselves to Europe, let us look at a few instances where this principle has prevailed, and see the effects to which it has led. . . . Is it to be expected then, that such a state of things can ever be endured in America? It appears to us that all reasons which could oppose it in other countries, apply with greater force here; and that the marked distinctions between us and the African, will increase ten fold all animosities which must be occasioned by the clashing of interests of people who, though inhabiting the safe soil, are perfectly distinct in their relations and political rights.

It seems to us, that in such a state of affairs, there would be two governments in our land, neither of them subordinate to the other, both equal, and what is worse, both supreme. Every thing in nature seems to oppose this divided dominion. It follows, almost of course, that when two equal powers are exerted in the same field, there they will be in opposition to each other. Even inanimate nature proves it to us. How then can it be expected that two nations inflamed by the remembrance of former servitude, on one side, and the remembrance of former dominion on the other, can ever be at rest in so close a proximity. Innumerable causes of jealousy will arise; and jealousy will even exist without cause, and every citizen will be placed on a mine, with countless thousands and millions of fiery sparks flying over and around it, any one of which should it happen to fall, will involve him, his country, his friend and his foe, in one indiscriminate and irretrievable equality of ruin.

It appears then to us, that until the African is relieved from the blighting presence of European Society and Institutions, he must continue to be the degraded and wretched being that he is. The Colonization Society points out the way, and, so far as its limited funds enable it, affords the means of effecting this change; and its plan is the only remaining one which appears to be practicable.

It is however objected that this offer is not made equally to all, to the slave as well as the freeman; and those who are determined to ruin the Society, *per fas aut nefas,* right or wrong, draw the very forced conclusion, that the Society is inimical to liberty. It avails not to assert, both in profession and in practice, that the freedom of the African is one of the dearest objects of the association. The charge is reiterated in the face of every fact, and in defiance of the characters of some of the greatest and best philanthropists in the Union, who have identified themselves with this Institution.

It is most true that the Colonization Society does not offer the opportunity of emigration directly to the slave, while he remains one, and for the simple reason, that such an offer is wholly out of its power. By the original compact formed between the people of the several States, and by subsequent legislation, the possession of negro slaves has been guaranteed to the Southern States. It is now too late for us to say whether the compact was a wise one, or whether, in the language used by a distinguished statesman in the last session of Congress, "it would be made if the bargain were to be struck again." It is manifest that, while the federal compact subsists in its present form, to make attacks upon slave property, is a violation of that compact. When it is rescinded, and then only, can we interfere with the Institutions of our neighbors.

As the Society places its hopes of ultimate success upon the popularity, the confidence, and the moral influence which it will one day obtain, it manifestly ought to do nothing to destroy that confidence, or to make any portion of the Union believe that it will act in violation of public order, or public law, or in subversion of the vested enjoyment of recognized property. It wishes to act under the sanction and within the pale of the laws of the land. It wishes to abolish slavery not by bloodshed, not by forcibly severing the slave from his master, but by the conviction on the mind of the master that it is for his interest to relinquish the slave.

Even were it practicable or lawful to emancipate by one act the whole of our slave population, still in our opinion it would be utterly inexpedient. The time is not yet ripe for total emancipation. Imagination can hardly conceive a greater evil that could befall our Southern brethren—not to mention our own case—than such a measure. Let us picture to ourselves nearly three millions of human beings without property, without education, suddenly left to their own resources, deprived by the same act of the means of subsistence, and of the right of demanding it from any other persons. What peace, what security can then exist, south of the Potomac. The demands of nature will and must be satisfied; and if a starving and lawless population cannot obtain food and shelter in any other way, they will turn every village into a desert, and every house into a funeral pyre, in the accomplishment of their object. Even their gladness for recovered freedom, would be sufficient to convert such a population into murderers. It is urged that a spirit of gratitude will keep the newly emancipated blacks in quiet. But such is not the course of nature. All bodies of men under sudden and immense changes are ungovernable. The fervid spirit of liberty worked so strongly, when the orderly people of Massachusetts were delivered from the comparatively easy burdens of the British supremacy, that it broke out in tumults and insurrections, which endangered the existence of the Commonwealth. And can it be expected that better rule may be kept with a people acknowledging no law but their own feelings, when disenthralled, and placed within the reach of those whom education and habit have ever taught them to consider as their direst foes?

We dread and deprecate, then, the extension of the principles of those who, opposed both to slavery and Colonization, would let loose the slaves like wild beasts, to desolate and possess the land. We have not arrived at such a sickly pitch of philanthropy, as to advocate a measure which would certainly lead to the extermination of one of the parties at the South, and would leave the other in a deplorable state of weakness and distress, merely because every man having an abstract right to freedom, that right should be carried into immediate fruition, be the consequences what they may. In point of fact, the whole composition of society is based upon the relinquishment or violation of abstract rights. The power of inheritance is in derogation of that abstract right of the living which takes all control of property from the dead; and leaves it for the enjoyment of the first occupant. Punishment also is a violation of the abstract right, in virtue of which no one man is answerable to others for his injustice to a third. But do we therefore, leave the criminal merely to the vengeance of God? Men always run into absurdities when they act on abstract principles, without taking into consideration the existing circumstances which modify or control them. If we insist on the enforcement of all abstract rights, we must go back to a state of nature, to which the only road lies through as many centuries of anarchy, as have been necessary to bring mankind from the state of nature to that of civilization.

For ourselves we have no fears of the difficulty of emancipation. We consider it one of the least obstacles with which the Society has to contend. We are willing to believe and hope, that slavery among the best and most intelligent Southern men, is looked upon as an enormous evil, and crying injustice; and that it is still supported because of the belief of the utter impracticability of getting rid of it. When the Colonization Society has sufficiently developed the means for obtaining this end, there can be no doubt that the southern masters will gladly contribute their aid to relieve themselves from their burdens. This is abundantly demonstrated by the experience of the last few years, as it is well known that the Colonization Society has been obliged to refuse hundreds of emancipated slaves offered to them by their masters for the purpose of transportation to Liberia, on account of the low state of their finances.

Until this difficulty is removed, the operations of the Society cannot be very much extended, and its success in its limited sphere will only serve to point out the way and demonstrate the practicability of rational, humane, and universal emancipation.

THE GENTEEL SCIENCE OF RACISM

Slavery in the Light of Ethnology

Samuel A. Cartwright was a prominent New Orleans physician and scientist. As an influential contributor to the pseudoscience of race, he presented "proof" of the Negroes' alleged inferiority from his research. He maintained that the distinctive characteristics of the black race proved that "subordination to the white race is its normal condition," that "social and political equality is abnormal to it, whether educated or not." He also concluded that the "same ordinance which keeps the spheres in their orbits and holds the satellites in subordination to the planets is the ordinance that subjects the negro race to the empire of the white man's will."

Cartwright, by accepting without question the theory of the origins of man, was impelled to concentrate the greater part of his "scientific" research on proving that the African, as a separate species, was the best suited of all beings for a permanently subservient role in white society.

Although there were numerous scientists, such as John H. Van Evrie, Josiah Nott and Louis Agassiz who engaged in similar research, Cartwright's book, Natural History of the Prognathous Species of Mankind *(1857), was one of the most*

Source: [4] Samuel Cartwright, "On the Caucasians and the Africans," reprinted in E. N. Elliott, *Cotton Is King, and Pro-Slavery Arguments* (Augusta, Ga., 1860), pp. 717–722.

blatant examples of racist-oriented science in the antebellum period.

. . . The Nilotic monuments furnish numerous portraits of the negro races, represented as slaves, sixteen hundred years before the Christian era. Although repeatedly drawn from their native barbarism and carried among civilized nations, they soon forget what they learn and relapse into barbarism. If the inherent potency of the prognathous type of mankind had been greater than it actually is, sufficiently great to give it the independence of character that the American Indian possesses, the world would have been in a great measure deprived of cotton and sugar. The red man is unavailable as a laborer in the cane or cotton field, or anywhere else, owing to the unalterable ethnical laws of his character. The white man can not endure toil under the burning sun of the cane and cotton field, and live to enjoy the fruits of his labor. The African will starve rather than engage in a regular system of agricultural labor, unless impelled by the stronger will of the white man. When thus impelled, experience proves that he is much happier, during the hours of labor in the sunny fields, than when dozing in his native woods and jungles. He is also eminently qualified for a number of employments, which the instincts of the white man regard as degrading. If the white man be forced by necessity into employments abhorrent to his instincts, it tends to weaken or destroy the sentiment or principle of honor or duty, which is the mainspring of heroic actions from the beginning of historical times to the present, and is the basis of everything great and noble in all grades of white society.

The importance of having these particular employments, regarded as servile and degrading by the white man, attended to by the black race, whose instincts are not repugnant to them, will be at once apparent to all those who deem the sentiment of honor or duty as worth cultivating in the human breast. It is utterly unknown to the prognathous race of mankind, and has no place in their language. When the language is given to them they can not comprehend its meaning, or form a conception of what is meant by it. Every white man, who has not been degraded, had rather be engaged in the most laborious employments, than to serve as a lacquey or body servant to another white man or being like himself. Whereas, there is no office which the negro or mulatto covets more than that of being a body servant to a real gentleman. There is no office which gives him such a high opinion of himself, and it is utterly impossible for him to attach the idea of degradation to it. Those identical offices which the white man instinctively abhors, are the most greedily sought for by negroes and mulattoes, whether slave or free, in preference to all other employments. North or South, free or slave, they are ever at the elbow, behind the table, in hotels and steamboats; ever ready, with brush in hand, to brush the coat or black the shoes, or to perform any menial service which may be required, and to hold out the open palm for the dime. The innate love to act as body servant or lacquey is too strongly developed in the negro race to be concealed. It admirably qualifies them for waiters and house servants, as their strong muscles, hardy frames, and the positive pleasure that labor in a hot sun confers on them, abundantly qualify them for agricultural employment in a hot climate.

Hence, the primordial cell germ of the Nigritians has no more potency than what is sufficient to form a being with physical power, when its dynamism becomes exhausted, dropping the creature in the wilderness with the mental organization too imperfect to enable him to extricate himself from barbarism. If nature had intended the prognathous race for barbarism as the end and object of their creation, they would have been like lions and tigers, fierce and untamable. So far from being like ferocious beasts, they are endowed with a will so weak, passions so easily subdued, and dispositions so gentle and affectionate, as readily to fall under subjection to the wild Arab, or any other race of men. Hence they are led about in gangs of a hundred or more by a single individual, even by an old man, or a cripple, if he be of the white race and possessed of a strong will. The Nigritian has such little command over his own muscles, from the weakness of his will, as almost to starve, when a little exertion and forethought would procure him an abundance. Although he has exaggerated appetites and exaggerated senses. calling loudly for their gratification, his will is too weak to command his muscles to engage in such kinds of labor as would readily procure the fruits to gratify them. Like an animal in a state of hibernation, waiting for the external aid of spring to warm it into life and power, so does the negro continue to doze out a vegeto-animal existence in the wilderness, unable to extricate himself therefrom—his own will being too feeble to call forth the requisite muscular exertion. His muscles not being exercised, the respiration is imperfect, and the blood is imperfectly vitalized. Torpidity of body and hebetude of mind are the effects thereof, which disappear under bodily labor, because that expands the lungs, vitalizes the blood, and wakes him up to a sense of pleasure and happiness unknown to him in the vegeto-animal or hibernating state. Nothing but will is wanting to transform the torpid, unhappy tenant of the wilderness into a rational and happy thing—the happiest being on earth, as far as sensual pleasures are concerned.

The white man has an exaggerated will more than he has use for; because it frequently drives his own muscles beyond their physical capacity of endurance. The will is not a faculty confined within the periphery of the body. It can not, like the imagination, travel to immeasurable distances from the body, and in an instant of time go and return from Aldabaran, or beyond the boundaries of the solar system. Its flight is confined to the world and to limits more or less restricted—the less restricted in some than in others. The will has two powers—direct and indirect. It is the direct motive power of the muscular system. It indirectly exerts a dynamic force upon surrounding objects when associated with knowledge. It gives to knowledge its power. Everything that is made was made by the Infinite Will associated with infinite knowledge. The will of man is but a spark of the Infinite Will, and its power is only circumscribed by its knowledge. A man possessing a knowledge of the negro character can govern a hundred, a thousand, or ten thousand of the prognathous race by his will alone, easier than one ignorant of that character can govern a single individual of that race by the whip or a club. However disinclined to labor the negroes may be, they can not help themselves; they are obliged to move and to exercise their muscles when the white man, acquainted with their character, *wills* that they should do so. They can not resist that will, so far as labor of body is concerned.

If they resist, it is from some other cause than that connected with their daily labor. They have an instinctive feeling of obedience to the stronger will of the white man, requiring nothing more than moderate labor. So far, their instincts compel obedience to will as one of his rights. Beyond that, they will resist his will and be refractory, if he encroaches on what they regard as their rights, viz: the right to hold property in him as he does in them, and to disburse that property to them in the shape of meat, bread and vegetables, clothing, fuel and house-room, and attention to their comforts when sick, old, infirm, and unable to labor; to hold property in him as a conservator of the peace among themselves, and a protector against trespassers from abroad, whether black or white; to hold property in him as impartial judge and an honest jury to try them for offenses, and a merciful executioner to punish them for violations of the usages of the plantation or locality.

With those rights acceded to them, no other compulsion is necessary to make them perform their daily tasks than *his will be done*. It is not the whip, as many suppose, which calls forth those muscular exertions, the result of which is sugar, cotton, breadstuffs, rice and tobacco. These are products of the white man's will, acting through the muscles of the prognathous race in our Southern States. If that will were withdrawn, and the plantations handed over as a gracious gift to the laborers, agricultural labor would cease for the want of that spiritual power called the will, to move those machines—the muscles. They would cease to move here, as they have in Hayti. If the prognathous race were expelled the land, and their place supplied with double their number of white men, agricultural labor in the South would also cease, as far as sugar and cotton are concerned, for the want of muscles that could endure exercise in the smothering heat of a cane or cotton field. Half the white laborers of Illinois are prostrated with fevers from a few days' work in stripping blades in a Northern corn field, owing to the confinement of the air by the close proximity of the plants. Cane and cotton plants form a denser foliage than corn—a thick jungle, where the white man pants for breath, and is overpowered by the heat of the sun at one time of day, and chilled by the dews and moisture of the plants at another. Negroes glory in a close, hot atmosphere; they instinctively cover their head and faces with a blanket at night, and prefer laying with their heads to the fire, instead of their feet. This ethnical peculiarity is in harmony with their efficiency as laborers in hot, damp, close, suffocating atmosphere—where instead of suffering and dying, as the white man would, they are healthier, happier, and more prolific than in their native Africa—producing, under the white man's will, a great variety of agricultural products, besides upward of three millions of bales of cotton, and three hundred thousand hogsheads of sugar. Thus proving that subjection to his will is normal to them, because, under the influence of his will, they enjoy life more than in any other condition, rapidly increase in numbers, and steadily rise in the scale of humanity.

The power of a stronger will over a weaker or the power of one living creature to act on and influence another, is an ordinance of nature, which has its parallel in the inorganic kingdom, where ponderous bodies, widely separated in space, influence one another so much as to keep up a constant interplay of action and reaction throughout nature's vast realms. The same ordinance which keeps the spheres in their orbits and holds the satellites in subordination to the planets, is the ordinance that subjects the negro race to the empire of the white man's will. From that ordinance the snake derives its power to charm the bird, and the magician his power to amuse the curious, to astonish the vulgar, and to confound the wisdom of the wise. Under that ordinance, our four millions of negroes are as unalterably bound to obey the white man's will, as the four satellites of Jupiter the superior magnetism of that planet. If individual masters, by releasing individual negroes from the power of their will, can not make them free or release them from subordination to the instinctive public sentiment or will of the aggregate white population, which as rigidly excludes them, in the so-called free States, from the drawing room and parlor as it does pots and kettles and other kinds of kitchen furniture. The subjugation of equals by artifice or force is tyranny or slavery; but there is no such thing in the United States, because equals are on a perfect equality here. The subordination of the Nigritian to the Caucasian would never have been imagined to be a condition similar to European slavery, if any regard had been paid to ethnology. Subordination of the inferior race to the superior is a normal, and not a forced condition. Chains and standing armies are the implements used to force the obedience of equals to equals—of one white man to another. Whereas, the obedience of the Nigritian to the Caucasian is *spontaneous* because it is normal for the weaker will to yield obedience to the stronger. The ordinance which subjects the negro to the empire of the white man's will, was plainly written on the heavens during our Revolutionary war. It was then that the power of the united will of the American people rose to its highest degree of intensity.

A Scientist on the Education of Blacks

John H. Van Evrie, Washington, D.C., physician and New York City publisher, subscribed to the scientific racist ideology of the mid-nineteenth century which affirmed that the Negro belonged to a lower order of man. In his major contribution to the literature of scientific racism, he suggested that what was needed instead of a defense of slavery was a demonstration "to the senses, as well as the reason, that the negro is a different and subordinate being."

In his book, Negroes and Negro "Slavery": The First an Inferior Race: The Latter Its Normal Condition *(1853), the well-known doctor discussed the various aspects of the alleged biological and mental inferiority of the black race. Although black intellectual achievement had been displayed in the poetry of Phyllis Wheatley, in the mathematics of Benjamin Banneker, and in the oratory of Frederick Douglass, Van Evrie concluded that the mental powers of the Negro were "unable to grapple with science or philosophy, or abstractions of any kind." Moreover, it "would be folly to suppose that he would be or could be interested in history or biography, in which his race, his*

Source: [5] John H. Van Evrie, *Negroes and Negro "Slavery": The First an Inferior Race: The Latter Its Normal Condition,* 2nd ed. (New York, 1861), pp. 215–222.

instincts, his wants have no share, record, or connection what-ever."

EDUCATION OF NEGROES

The *fact* that the negro is a negro, carries with it the inference or the necessity that his education—the cultivation of his faculties, or the development of his intelligence—must be in harmony with itself, and therefore must be an entirely different thing from the education of the Caucasian. The term education, in regard to our own race, has widely different significations. It may be the mere development of the mind, or it may mean, with the cultivation of the intellect, the formation of the character, as Pope says:

'Tis education forms the common mind;
Just as the twig is bent, the tree's inclined.

But within restricting the term to the former limit—the development of the intelligence—it will be found that the education of the negro at the South is in entire harmony with his wants, the character of his mind, the necessities of his mental organism; and that they are the best educated negro population ever known in human experience.

Common sense and experience teach us to educate all creatures committed to our charge in accordance with their wants. No one would presume to teach a horse as he would a dog, or any other animal. We have our schools for girls as well as for boys, and the education varies continually as the child changes into youth, adolescence, and finally into manhood. The nature and condition of the pupil are the great central facts—whether a horse, or a dog, a boy or a girl, a youth or a man, a negro or a Caucasian; the education must, if natural and proper, always hinge on this central fact. The negro brain and mental character, as has been shown, differs from our own both in degree and in quality, in the extent of its powers and the form or modes of mental action. As still more strikingly manifest among animals, the negro child has more intelligence than the white of the same age. This is in harmony with the great fundamental law which renders the most perfectly organized beings most dependent on reason—in the parents, if not that of the offspring. The calf or pig of a month has more intelligence than the child of that age; the negro child has more than that of the Caucasian, but the character of this intelligence, of course, varies in each and every case. In the lower animals it is instinct; in the case of the negro child it is more than instinct, but it is also radically different from that nascent rationality peculiar to the white child. Nevertheless, it is intelligence, and, as observed, more active in the negro child than in that of the white of the same age—an intelligence which enables it to preserve life where the former would, perhaps, perish, and thus to preserve the race amid the exigencies of savagism and the absence of care and forethought in the parents. It is this smartness of the negro child that has often deceived and deluded those perverse and deluded people of our own race, who get up negro schools. They see, or rather think they see, in this smartness the proof of their theories in regard to negroes, and parade their pets to admiring visitors with the utmost confidence in the justice and humanity of their exertions in behalf of an "oppressed and down-trodden race." But a few years more of these negro pupils would be sufficient (if any thing could be) to open the eyes of these perverted people, who, shutting their eyes and closing their ears to the ignorance and miseries of their own race, waste their money and time on a different one; indeed worse than waste, for they inflict much evil on the mistaken objects of their labors, evils though perhaps not traceable, that must necessarily attend every one of these negro pupils thus forced into a development opposed to the laws of their organism, and in contradiction to the negro nature.

The cultivation and development of the mental faculties, the mode or modes of education, are instinctive with our race, though constantly improved and perfected by reason resting on experience. The Greeks, Egyptians, and other ancient nations practiced substantially the system now common to modern times—that is, they taught their children by abstract lessons as well as oral instructions. They studied arithmetic, or the science of numbers, grammar, history, etc., under the direction of parents or guardians, as well as listened to lectures on rhetoric and philosophy in the "groves of the academy." History and biography were the legends and traditions of gods and goddesses, it is true, but modern history is mainly that of kings and queens, and as the former were once human, the only substantial difference consists in the greater accuracy of the latter.

The Mongol mind has its specific tendencies in this respect; that is, children are taught, not by abstract lessons but by material emblems which represent *their* ideas. They have no history, in our sense of the term. It is utterly impossible that the Mongol mind can trace back events beyond a certain number of generations, and the crude and contradictory mass of nonsense which passes for Chinese history or the "annals of China," is the work of Caucasian Tartars or those of predominating Caucasian innervation.

The negro has never taken one step towards mental development, as we understand it. He has never invented an alphabet—that primal starting point in mental cultivation—he has never comprehended even the simplest numerals—in short, has had no instruction and can give no instruction except that which is verbal and imitated, which the child copies from the parents, which is limited to the existing generation, and therefore the present generation are in the same condition that their progenitors occupied thousands of years ago. But the Almighty has adapted him to a very different condition from this fixed and non-progressive savagism. All the subordinate races have a certain capacity for imitating the higher habitudes of the Caucasian, unless it be the Mongol, which, perhaps, does not possess this faculty. The English have been masters in Hindostan for more than a century—their power rests on the same tenure of force on which it was founded—they have made no impression whatever on the habitudes of the Hindostanee—their language, their schools, their religion, their mental habits, are untouched, and it may be doubted if God ever designed that they should be in juxtaposition or made subject to a superior race.

In regard to the negro, there can be no doubt, not merely because, by himself, he is a non-producing and non-advancing savage, but because his entire structure, mental and physical, is adapted to juxtaposition. All the other races have a certain specific character to overcome first, or to be understood and properly harmonized, but the negro is a blank, a wilderness, a barren waste, waiting for the husbandman or the Caucasian teacher to develop his real worth, and gifted with his wonderful imitative powers, he not only never resists, but reaching forth his hands for guidance and protection, at once accepts his teacher, and submits himself to his control. Of the four millions now in our midst, a considerable proportion are the children of native Africans, indeed, there are not a few natives still among us, and yet everything connected with Africa—their traditions, language, religion, even their names have wholly disappeared. The Normans conquered the Saxons eight centuries ago, but the Saxon names, and even their language, are now as entirely Saxon as if a Norman had never landed on the shores of England. This blank, this feeble mental capacity and readiness of the negro nature to imitate the habits, bodily or mental of the superior race, adapts the negro to his subordinate social position, and the purposes to which Providence has assigned him. The child-like intellect does not resist the strong and enduring mental energies of the Caucasian—its first impressions pass away in a few years, while its imitative capacities sit so gracefully on the negro nature that multitudes of ignorant people confound the real with the borrowed, and actually suppose that the "smart" negroes to be met with occasionally at the North are examples of native capacity. Of course, the borrowed intelligence is equally short-lived, and were our negroes carried back to Africa, they would lose what they had acquired here with the same rapidity that they have parted with their original Africanism, and names among them now celebrated would be as utterly lost a hundred years hence as their African names have disappeared here. These things being so, it obviously follows that negro "education" must be oral and verbal, or, in other words, that the negro should be placed in the best position possible for the development of his imitative powers— to call into action that peculiar capacity for copying the habits, mental and moral, of the superior Caucasian. It may be said that all mental instruction is through the imitative capacity, or that our own children are thus educated, but the negro mind, in essential respects, is always that of a child. The intelligence, as observed, is more rapidly developed in the negro child— those faculties more immediately connected with sensation, perception and perhaps memory, are more energetic, but when they reach twelve and fifteen they diverge, the reflective faculties in the white are now called into action, the real Caucasian character now opens, the mental forces are fairly evolved, while the negro remains stationary—a perpetual child. The negro of forty or fifty has more experience or knowledge, perhaps as the white man of that age has a more extended knowledge than the man of twenty-five, but the intellectual calibre, the actual mental capacity in the former case is no greater than it was at fifteen; when its utmost limits were reached—its entire power in full development.

The universal experience which, in this as many other instances, usually rests upon truth, leads the people of the South to designate the negro of any age as a "boy"—an expression perfectly correct, in an intellectual sense, as the negro reaches his mental maturity, at twelve or fifteen, and viewed from our stand-point, is, therefore, always a boy. Indeed, this psychological fact, together with his imitative instinct, constitute the specific character of the face, and present the landmarks necessary for our guidance when dealing with the mental and moral wants of the negro. Intellectually considered, he is always a boy—a perpetual child—needing the care and guidance of his master, and his instinctive tendencies to imitate him, therefore, demand that, as in the case of children, the master should present him a proper example. His mental wants, it is believed, are provided for, and his capabilities in these respects fully developed at the South. They are in pretty extensive intercourse with the white people; even on the large plantations, they have the master's family or that of the overseer to copy after and to guide them, and though it may be that something more is needed, that a better mental training is possible in the future, it is, at all events, certain that this verbal instruction is better adapted to their wants than the schools and colleges of a different and vastly superior race. If any one should propose to teach children of five the branches proper to those of ten and twelve years of age, or the latter those that occupy young men in the universities, it would be seen at a glance that this teaching was unnatural and improper. And our every-day experience will show that it is injurious, not alone to the mental, but to the bodily health of the pupil. The same or similar results must attend the school education of negroes. It is, perhaps, difficult to trace the consequences of negro education at the North. There are but few negroes, and the mulattoes and mongrels who pass for such must pay a penalty for this education according, doubtless, to their proportion of negro blood.

The mongrels, and possibly some negroes at the North, often seem as well educated as white men, but it must be at the expense of the body, shortening the existence, just as we sometimes witness in the case of children when the pride, vanity, or ignorance of parents have stimulated their minds, and dwarfed or destroyed their bodies. An "educated" negro, like a "free negro," is a social monstrosity, even more unnatural and repulsive than the latter.

It is creditable to the people of the South that no such outrage on nature and common sense is found in all her borders. God has made the negro an inferior being, not in most cases, but all cases, for there are no accidents or exceptions in His works. There never could be such a thing as a negro equaling the standard Caucasian in natural ability. The same Almighty Creator has also made all white men equal—for idiots, insane people, etc., are not exceptions, they are results of human vices, crimes, or ignorance, immediate or remote. What a false and vicious state of society, therefore, when human institutions violate this eternal order, and by withholding education from their own brethren, educate the inferior negro, and in a sense make him superior to white men, by setting aside the law of God!

Some of the States have passed laws against teaching negroes to read; a more extended and enlightened knowledge of the negro will, doubtless, some day govern this matter through public opinion, and without governmental interference. The negro learns from his master all he needs to know, all that he can know, in a proper sense, all that is essential to the performance of his duties, or necessary to his happiness and the fulfillment of the purposes to which nature has adapted him; and though there might, perhaps, be no good reason given why he should be prohibited from learning to read, it is sufficient to say that it is absurd, as well as a waste of time that should be carefully employed. His mental powers are unable to grapple with science or philosophy, or abstractions of any kind, and it would be folly to suppose that he would be or could be interested in history or biography, in which his race, his instincts, his wants have no share, record or connection whatever.

All this applies, of course, to the South—to negroes in their normal condition and natural relation to the superior race. It may be well enough at the North, as long as they have mongrels and free negroes, to provide schools for them, as they have no other guide or protector but the State itself, but though they thus acquire a certain kind of mental activity, as observed, it is at the expense of the vital forces, and another of those incidental causes that tend to the final extinction of this abnormal element. It is, however, a disgrace, and, to a certain extent, a crime in any State to educate negroes or mongrels, so long as they have one single uneducated white man within their limits. The proof of this is seen every day in the *fact,* that however educated, or whatever the seeming mental superiority of the "colored" man, the uneducated white man tolerates no equality. Thus nature vindicates her rights, and whatever the ignorance, delusion, or crimes of society, the eternal order fixed by the hand of God is inevitable and everlasting.

THE AMERICAN INDIAN: PRELUDE
TO GENOCIDE AND ISOLATION

Andrew Jackson and the Removal
of the Indians

On December 8, 1829, President Andrew Jackson in his first annual message to the nation officially endorsed the removal

Source: [6] Andrew Jackson, "The Condition & Ulterior Destiny of the Indian Tribes," from First Annual Message, *A Compilation of the Messages & Papers of the Presidents: 1789–1897,* J. D. Richardson, ed., Wash., D.C., 1907, pp. 456–459.

of the Cherokee Indians from Georgia and Alabama to "west of the Mississippi [River], and without the limits of any state or territory." Supporting the proposed removal were the Indian-haters, who asserted that "civilized states [specifically Georgia] have a right to extend their jurisdiction over tribes of savages living within their limits." They concluded, moreover, that the practical assertion of [this] jurisdiction . . . is necessary due to their [Indians'] ignorance and superior intelligence of the whites." Subsequent to all this, the Cherokee Nation was successfully removed.

. . . The Condition and ulterior destiny of the Indian tribes within the limits of some of our States have become objects of much interest and importance. It has long been the policy of Government to introduce among them the arts of civilization, in the hope of gradually reclaiming them from a wandering life. This policy has, however, been coupled with another wholly incompatible with its success. Professing a desire to civilize and settle them, we have at the same time lost no opportunity to purchase their lands and thrust them farther into the wilderness. By this means they have not only been kept in a wandering state, but been led to look upon us as unjust and indifferent to their fate. Thus, though lavish in its expenditures upon the subject, Government has constantly defeated its own policy, and the Indians in general, receding farther and farther to the west, have retained their savage habits. A portion, however, of the Southern tribes, having mingled much with the whites and made some progress in the arts of civilized life, have lately attempted to erect an independent government within the limits of Georgia and Alabama. These States, claiming to be the only sovereigns within their territories, extended their laws over the Indians, which induced the latter to call upon the United States for protection.

Under these circumstances the question presented was whether the General Government had a right to sustain those people in their pretensions. The Constitution declares that "no new State shall be formed or erected within the jurisdiction of any other State" without the consent of its legislature. If the General Government is not permitted to tolerate the erection of a confederate State within the territory of one of the members of this Union against her consent, much less could it allow a foreign and independent government to establish itself there. Georgia became a member of the Confederacy which eventuated in our Federal Union as a sovereign State, always asserting her claim to certain limits, which, having been originally defined in her colonial charter and subsequently recognized in the treaty of peace, she has ever since continued to enjoy, except as they have been circumscribed by her own voluntary transfer of a portion of her territory to the United States in the articles of cession of 1802. Alabama was admitted into the Union on the same footing with the original States, with boundaries which were prescribed by Congress. There is no Constitutional, conventional, or legal provision which allows them less power over the Indians within their borders than is possessed by Maine or New York. Would the people of Maine permit the Penobscot tribe to erect an independent government within their State? And unless they did would it not be the duty of the General Government to support them in resisting such a measure? Would the people of New York permit each remnant of the Six Nations within her borders to declare itself an independent people under the protection of the United States? Could the Indians establish a separate republic on each of their reservations in Ohio? And if they were so disposed would it be the duty of this Government to protect them in the attempt? If the principle involved in the obvious answer to these questions be abandoned, it will follow that the objects of this Government are reversed, and that it has become a part of its duty to aid in destroying the States which it was established to protect.

Actuated by this view of the subject, I informed the Indians inhabiting parts of Georgia and Alabama that their attempt to establish an independent government would not be countenanced by the Executive of the United States, and advised them to emigrate beyond the Mississippi or submit to the laws of those States.

Our conduct toward these people is deeply interesting to our national character. Their present condition, contrasted with what they once were, makes a most powerful appeal to our sympathies. Our ancestors found them the uncontrolled possessors of these vast regions. By persuasion and force they have been made to retire from river to river and from mountain to mountain, until some of the tribes have become extinct and others have left but remnants to preserve for a while their once terrible names. Surrounded by the whites with their arts of civilization which by destroying the resources of the savage doom him to weakness and decay, the fate of the Mohegan, the Narragansett, and the Delaware is fast overtaking the Choctaw, the Cherokee, and the Creek. That this fate surely awaits them if they remain within the limits of the States does not admit of a doubt. Humanity and national honor demand that every effort should be made to avert so great a calamtiy. It is too late to inquire whether it was just in the United States to include them and their territory within the bounds of new States, whose limits they could control. That step can not be retraced. A State can not be dismembered by Congress or restricted in the exercise of her constitutional power. But the people of those States and every State, actuated by feelings of justice and a regard for our national honor, submit to you the interesting question whether something can not be done, consistently with the rights of the States, to preserve this much-injured race.

As a means of effecting this end I suggest for your consideration, the propriety of setting apart an ample district west of the Mississippi, and without the limits of any State or Territory now formed, to be guaranteed to the Indian tribes as long as they shall occupy it, each tribe having a distinct control over the portion designated for its use. There they may be secured in the enjoyment of governments of their own choice, subject to no other control from the United States than such as may be necessary to preserve peace on the frontier and between the several tribes. There the benevolent may endeavor to teach them the arts of civilization, and, by promoting union and harmony among them, to raise up an interesting commonwealth, destined to perpetuate the race and to attest the humanity and justice of this Government.

This emigration should be voluntary, for it would be as cruel as unjust to compel the aborigines to abandon the graves of their fathers and seek a home in a distant Land. But they should be distinctly informed that if they remain within the limits of the States they must be subject to their laws. In return for their obedience as individuals they will without doubt be protected in the enjoyment of those possessions which they have improved by their industry. But it seems to me visionary to suppose that in this state of things claims can be allowed on tracts of country on which they have neither dwelt nor made improvements, merely because they have seen them from the mountain or passed them in the chase. Submitting to the laws of the States, and receiving, like other citizens, protection in their persons and property, they will ere long become merged in the mass of our population.

The Indian and "Manifest Destiny"

Thomas Hart Benton, a politically powerful Missouri Senator, was a staunch advocate of America's westward expansion. As a promoter of the myth of Anglo-Saxon superiority, he regarded the Indian as an obstacle to the settlement of the vast western territory. Asserting his belief that the "removal system" of Andrew Jackson was no longer viable, he suggested in a speech on the settlement of Oregon that the Indian accept civilization or be eliminated. This proposition advanced by Benton, was, for the first time, seriously considered as a solution to the problem.

In his address to the Senate, Benton reported that the advance of civilization had driven the Indian "from the Atlantic coast" and that the tribes who resisted had met with a justifiable "extinction." The elimination of the Indian was no cause for lamentation, however, for, according to Benton, it was "the effect of divine law." Moreover, he praised the destruction of the tribes because it enabled a Christian people to replace "the savages." He further concluded that "civilization, or extinction, has been the fate of all people who have found them-

Source: [7] *United States Congressional Globe,* 29th Cong., 1st Sess., pp. 917–918.

selves in the track of advancing whites," and ". . . extinction [of Indians] has followed as a consequence of its resistence."

With this rationale, Benton and his followers exonerated the subsequent genocide and incarceration of the American Indian.

. . . The effect of the arrival of the Caucasian, or White race, on the western coast of America, opposite the eastern coast of Asia, remains to be mentioned among the benefits which the settlement of the Columbia [River] will produce; and that a benefit, not local to us, but general and universal to the human race. Since the dispersion of man upon earth, I know of no human event, past or to come, which promises a greater, and more beneficent change upon earth than the arrival of the van of the Caucasian race (the Celtic-Anglo-Saxon division) upon the border of the sea which washes the shore of the eastern Asia. The Mongolian, or Yellow race, is there, four hundred millions in number, spreading almost to Europe; a race once the foremost of the human family in the arts of civilization, but torpid and stationary for thousands of years. It is a race far above the Ethiopian, or Black—above the Malay, or Brown, (if we must admit five races)—and above the American Indian, or Red: it is a race far above all these, but still, far below the White; and, like all the rest, must receive an impression from the superior race whenever they come in contact. It would seem that the White race alone received the divine command, to subdue and replenish the earth! For it is the only race that has obeyed it—the only one that hunts out new and distant lands, and even a New World, to subdue and replenish. Starting from western Asia, taking Europe for their field, and the Sun for their guide, and leaving the Mongolians behind, they arrived, after many ages, on the shores of the Atlantic, which they lit up with the lights of science and religion, and adorned with the useful and the elegant arts. Three and a half centuries ago, this race, in obedience to the great command, arrived in the New World, and found new lands to subdue and replenish. For a long time it was confined to the border of the new field, (I now mean the Celtic-Anglo-Saxon division;) and even fourscore years ago the philosophic [Edmund] Burke was considered a rash man because he said the English colonists would top the Alleganies, and descend into the valley of the Mississippi, and occupy without parchment if the Crown refused to make grants of land. What was considered a rash declaration eighty years ago, is old history, in our country, at this day. Thirty years ago I said the same thing of the Rocky Mountains and the Columbia; it was ridiculed then: it is becoming history today. The venerable Mr. Macon has often told me that he remembered a line low down in North Carolina, fixed by a royal governor as a boundary between the whites and the Indians; where is that boundary now? The van of the Caucasian race now top the Rocky Mountains, and spread down to the shores of the Pacific. In a few years a great population will grow up there, luminous with the accumulated lights of European and American civilization. Their presence in such a position cannot be without its influence upon eastern Asia. The sun of civilization must shine across the sea; socially and commercially, the van of the Caucasians, and the rear of the Mongolians, must intermix. They must talk together, and trade together, and marry together. Commerce is a great civilizer —social intercourse as great—and marriage greater. The White and Yellow races can marry together, as well as eat and trade together. Moral and intellectual superiority will do the rest; the White race will take the ascendant, elevating what is susceptible of improvement—wearing out what is not. The Red race has disappeared from the Atlantic coast: the tribes that resisted civilization, met extinction. This is a cause of lamentation with many. For my part, I cannot murmur at what seems to be the effect of divine law. I cannot repine that this Capitol has replaced the wigwam—this Christian people, replaced the savages—white matrons, the red squaws—and that such men as Washington, Franklin, and Jefferson have taken the place of Powhattan, Opechonecanough, and other red men, howsoever respectable they may have been as savages. Civilization, or extinction, has been the fate of all people who have found themselves in the track of the advancing Whites, and civilization, always the preference of the Whites, has been pressed as an object, while extinction has followed as a consequence of its resistence. The Black and the Red races have often felt their ameliorating influence. The yellow race, next to themselves in the scale of mental and moral excellence, and in the beauty of form, once their superiors in the useful and elegant arts, and in learning, and still respectable though stationary; this race cannot fail to receive a new impulse from the approach of the Whites, improved so much since so many ages ago they left the western borders of Asia. The apparition of the van of the Caucasian race, rising upon them in the east after having left them on the west, and after having completed the circumnavigation of the globe, must wake up and reanimate the torpid body of old Asia. Our position and policy will commend us to their hospitable reception; political considerations will aid the action of social and commercial influences. Pressed upon by the great Powers of Europe—the same that press upon us—they must in our approach hail the advent of friends, not of foes—of benefactors not of invaders. The moral and intellectual superiority of the White race will do the rest; and thus, the youngest people, and the newest land, will become the reviver and the regenerator of the oldest.

It is in this point of view, and as acting upon the social, political, and religious condition of Asia, and giving a new point of departure to her ancient civilization, that I look upon the settlement of the Columbia River by the van of the Caucasian race as the most momentous human event in the history of man since his dispersion over the face of the earth.

ATTITUDES TOWARD THE OUTGROUP: NATIVISM AND RACE

Samuel F. B. Morse on the "Imminent Dangers" of Foreign Immigration

The most prominent American figure in the pre-Civil War nativist movement was the inventor and artist, Samuel F. B. Morse. Morse wrote extensively on nativism, and was especially concerned with an alleged papal plot to conquer the United States. In the early 1830's, the anti-Catholic press in the United States was alarmed by the activities of the Leopold Association, a Catholic missionary society, which had been founded with the avowed intention of strengthening Catholicism in America. In a series of letters published by a leading Protestant weekly—the New York Observer—*Morse himself claimed to have "performed the important task of linking immigration and Catholicism and making both equally objectionable in American eyes." The material, which was entitled "A Foreign Conspiracy against the Liberties of the United States," was widely reprinted in nativist and religious newspapers; the concept of a vast international subversive conspiracy directed against American institutions has always had great popular appeal in the United States, and so it went with Morse's article. Morse was so encouraged by the reception of "A Foreign Conspiracy" that he decided expatiate on the role of the immigrants in the alleged papal subjugation of this country. Consequently, Morse wrote another series of letters, this time entitled "Imminent Dangers to the Free Institutions of the*

Source: [8] Samuel F. B. Morse, *Imminent Dangers to the Free Institutions of the United States Through Foreign Immigration and the Present State of the Naturalization Law* (New York, 1835), pp. 6–11.

*United States Through Foreign Immigration," for New York
City's leading businessman's newspaper,* The Journal of Commerce.

. . . I have set forth in a very brief and imperfect manner the
evil, the great and increasing evil, that threatens our free institutions from *foreign interference.* Have I not shown that there
is real cause for alarm? Let me recapitulate the facts in the
case, and see if any of them can be denied; and if not, I submit
it to the calm decision of every American, whether he can still
sleep in fancied security, while incendiaries are at work; and
whether he is ready quietly to surrender his liberty, civil and
religious, into the hands of foreign powers.

1. It is a fact, that in this age the subject of civil and religious liberty agitates in the most intense manner the various
European governments.

2. It is a fact, that the influence of American free institutions in subverting European despotic institutions is greater
now than it has ever been, from the fact of the greater maturity,
and long-tried character, of the American form of government.

3. It is a fact, that Popery is opposed in its very nature to
Democratic Republicanism; and it is, therefore, as a political
system, as well as religious, opposed to civil and religious liberty, and consequently to our form of government.

4. It is a fact, that this truth, respecting the intrinsic character of Popery, has lately been clearly and demonstratively
proved in public lectures, by one of the Austrian Cabinet, a
devoted Roman Catholic, and with the evident design (as subsequent events show) of exciting the Austrian government to a
great enterprise in support of absolute power.

5. It is a fact, that this Member of the Austrian Cabinet, in
his lectures, designated and proscribed this country by name,
as the *"great nursery of destructive principles; as the Revolutionary school for France and the rest of Europe,"* whose con-
tagious examples of Democratic liberty had given, and would
still give, trouble to the rest of the world, unless the evil were
abated.

6. It is a fact, that very shortly after the delivery of these
lectures, a Society was originated in the Austrian capital, called

the St. Leopold Foundation, for the purpose "of promoting the greater activity of Catholic Missions in America."

7. It is a fact, that this Society is under the patronage of Emperor of Austria—has its central direction at Vienna—is under the supervision of Prince Metternich—that it is an extensive combination, embodying the civil, as well as ecclesiastical *officers,* not only of the *whole Austrian Empire,* but of the neighboring Despotic States—that it is actively at work, collecting moneys, and sending agents to this country, to carry into effect its designs.

8. It is a fact, that the agents of these foreign despots, are, for the most part, *Jesuits.*

9. It is a fact, that the effects of this society are already apparent in the otherwise unaccountable increase of Roman Catholic cathedrals, churches, colleges, convents, nunneries, etc., in every part of the country; in the sudden increase of Catholic emigration: in the increased clannishness of the Roman Catholics, and the boldness with which their leaders are experimenting on the character of the American people.

10. It is a fact, that an unaccountable disposition to riotous conduct has manifested itself within a few years, when exciting topics are publicly discussed, wholly at variance with the former peaceful, deliberative character of our people.

11. It is a fact, that a species of police, unknown to our laws, has repeatedly been put in requisition to keep the peace among a certain class of foreigners, who are Roman Catholics, viz. Priest-police.

12. It is a fact, that Roman Catholic priests have interfered to influence our elections.

13. It is a fact, that politicians on both sides have propitiated these priests, to obtain the votes of their people.

14. It is a fact, that numerous Societies of Roman Catholics, particularly among the Irish foreigners, are organized in various parts of the country, under various names, and ostensibly for certain benevolent objects; that these societies are united together by correspondence, all which may be innocent and praiseworthy, but viewed in connexion with the recent aspect of affairs, are at least suspicious.

15. It is a fact, that an attempt has been made to organize

a military corps of Irishmen in New York, to be called the O'Connell Guards; thus commencing a military organization of foreigners.

16. It is a fact, that the greater part of the foreigners in our population is composed of Roman Catholics.

Facts like these I have enumerated might be multiplied, but these are the most important, and quite sufficient to make every American settle the question with himself, whether there is, or is not, danger to the country from the present state of our Naturalization laws.

. . . Few, out of the great cities, are aware what sophistry has of late been spread among the more ignorant class of foreigners, to induce them to clan together, and to assert what they are pleased to call their rights. The ridiculous claim to superior privileges over native citizens, which I have noticed, is a specimen; one of many, in which Jesuit sophistry is at work to keep the slaves of superstition and ignorance still bound in their chains. . . . Jesuitism is full of expedients of the kind I have alluded to, and as we have Jesuits avowedly, and systematically, and diligently at work in our society, in the pay and interest of foreign powers, we ought to be watchful of all their movements. There are no greater enemies of the emigrant population than these Holy Alliance emissaries. Already they have done them irreparable injury. Already are witnessed the fruits of their disorganizing efforts. Already has the influence of bad councils led the deluded emigrant, particularly the Irish emigrant, to adopt such a course as to alienate from him the American people. Emigrants have been induced to prefer such arrogant claims, they have nurtured their foreign feelings and their foreign nationality to such a degree, and manifested such a determination to create and strengthen a separate and a foreign interest, that the American people can endure it no longer, and a direct hostile interest is now in array against them. This is an effect natural from such a cause; it is one long ago predicted in the hope of averting the evil. If evil is the consequence, the writer at least washes his hands of the guilt. The name and character of foreigner has, by this conduct of emigrants and their advocates, become odious, and the public voice is becoming louder and louder, and it will increase to unanimity, or at least so far as real American feeling pervades the hearts of Americans, until its language will be intelligible and audible even to those deaf ears, who now affect neither to hear, nor to heed it. When I say that the name of foreigner has become odious, I speak of a fact, not in approval of the fact. No one more than the writer can lament the apparent, (for it is only apparent,) indiscriminate censure of innocent and guilty together, which is unavoidable in combating an evil of this magnitude and character; he has no fears that the severity of any strictures which truth compels him to make upon *foreigners collectively* will give umbrage to a single intelligent and really naturalized citizen. For such a citizen, if he has been long a citizen, must be fully as conscious as the writer, that the habitual and almost *time-sanctioned* abuses of naturalization, have now reached an important and most dangerous crisis. The naturalized citizen who conducts consistently, who has become an American in reality, and not merely by profession, is not touched by any censure of mine. Neither is the foreigner who is temporarily or officially here; he is professedly an alien, and meddles not, (at least legally,) with our politics. It is that anomalous, nondescript, *hermaphrodite,* Jesuit thing, neither foreigner nor native, yet a moiety of each, now one, now the other, both or neither, as circumstances suit, against whom I war; a naturalized *foreigner,* not a naturalized *citizen,* a man who from Ireland, or France, or Germany, or other foreign lands, renounces his native country and adopts America, professes to become an American, and still, being received and sworn to be a citizen, talks, (for example,) of Ireland as "his home," as "his beloved country," resents any thing said against the Irish as said against him, glories in being Irish, forms and cherishes an Irish interest, brings hither Irish local feuds, and forgets, in short, all his new obligations as an American, and retains both a name and a feeling and a practice in regard to his adopted country at war with propriety, with decency, with gratitude, and with true patriotism. I hold no parley with such contradictions as Irish fellow-citizens, French fellow-citizens, or German fellow-citizens. With as much consistency might we say *foreign natives,* or *hostile friends.* But the present is no time either for compliment or nice discrimination. When the country is invaded by an army, it is not the moment to indulge in pity towards the deluded soldiers of the various hostile corps, who act as they are commanded by their superior officers. It is then no time to make distinctions among the officers, lest we injure those who are involuntarily fighting against us, or who may be friends in the enemy's camp. The first thing is to bring the whole army to unconditional surrender, and when they have laid down their arms in a body, and acknowledged our sovereignty, then good fellowship, and courtesy, and pity will have leisure to indulge in discriminating friends from foes, and in showing to each their respective and appropriate sympathies.

We have now to resist the *momentous* evil that threatens us from *Foreign Conspiracy*. The *Conspirators* are in the *foreign importations*. Innocent and guilty are brought over together. We must of necessity suspect them all. That we are most seriously endangered, admits not of the slightest doubt; we are experiencing the natural reaction of European upon American principles, and it is infatuation, it is madness not to see it, not to guard against it. A subtle attack is making upon us by foreign powers. The proofs are as strong as the nature of the case allows. They have been adduced again and again, and they have not only been uncontradicted, but silently acquiesced in, and have acquired fresh confirmation by every day's observation. The arbitrary governments of Europe—those governments who keep the people in the most abject obedience at the point of the bayonet, with Austria at their head, have combined to attack us in every vulnerable point that the nation exposes to their assault. They are impelled by self-preservation to attempt our destruction—they must destroy democracy. It is with them a case of life and death—they must succeed or perish. If they do not overthrow American liberty, American liberty will overthrow their despotism. They know this fact well. They have declared it. They are acting in accordance with their convictions, and declarations, and they are acting wisely. They have already sent their chains, and oh! to our shame to be it spoken, are fastening them upon a *sleeping* victim. Americans, you are marked for their prey, not by foreign bayonets, but *by weapons surer of effecting the conquest of liberty* than all the munitions of physical combat in the military or naval storehouses of Europe. Will you not awake to the apprehension of the reality and extent of your danger? Will you be longer deceived by the pensioned Jesuits, who having surrounded your press, are now using it all over the country to stifle the cries of danger, and lull your fears by attributing your alarm to a false cause. Up! up! I beseech you. Awake! To your posts! Let the tocsin sound from Maine to Louisiana. Fly to protect the vulnerable places of your Constitution and Laws. Place your guards; you will need them, and quickly too. And first, shut your gates. Shut the open gates. The very first step of safety is here. It is the beginning of defence. Your enemies, in the guise of friends, by thousands, are at this moment rushing in to your ruin through the open portals of *naturalization*. Stop them, or you are lost, irrevocably lost. The first battle is here at the gates. Concentrate here. And be sure your enemy will here show his strength; you here can test his force or his existence, if you indeed doubt his existence. He will dispute this entrance inch by inch. Already is he alarmed, already has he set in motion his troops to resist. Will you despise the cry of danger? Well, be it so. Believe the foreign Jesuit rather than your own countrymen. Open wide your doors. Yes, throw down your walls. Invite, nay allure, your enemies. Enlarge your alms-houses and your prisons; be not sparing of your money; complain not of the outrages in your streets, nor the burden of your taxes. You will be repaid in praises of your toleration and liberality. What though European despots have compelled you to be the nurses of their halt, and blind, and naked, and the keepers of their criminals; what though they have compelled you to the necessity of employing your lives in toiling and providing for their outcast poor, and have caused you to be vexed, and your habits outraged by the expatriated turbulence of their cities, instead of allowing you to rejoice in the prosperity, and happiness, and peaceful neighborhood of your own well-provided, well-instructed children.

Have you no reward? Oh, yes; your country is filling with a noble foreign population, all friends of liberty, all undoubted Democrats, taught in the school of Democratic Europe, accustomed to huzza with one voice for liberty, and under the guidance of Jesuit leaders well trained; far famed, long tried friends of Democracy; and to make assurance doubly sure, selected with the greatest care by Austria's Democratic Emperor, and Rome's Democratic Pope, who watch them with jealous eyes, and if not faithful in *upholding Democracy,* will deprive them of their stipulated wages, and recall them home, to receive their merited punishment—an Archbishop's see, or a Cardinal's hat. Democracy is safe with such keepers. The country is in no danger. Sleep on.

The "Greatest of the Nativistic Propaganda Works"

Described by the historian Ray Allen Billington as the "greatest of the nativistic propaganda works," Maria Monk's Awful Disclosures of the Hotel Dieu Nunnery of Montreal *was first published in 1836 and had numerous subsequent printings. Allegedly raised as a Protestant, the authoress, Maria Monk, recounted her experiences as a student and nun in a Montreal nunnery. Her book contains a fantastic story of infanticide, murder, and licentiousness. Claiming to have escaped from the convent, Maria came to New York City to publish her tale. Most authorities agree that the work was ghost-written, and moreover, was part of a hoax intended to inflame anti-Catholic passions. The widespread acceptance and popularization of the "disclosures" involving the sinful lives of priests and nuns, however, has given the work historical significance.*

Portions of chapters XVI and XVII, which are reprinted here, served to incite anti-Catholic gossip. Maria describes the alleged freedom with which priests were able to visit nuns, and the ruses the clerics employed to seduce the sisters. Most shocking of all are her depictions of the baptism and murder of babies which she claimed to have witnessed in the "Black Nunnery."

Source: [9] Maria Monk, *Awful Disclosures of the Hotel Dieu Nunnery of Montreal* (New York, 1836), pp. 167–170, 174–180.

Some of the priests from the Seminary were in the nunnery every day and night, and often several at a time. I have seen nearly all of them at different times, though there are about one hundred and fifty in the district of Montreal. There was a difference in their conduct; though I believe every one of them was guilty of licentiousness; while not one did I ever see who maintained a character any way becoming the profession of a priest. Some were gross and degraded in a degree which few of my readers can ever have imagined; and I should be unwilling to offend the eye, and corrupt the heart of any one, by an account of their words and actions. Few imaginations can conceive deeds so abominable as they practised, and often required of some of the poor women, under the fear of severe punishment, and even of death. I do not hesitate to say with the strongest confidence, that although some of the nuns became lost to every sentiment of virtue and honour, especially one from the Congregational Nunnery whom I have before mentioned, Saint Patrick, the greater part of them loathed the practices to which they were compelled to submit, by the Superior and priests, who kept them under so dreadful a bondage.

. . . The priests are liable, by their dissolute habits, to occasional attacks of disease, [venereal disease] which render it necessary, or at least prudent, to submit to medical treatment.

In the Black Nunnery they find private accommodations, for they are free to enter one of the private hospitals whenever they please; which is a room set apart on purpose for the accommodation of the priests; and is called a retreat-room. But an excuse is necessary to blind the public, and this they find in the pretence they make of being in a "Holy Retreat." Many such cases have I known; and I can mention the names of priests who have been confined in this Holy Retreat. They are carefully attended by the Superior and old nuns, and their diet mostly consists of vegetable soups, etc., with but little meat, and that fresh. I have seen an instrument of surgery laying upon the table in that holy room, which is used only for particular purposes.

. . . It will be recollected that I was informed immediately after receiving the veil, that infants were occasionally murdered in the Convent. I was one day in the nuns' private sick-room, when I had an opportunity, unsought for, of witnessing deeds of such a nature. It was, perhaps, a month after the death of Saint Francis. Two little twin babes, the children of Sainte Catharine, were brought to a priest, who was in the room, for baptism. I was present while the ceremony was performed, with the Superior and several of the old nuns, whose names I never knew, they being called Ma tant, Aunt.

The priests took turns in attending to confession and cate-chism in the Convent, usually three months at a time, though sometimes longer periods. The priest then on duty was Father Larkin. He is a good-looking European, and has a brother who is a professor in the college. He first put oil upon the heads of the infants, as is the custom before baptism. When he had bap-tised the children, they were taken, one after another, by one of the old nuns, in the presence of us all. She pressed her hand upon the mouth and nose of the first, so tight that it would not breathe, and in a few minutes, when the hand was removed, it was dead. She then took the other and treated it in the same way. No sound was heard, and both the children were corpses. The greatest indifference was shown by all present during this operation; for all, as I well knew, were long accustomed to such scenes. The little bodies were then taken into the cellar, thrown into the pit I have mentioned, and covered with a quan-tity of lime.

I afterward saw another new-born infant treated in the same manner, in the same place: but the actors in this scene I choose not to name, nor the circumstances as everything connected with it is of a peculiarly trying and painful nature to my own feelings.

These were the only instances of infanticide I witnessed; and it seemed to be merely owing to accident that I was then present. So far as I know, there were no pains taken to preserve secrecy on this subject; that is, I saw no attempt made to keep any of the inmates of the Convent in ignorance of the murder of children. On the contrary, others were told, as well as my-self, on their first admission as veiled nuns, that all infants born in the place were baptized and killed, without loss of time;

and I had been called to witness the murder of the three just mentioned, only because I happened to be in the room at the time.

That others were killed in the same manner during my stay in the nunnery, I am well assured.

How many there were I cannot tell, and having taken no account of those I heard of, I cannot speak with precision; I believe, however, that I learnt through nuns, that at least eighteen or twenty infants were smothered, and secretly buried in the cellar, while I was a nun.

. . . Several nuns died at different times while I was in the Convent, how many I cannot say, but there was a considerable number; I might rather say many in proportion to the number in the nunnery. The proportion of deaths I am sure was very large. There was always some in the nuns' sick-rooms, and several interments took place in the chapel.

When a Black nun is dead, the corpse is dressed as if living, and placed in the chapel in a sitting posture, within the railing round the alter, with a book in the hand, as if reading. Persons are then freely admitted from the street, and some of them kneel and pray before it. No particular notoriety is given, I believe, to this exhibition out of the Convent, but such a case usually excites some attention.

The living nuns are required to say prayers for the delivery of their deceased sister from purgatory, being informed, as in all other such cases, that if she is not there, and has no need of our intercession, our prayers are in no danger of being thrown away, as they will be set down to the account of some of our departed friends, or at least to that of the souls which have no acquaintances to pray for them.

It was customary for us occasionally to kneel before a dead nun thus seated in the chapel, and I have often performed this task. It was always painful, for the ghastly countenance being seen whenever I raised my eyes, and the feeling that the position and dress were entirely opposed to every idea of propriety in such a case, always made me melancholy.

. . . One of the most remarkable and unaccountable things that happened in the Convent, was the disappearance of the old Superior. She had performed her customary part during the day, and had acted and appeared just as usual. She had shown no symptoms of ill health, met with no particular difficulty in conducting business, and no agitation, anxiety, or gloom had been noticed in her conduct. We had no reason to suppose that during that day she had expected any thing particular to occur, any more than the rest of us. After the close of our customary labours and evening lecture, she dismissed us to retire to bed, exactly in her usual manner. The next morning the bell rang, we sprang from our beds, hurried on our clothes as usual, and proceeded to the community room, in double line, to commence the morning exercise. There, to our surprise, we found Bishop Lartigue; but the Superior was no where to be seen. The Bishop soon addressed us, instead of her, and informed us, that a lady near him, whom he presented us, was now the Superior of the Convent, and enjoined upon us the same respect and obedience which we had paid to her predecessor.

The lady he introduced us to was one of our oldest nuns, Saint Du****, a very large, fleshy woman, with swelled limbs, which rendered her very slow in walking, and often gave her great distress. Not a word was dropped from which we could conjecture the cause of this change, nor of the fate of the old Superior. I took the first opportunity to inquire of one of the nuns whom I dared talk to, what had become of her; but I found them as ignorant as myself, though suspicious that she had been murdered by the orders of the Bishop. Never did I obtain any light on her mysterious disappearance. I am confident, however, that if the Bishop wished to get rid of her privately and by foul means, he had ample opportunities and power at his command. Jane Ray, as usual, could not allow such an occurrence to pass by without intimating her own suspicions more plainly than any other of the nuns would have dared to do. She spoke out one day, in the community-room, and said, "I'm going to have a hunt in the cellar for my old Superior."

PART 4

**Emancipation and Equality:
Racist Reflections During
the Civil War**

INTRODUCTION

At the beginning of the Civil War, most Americans were aware that slavery was the root cause of the conflict. They recognized that in order for the Union to survive, the institution had to be abolished. Nevertheless, strong anti-Negro sentiment in white America was a more than adequate adhesive to bind the emerging ideological divisions. This hostility, shared by most Americans and a keystone in the philosophy of the major political parties, led, during the duration of the war, to the blatant practice of racism.

The reality of anti-black enmity became manifest when the suggestion was made to emancipate the slaves and recruit blacks for the Union army. This proposal only served to ignite existing racial tensions. Responding to the demand for black troops, congressional leaders asserted that it was a "white man's war." They maintained that the presence of blacks would increase desertions, discourage enlistments and degrade the white soldier.

Underlying these "practical" considerations, however, was the fear that the presence of Negro troops would engender racial equality within the military structure. It was claimed that if blacks were given equality with white soldiers, the situation would lead to demands for the same treatment in civilian life.

Thus, the opposition to an integrated army was in reality motivated by the anticipation of black demands for an integrated nation. The manic fear inspired by the mere implication of a society based on equality caused opposition to all attempts to enlist black soldiers. Nevertheless, despite this racist background, in January 1863, Negroes were accepted into the armed forces.

Most Unionists agreed that the freedom of blacks posed a threat to white civilization. With hordes of ex-slaves expected to inundate the North, racist hysteria reached peak proportions in the years 1862–1863. With a reasoning grounded in fear and clouded by three hundred years of anti-black declamations, northern leaders warned of the impending "Africanization" and "mongrelization" of the Anglo-Saxon people.

In addition, bigots played on the insecurity and fears of the labor force. Suggesting that the massive black migration would cause a reduction of wages, a loss of jobs and a lowering of the standard of living, racially intolerant political leaders convinced the working class of the economic threat posed by the influx into their ranks of millions of ex-slaves.

Finding overwhelming support for their anti-black campaigns among the new immigrant labor groups, ironically, the racists established an alliance with the same people whom they had previously attacked in the nativist movements of 1820–1860. Thus, the Irish and German Catholics, who had themselves been the victims of intolerance and hatred, were among the most outspoken activists in the fight against emancipation.

With the military success of the Union army, and the subsequent realization that massive numbers of blacks would not "invade" the North, the supporters of the use of Negro soldiers and emancipation were vindicated. Likewise, the growing national economy and the successful integration of Freedom into the labor force served to temporarily alleviate much of the anti-black sentiment.

Although the results of the war brightened the outlook for the Negro, he was not yet destined to be accepted as an equal by his fellow Americans. By proclaiming that the war had not been a crusade for freedom, whites clearly made it known that the black man was still an "alien" in the land of his birth.

Is Ohio to Be Africanized?

When Abraham Lincoln's preliminary draft of the Emancipa-
tion Proclamation was read to his Cabinet on July 22, 1862,
a manic fear of massive black migration to the northern states
(especially the Midwest) became manifest. Echoing this
anxiety, numerous public officials, newspaper editors, and loyal
Union citizens repeated the sentiments of the most outspoken
bigots of the decade.

Although Lincoln justified the proposed policy as a military
necessity, many Americans refused to accept emancipation as
anything other than a threat to "Africanize" their homes. With
the abolition of slavery, most whites envisioned millions of un-
controlled blacks destroying the basic fabric of their society.

Foremost in opposition to any scheme of manumission was
Ohio Congressman Samuel Sullivan Cox. In one of his numer-
ous tirades against Lincoln's proposal, Cox maintained that it
was "neither convenient nor advantageous to the State of Ohio
to have this influx of blacks." In addition, he declared that
"even if there were no prejudices or instincts against color or
race in our midst, a true State policy would forbid such a horde
of Africans as emancipation would send to Ohio."

Furthermore, he warned that if abolition were successful,
"Ohio [troops might not] fight at all, if the result [should] be
the flight and movement of the black race by millions to their
own state."

Mr. Speaker: At the beginning of our civil conflict this House
passed almost unanimously a resolution offered by the gentleman from Kentucky (Mr. Crittenden) as to the character of
the war. It was a pledge that the war should not be waged in

Source: [1] Samuel Sullivan Cox, "Emancipation and Its Results—Is
Ohio To Be Africanized?" *Speech of Hon. S. S. Cox, of Ohio, Delivered
in the House of Representatives, June 6, 1862* (Washington, D.C.,
1862), pp. 1–16.

hostility to the institutions of any of the States. On the faith of its pledge men and money were voted. Since then that pledge has been broken both in this House and out of it.

Sir, I have watched with anxiety the conduct of this House. No heed is given here to the warning of loyal Union men from the slave states. Their advice is met with the cry "oh, they are for slavery; and no pro-slavery man can be loyal." No attention is paid to old-time political opponents, whose friends are the majority in the field. For aiding to preserve the Union, which they have been taught by their party canons to revere, they are treated to taunts and slander.

Measures like those from Massachusetts, which hold States as conquered fiefs; which would recognize republics abroad because they are black; which would create equality of black and white, such as passed the Senate, in carrying the mails; which abolished slavery in this District; which, like the acts of confiscation and emancipation here urged are to free the whole or a portion of the black population; all these measures, sir, are subversive of the institutions of the States, and have created apprehension and distrust.

. . . There is something needed in making successful civil war besides raising money and armies. You must keep up the confidence and spirit of the people. It must not only be animated by a noble passion at the outset, but it must be sustained by confidence in the cause. You dispirit the army and destroy its power, if you give forth an uncertain sound. Is there a member here who dare say that Ohio troops will fight successfully or fight at all, if the result shall be the flight and movement of the black race by millions northward to their own state? Our soldiers will endure great sacrifices, if they think that they are planting the flag over States where it has been shamelessly dishonored, and if they believe that the United States, as they have been made by our Constitution and constellated by time, are to be again enstarred in full brilliancy. But when you make men homeless, when you crape the doors and bedew the eyes of the bereaved—when bloody calamity darkens the hearth and heavy taxes oppress labor, there must be no ambiguity of policy.

. . . One thing is sure . . . the tendency of legislative action here is to free the slaves of the South and hurl them in hordes upon the North. Events, says [Wendell] Phillips, are grinding out the freedom of the negro; and these abolition bills are events. The confiscation bill passed last week, and the emancipation bill resurrected by a majority of four after its temporary death, have this meaning.

. . . But, sir, my opposition to such bills proceeds mainly from other and more conclusive reasoning. Granting that these bills are constitutional, and that they are according to the law of nations, a more momentous question arises. It is no less than the *preservation of the people and society of the North*. You free the slaves to punish treason; you free the slaves because you hate slavery. But what if the punishment falls upon the loyal North? Shall Ohio suffer because South Carolina rebels? Shall the North be destroyed or impaired in its progressive prosperity, by your projects of wholesale freedom of the slaves, because it will punish, cripple, or destroy slavery or the South!

It is beyond doubt that a large number of the four millions of slaves will be freed incidentally by the war. Already ten thousand are freed in South Carolina; as many more in Virginia; and perhaps as many more in the West. It has been computed that already some 70,000 blacks are freed by the war. I see it stated authoritatively that more contrabands followed Gen. Banks' retreat down the Virginia Valley than his troops numbered. These are being scattered North, are becoming resident in this District and supported by the largesses of the federal treasury. It is said that 18,000 rations are daily given out to negroes by our government. This is but a small number of those who are freed, or to be freed, by these bills. The mildest confiscation bill proposed will free not less than 700,000 slaves. The bill which is before us frees three millions, at least. The bills which receive the favor of the majority of the Republican party will free four millions. Nothing less will satisfy this Congress. That is now apparent. If you do not free all, say the extremists, your war is rose-water. If not all, no peace is possible.

. . . The right and power to exclude Africans from the States North, being compatible with our system of State sovereignty and federal supremacy, I assert that it is impolitic, dangerous, degrading, and unjust to the white men of Ohio and of the North, to allow such immigration.

By the census of 1860, in Ohio, we have 36,225 colored persons out of a population of 2,339,559. As a general thing, they are vicious, indolent, and improvident. They number as yet one black to about sixty-three whites; but their ratio of increase, during the last ten years, has been 43.30 percent, while that of the white increase is only 17.82 percent.

About one-tenth of our convicts are negroes. I gather from the census of 1850, that four-tenths of the female prisoners are blacks, although they compose but one-eighteenth of the female population of Ohio. In Massachusetts the convicts in the penitentiary are one-sixth black; Connecticut, one-third; New York, one-fourth. In Ohio the blacks are not agriculturalists. They soon become waiters, barbers, and otherwise subservient to the whites. They have just enough consequence given to them by late events to be pestilent. The resistance of the abolitionists to the Federal authority in Ohio, within the past three years, was abetted by colored men, some of whom had received schooling enough at Oberlin [college] to be vain and ostentatiously seditious.

The last Legislature of Ohio, by their committee, gave their proteges this certificate of character in their report:

> The negro race is looked upon by the people of Ohio as a class to be kept by themselves—to be debarred of social intercourse with the whites—to be deprived of all advantages which they cannot enjoy in common with their own class.
>
> Deprived of the advantages here enumerated, it could not be expected that he should attain any great advancement in social improvement. Generally, the negro in Ohio is lazy, ignorant, and vicious.

If this be true, it would be well to inquire why energetic legislation was not had, in view of the emancipation schemes here impending, to prevent this lazy, ignorant, and vicious class from overrunning our State. Such legislation was asked and refused.

If further testimony is needed as to the feeling of the people of Ohio and the northwest as to the blacks, I refer you to the speech of an Ohio Senator [Mr. Sherman]. Speaking in favor of emancipation in this District, he balanced himself on the slackwire after this fashion:

> This is a good place to begin emancipation for another reason. *This is a very Paradise for free negroes.* Here they enjoy more social equality than they do anywhere else. In the State where I live we do not like negroes. We do not disguise our dislike. As my friend from Indiana [Mr. Wright] said yesterday, the whole people of the north-western States are, for reasons, whether correct or not, opposed to having many negroes among them, and that principle or prejudice has been engrafted in the legislation of nearly all the northwestern States.

It is a fine thing, the Senator thinks, to free the negroes here; not so good in Ohio. Here they have a paradise; in Ohio, its opposite, I suppose. If the Senator could visit Green's Row, within the shadow of this Capitol, henceforth "Tophet and black Gehenna called, the type of hell," and note the squalor, destitution, laziness, crime, and degradation there beginning to fester; if he could visit the alleys in whose miserable hovels the blacks congregate, he would hardly be reminded of the paradise which Milton sang, with its amaranthine flowers [laughter], its blooming trees of life, its golden fruitage, its amber rivers rolling o'er elysian flowers, its hills and fountains and fresh shades, its dreams of love, and its adoration of God. Alas! he would find nothing here to remind him of that high estate in Eden, save the fragrance of the spot and the nakedness of its inhabitants [laughter].

If the rush of free negroes to this paradise continues, it would be a blessing if Providence should send Satan here in the form of a serpent, and an angel to drive the descendants of Adam and Eve into the outer world. If it continues, you will have no one here but Congressmen and negroes, and that will be punishment enough [laughter]. You will have to enact a fugitive law, to bring the whites to their capital [laughter].

The condition of the negroes here is not unlike their condition in Ohio. Perhaps it is worse here than in Ohio, for their numbers are so much more here in proportion to the population.

This population already on our hands in Ohio we can take care of; but if we cannot stop more from coming into Ohio, there is no sense in beginning to colonize the free blacks which we have on hand. I make no proposition as to them now. They do not, except in certain localities, interfere greatly either with our laws or our labor. But the question of allowing more to come in, is the question I discuss, not as to what we shall do with what we have. This is a question as gigantic as the schemes of emancipation. It is a practical question, as the war is already throwing them within our borders in great numbers.

Slavery may be an evil, it may be wrong for southern men to use unpaid labor, but what will be the condition of the people of Ohio when the free jubilee shall have come in its ripe and rotten maturity. If slavery is bad, the condition of the State of Ohio, with an unrestrained black population, only double what we now have, partly subservient, partly slothful, partly criminal, and all disadvantageous and ruinous, will be far worse.

. . . The mixture of the races tends to deteriorate both races. Physiology has called our attention to the results of such intermarriages or connections. These results show indifferences in stature and strength, depending on the parentage, with a corresponding difference in the moral character, mental capacity, and worth of labor. The mulatto is not long lived. It is a fact that no insurance company will insure their lives. In New England there is one blind negro for every 807, while at the South there is one for every 2,635. In New England there is one insane negro for every 980, while in the South one for every 3,080. If they were the only insane persons there I would not complain. They catch it there from the whites [laughter]. It is neither philanthropic nor congenial to send the negro to the North, where he wilts, when at the congenial South he increases in numbers even in slavery! Our statistician boasts that Ohio has men of greater height, by actual measurement, than England, Belgium, or Scotland, and in breadth of chest nearly equal to that of Scotland, and above all others. I do not offer myself as a specimen [laughter]. But how long before the manly, warlike people of Ohio of fair hair and blue eyes, in a large proponderance, would become, in spite of Bibles and morals, degenerate under the wholesale emancipation and immigration favored by my colleague?

The free negroes will become equal, or will continue unequal to the whites. Equality is a condition which is self-protective, wanting nothing, asking nothing, able to take care of itself. It is an absurdity to say that two races as dissimiliar as black and white, of different origin, of unequal capacity, can succeed in the same society when placed in competition. There is no such example in history of the success of two separate races under such circumstances.

Less than sixty-years ago, Ohio had thousands of an Indian population. She has now but thirty red men in her borders. The negro, with a difference of color indelible, has been freed under every variety of circumstances; but his freedom has too often been nominal.

Prejudice, stronger than all principles, though not always stronger than lust, has imperatively separated the whites from the blacks. In the school-house, the church or the hospital, the black man must not seat himself beside the white; even in death and at the cemetery the line of distinction is drawn.

To abolish slavery the North must go still further and forget that fatal prejudice of race which governs it, and which makes emancipation so illusory. To give men their liberty, to open to them the gates of the city, and then say, "There, you shall live among yourselves, you shall marry among yourselves, you shall form a separate society in society," is to create a cursed caste and replace slaves by pariahs.

Again, it is neither convenient nor advantageous to the State of Ohio to have this influx of blacks. It may be abstractly wrong to debar them from our State; but some one has wisely said that "the abstract principles of right and wrong we know, but not the processes, nor the duration of their working out in history. All the white handkerchiefs in Exeter Hall will not force the general Congress of Nations to decide questions otherwise than by the laws of convenience and advantage."

Were there no prejudices or instincts against the color or race in our midst, a true State policy would forbid such a horde of Africans as emancipation would send to Ohio. Ohio has a larger circuit of slave territory abutting on her border, than any other Northern State. The Ohio River runs over 500 miles along our border, dividing us from Kentucky and Virginia. Illinois and Indiana forbid all negroes from their states. Since 1850 Iowa and Wisconsin have had the same policy. Is Ohio to be the only asylum for the slaves of Virginia and Kentucky and the other States south? Suppose these schemes of emancipation succeed; or suppose they do not, and the emancipation incident to the war goes on, what proportion of the slaves of the South will cross into Ohio? They will not go to Canada, not now. They will move into lower Ohio, with the consuming power of the army worm. By the census, in Virginia and Kentucky alone, the colored people number 790,102!

How many of these blacks would come to Ohio! Is it high to calculate that one half of these in Virginia and Kentucky, and one-fourth of those south of Kentucky and Virginia will find a lodgment in Ohio? If the philanthropy of my colleague [Mr. Bingham] obtains, such will be the result.

In spite, however, of the laws of Illinois, Indiana and other Western States, the slaves of the Mississippi valley will, if freed, seek the Northwest. They will slip through into Illinois, Iowa, Kansas and Indiana. The gentleman from Indiana [Mr. Julian] the other day, said that in his part of the State, the law was a dead letter. He is no doubt partially correct.

In the past ten years the ratio of increase of free colored people in the United States has been 10.97 per cent, that of the slaves 23.38 per cent, and that of the white 38.12 per cent. In California the negroes have increased 296.67 per cent, compared to the white increase of 310.84 per cent. There are no laws of prohibition in California; while in Oregon, where such laws exist, the whole ratio of increase is 299.96 per cent, compared with a *loss* of 41.54 per cent of blacks! In other States there is this ratio: Illinois, white increase 101.49, black only 30.04; Iowa, white increase 251.22, black increase 207.21; Indiana, white increase 37.14, black *loss* 3.49; Wisconsin, white increase 154.10, black 133.22. In these States the law forbids blacks; but in spite of it they get in, but not to that extent which they do in Ohio and Michigan, where such laws do not exist. In the latter State the white increase is 87.89 per cent, the black is double, viz: 164.15! It will be perceived by an examination of the census, that it is in the Northwest, that the black race is increasing; while in other States further east and north, they do not increase in the same ratio. It is the Northwest which will be Africanized by the schemes here proposed.

The slaves in the Mississippi valley alone, in the States of Arkansas, Kentucky, Louisiana, Mississippi, Missouri and Tennessee, number 1,499,079. This does not include the free blacks, who would be compelled to share the exodus. Then Kansas, Nebraska, Iowa, Minnesota, Wisconsin, Michigan, Illinois, Indiana and Ohio, would be their asylum, but as the States west of Ohio are in advance of us in preventing this vicious immigration, Ohio, under the welcome of my colleague and his friends would have more than her fair quota.

. . . What shall be done? I answer, Representatives! that our duty is written in our oath! It is in the Constitution of the United States! Leave to the States their own institutions where that instrument leaves them, keep your faith to the Crittenden resolution, be rid of all ambiguous schemes and trust under God, for the revelation of His will concerning these black men in our land, and the overthrow by our power of this rebellion. Have you no faith in God, who writes the history of nations? Great as is our power, wise as is our system of government, brave as are our soldiers, unequalled as are our fleets of iron, it is only for Him to breath upon us,—and our power will fade. I know that His power can solve these dark problems of our fate. Let us do our duty to the order established by our fathers, under His wise inspiration, and all may be well.

Abraham Lincoln and Black Colonization

In anticipation of a successful Union victory at the conclusion of the American Civil War, Abraham Lincoln took preliminary

Source: [2] Abraham Lincoln, "Address on Colonization to a Deputation of Negroes," New York *Tribune*, August 15, 1862.

*steps toward "solving" America's racial difficulties. Faced with
a somewhat hostile Congress and an even more racially intolerant population (due to the fear of a mass black migration
to the North), he recognized that the freedom of four million
slaves in addition to the 500,000 free blacks, would create an
even deeper schism in the nation.*

*Thus, Lincoln who had stated in 1857 that a "separation of
the races [was] the only perfect prevention of amalgamation,"
advanced the idea of colonization before a group of prominent
free black citizens.*

*On August 14, 1862, he "gave audience to a committee of
colored men at the White House" and suggested that the site
of black settlement be in Central America. His rationale for
the proposal was based on the fact that "there [was] an unwillingness on the part of our people [whites], harsh as it may be,
for you free colored people to remain with us."*

*Subsequently, however, the negative reaction of black
leaders, the difficulties surrounding the mass deportation of
an entire people, and Lincoln's assassination, buried the colonization idea as a "solution" to the black-white confrontation.*

This afternoon the President of the United States gave audience to a Committee of colored men at the White House. . . .
Having all been seated, the President, after a few preliminary
observations, informed them that a sum of money had been
appropriated by Congress, and placed at his disposition for the
purpose of aiding the colonization in some country of the
people, or a portion of them, of African descent, thereby making it his duty, as it had for a long time been his inclination,
to favor that cause; and why, he asked, should the people of
your race be [colonized], and where? Why should they leave
this country? This is, perhaps, the first question for proper consideration. You and we are different races. We have between
us a broader difference than exists between almost any other
two races. Whether it is right or wrong I need not discuss, but
this physical difference is a great disadvantage to us both, as
I think your race suffer very greatly, many of them living among
us, while ours suffer from your presence. In a word we suffer

on each side. If this is admitted, it affords a reason at least why we should be separated. You here are freemen I suppose.

A Voice: Yes, sir.

The President: Perhaps you have long been free, or all your lives. Your race are suffering, in my judgment, the greatest wrong inflicted on any people. But even when you cease to be slaves, you are yet far removed from being placed on an equality with the white race. You are cut off from many of the advantages which the other race enjoy. The aspiration of men is to enjoy equality with the best when free, but on this broad continent, not a single man of your race is made the equal of a single man of ours. Go where you are treated the best, and the ban is still upon you.

I do not propose to discuss this, but to present it as a fact with which we have to deal. I cannot alter it if I would. It is a fact about which we all think and feel alike, I and you. We look to our condition, owing to the existence of the two races on this continent. I need not recount to you the effects upon white men, growing out of the institution of slavery. I believe in its general evil effects on the white race. See our present condition—the country engaged in war!—our white men cutting one another's throats, none knowing how far it will extend; and then consider what we know to be the truth. But for your race among us there could not be war, although many men engaged on either side do not care for you one way or the other. Nevertheless, I repeat, without the institution of Slavery and the colored race as a basis, the war could not have an existence.

It is better for us both, therefore, to be separated. I know that there are free men among you, who even if they could better their condition are not as much inclined to go out of the country as those, who being slaves could obtain their freedom on this condition. I suppose one of the principal difficulties in the way of colonization is that the free colored man cannot see that his comfort would be advanced by it. You may believe you can live in Washington or elsewhere in the United States the remainder of your life, perhaps more so than you can in any foreign country, and hence you may come to the conclusion that you have nothing to do with the idea of going to a foreign country. This is (I speak in no unkind sense) an extremely selfish view of the case.

But you ought to do something to help those who are not so fortunate as yourselves. There is an unwillingness on the part of our people, harsh as it may be, for you free colored people to remain with us. Now, if you could give a start to white people, you would open a wide door for many to be made free. If we deal with those who are not free at the beginning, and whose intellects are clouded by Slavery, we have very poor materials to start with. If intelligent colored men, such as are before me, would move in this matter, much might be accomplished. It is exceedingly important that we have men at the beginning capable of thinking as white men, and not those who have been systematically oppressed.

There is much to encourage you. For the sake of your race you should sacrifice something of your present comfort for the purpose of being as grand in that respect as the white people. It is a cheering thought throughout life that something can be done to ameliorate the condition of those who have been subject to the hard usage of the world. It is difficult to make a man miserable while he feels he is worthy of himself, and claims kindred to the great God who made him. In the American Revolutionary war sacrifices were made by men engaged in it; but they were cheered by the future. Gen. Washington himself endured greater physical hardships than if he had remained a British subject. Yet he was a happy man, because he was engaged in benefiting his race—something for the children of his neighbors, having none of his own.

The colony of Liberia has been in existence a long time. In a certain sense it is a success. The old President of Liberia, Roberts, has just been with me—the first time I ever saw him. He says they have within the bounds of that colony between 300,000 and 400,000 people, or more than in some of our old States, such as Rhode Island or Delaware, or of our newer States, and less than in some of our larger ones. They are not all American colonists, or their descendants. Something less than 12,000 have been sent thither from this country. Many of the original settlers have died, yet, like people elsewhere, their offspring outnumber those deceased.

The question is if the colored people are persuaded to go anywhere, why not there? One reason for an unwillingness to do so is that some of you would rather remain within reach of the country of your nativity. I do not know how much attachment you may have toward our race. It does not strike me that you have the greatest reason to love them. But still you are attached to them at all events.

The place I am thinking about having for a colony is in Central America. It is nearer to us than Liberia—not much more than one-fourth as far as Liberia, and within seven days' run by steamboat. Unlike Liberia it is on a great line of travel— it is a highway. The country is a very excellent one for any people, and with great natural resources and advantages, and especially because of the similarity of climate with your native land—thus being suited to your physical condition.

The particular place I have in view is to be a great highway from the Atlantic or Caribbean Sea to the Pacific Ocean, and this particular place has all the advantages for a colony. On both sides there are harbors among the first in the world.

. . . You have been talked to upon this subject, and told that a speculation is intended by gentlemen, who have an interest in the country . . . We have been mistaken all our lives if we do not know whites as well as blacks look to their self-interest. Unless among those deficient of intellect everybody you trade with makes something. You meet with these things here as elsewhere.

. . . I shall, if I get a sufficient number of you engaged, have provisions made that you shall not be wronged. If you will engage in the enterprise I will spend some of the money intrusted to me. I am not sure you will succeed. . . . The political affairs in Central America are not in quite as satisfactory condition as I wish. There are contending factions in that quarter; but it is true all the factions agreed alike on the subject of colonization, and want it, and are more generous than we are here. To your colored race they have no objection. Besides, I would endeavor to have you made equals, and have the best assurance that you should be the equals of the best.

The practical thing I want to ascertain is whether I can get a number of able-bodied men, with their wives and children,

who are willing to go, when I present evidence of encouragement and protection. Could I get a hundred tolerably intelligent
men, with their wives and children, to "cut their own fodder,"
so to speak? Can I have fifty? If I could find twenty-five able-
bodied men, with a mixture of women and children, good
things in the family relation, I think I could make a successful
commencement.

I want you to let me know whether this can be done or not.
This is the practical part of my wish to see you. These are the
subjects of very great importance, worthy of a month's study,
[and not] of a speech delivered in an hour. I ask you then to
consider seriously not pertaining to yourselves merely, nor for
your race, and ours, for the present time, but as one of the
things, if successfully managed, for the good of mankind—not
confined to the present generation, but as

"From age to age descends the lay,
     To millions yet to be,
Till far its echoes roll away,
     Into eternity."

The above is merely given as the substance of the President's
remarks.

The Chairman of the delegation briefly replied that "they
would hold a consultation and in a short time give an answer."
The President said: "Take your full time—no hurry at all."
The delegation then withdrew.

Miscegenation and the Re-election of Lincoln

*Although the word miscegenation was not to be found in any
dictionary of the 1860's, it was used to describe the illegal sexual union of white and black. And the topic of miscegenation
became an important emotional issue in the election of 1864.
In an attempt to discredit the Republican Party and reverse*

Source: [3] L. Seaman, LL.D., *What Miscegenation Is! and What We
Are To Expect Now that Mr. Lincoln Is Re-elected* (New York, 1864),
pp. 3–8.

their "pro-black" policies, the "Negro-haters" organized and promoted a campaign based on the fear and anxiety associated with racial amalgamation.

Thus, the racial extremists warned the nation that the re-election of Lincoln would be a direct step toward the "mongrelization" of the United States. The military victories of the Union, however, overshadowed the racist pleas. With the political victory of the Republicans, the bigots observed that "Since the re-election of Mr. Lincoln, the Blood Royal of Africa—the Creme de la creme of colored society [were] extremely jubilent."

"What is Miscegenation?"

It is unnecessary for us to enter into a lengthy definition of the word as the artist who engraved our frontpiece portrays that which our pen fails to accomplish. Our illustration represents an "intelligent gentleman of color" affectionately saluting [kissing] a pretty white girl of sixteen, with auburn hair and *light* complexion; the different shades of complexion of the two contrasting beautifully and lending enchantment to the scene. The thick tufts of wool of the one lends beauty to the long, waving auburn hair of the other, and the sweet, delicate little Roman nose of the one does not detract from the beauty of the broad, flat nose, with expanded nostrils of the other—while the intellectual, bold and majestic forehead of the one forms an unique, though beautiful contrast to the round, flat head, resembling a huge gutter mop, of the other. Contrast is the order of the day; a desire for sameness was an hallucination of the ancients, but we of the Nineteenth Century are going to bring about a new order of things.

Miscegenation is a coined word—coined in New England, and for the times. Amalgamationists not finding words sufficient in the English language to express their peculiar ideas, have manufactured it, and we need hardly say, it answers its purpose admirably. "Amalgamation," done very well for a time as a hobby but it soon lost its effect, and something new was needed to take its place. Accordingly the agitators got their heads together and invented the word "miscegenation" as best suited to define their cause and at once declared themselves

"Miscegenationists." A large and flourishing society soon sprang up under the appropriate title of the "Modern Order of Miscegenationists." The first society being formed in Boston, others sprang up rapidly throughout the State of Massachusetts, and from thence the contageon spread throughout all New England and by some ill wind that blows no one good, was wafted from Maine to Oregon, carrying everything before it, and by its fell swoop, upheaving and disorganizing society, respecting nothing but the negro. So complete was the organization and sway of the "Modern Order," when the late Presidential election took place, not only New England, but many of the Western and North Western States stood in solid phalanx for Miscegenation, and Mr. Lincoln was triumphantly re-elected.

Actual miscegenationists were first discovered in the South, but the atrocious crime was not popular although it was committed to a considerable extent, and men have been known to sell their own children into slavery, simply because of the supposed attainment of the offspring from its mother. But such beasts are only to be found in the South. Here in the North, we have a finer sense of the beautiful. Dark blood, in the estimation of the Northmen, instead of *attainting purifies*. A man whose veins are coursed by a certain amount of dark blood, and whose skin is correspondingly dark, is believed to be a superior being.

Many of our best orators have been advocating this mixture for some time. Wendell Phillips can't see why a negro is not the equal of a white man, and, in many instances, why he has not proved himself superior. When coalescesion takes place he believes that the excellent properties of Sambo's component parts are intensified and the sluggish material of the white man purified and renovated.

Cuffy's good time is come—his millennium is at hand. Millions of treasure is expended daily for his benefit. The blood of whitemen is shed in torrents for him. Mr. Lincoln says the war must be prosecuted until slavery is abolished. Henry Ward Beecher said in his Fifth Avenue Hotel speech, in reply to [Benjamin] Butler, that "when this war ceases slavery will be gone. It will be out of the way." He considered that "every drop of blood spilt without accomplishing that certainty squandered." Of course Mr. Beecher must believe the war is for the negro, and Mr. Lincoln declares that the war will stop when slavery is eradicated—hence our conclusion that Sambo's good time is come—that his millenium is at hand—that his star is in the ascendant. White men, just stand back and let the conquering heroes pass.

When the war was first inaugurated Miscegenation was but little spoken of and little thought of. Abolitionists were considered bad citizens. Amalgamationists were reviled and their names bid fair to be handed down to the execrations of posterity. But how is it now in the year of our Lord and Savior, one thousand eight hundred and sixty-four? Behold what a change! What a change has taken place in Israel! Those among us who were the greatest have become the least, and those who were the least have become the greatest! Gradually, for the past four years, public sentiment has been setting in Pompey's favor, and if it continues thus, at the same ratio, at the end of the next four years, dark complexions will be fashionable— white and pale faces will be discarded. The ladies, instead of applying white chalk to their faces, will use char-coal with profusion; instead of a small delicate foot being the rage, big flat understandings, with projecting heels will be all the go; instead of puckering up their lips to make their mouths look small they will be turning them inside out to resemble Dianah's ruby lips. Already the ladies of Washington have commenced to friz their hair *à la d'Afrique*. The front seats in places of amusement will be reserved, invariably, for colored folks. Congress will soon pass a law making the colored man a legal voter, and declaring him eligible to office; he will occupy public positions, from policeman up to president. We shall have the colored man in our Boards of Aldermen. Pompey will be Mayor, Judge, and Governor. Our legislators will be of the thick-lipped and wooley-headed fraternity. Colored men will be the occupants of brown stone fronts, and reside in our Clinton and Fifth Avenues. They will ride in their carriages with a white man on top as driver, and perhaps have another on behind. Things are changing. They are being reversed. It will be fashionable for a colored "gemman" to have a white driver upon the same grounds that it has, heretofore, been fashionable for *white* men to have *negro* drivers. 'Tother man is going to be the gentleman; that's all.

FRONT SEATS FOR COLORED FOLKS

The Trustees of Dr. Z. P. Lathrop's Church, Boston, have reserved their front seats for colored folks! White people are to be kept back under the gallaries and in the vestibule. This arrangement created a little hard feeling among the devoted members of the church, especially the female portion, but they soon became reconciled to the new order of things like good christians.

This surely is a bold step toward the "elevation of the negro," and merits the approbation of the Beechers and Cheevers. Boston is always ahead in every worthy enterprise, but in this instance, if rumor is to be believed, she will not be much ahead of Brooklyn. Already, we understand, the matter of reserving front seats for colored people in some of our first class churches is being seriously considered. The movement will be inaugurated on the Heights, and probably extend to Fleet street, Hanson Place, Lafayette avenue, Pacific street, Johnson street and Sand street.*

We are led to the conclusion that the colored people are to be favored with front seats from the tenor of the speeches delivered by some of the first men of Brooklyn on the occasion of a

GRAND MISCEGENATION JUBILEE,

held on Brooklyn Heights in the mansion of J. Walter Stuben, Esq., directly after the late election. The speakers in question thought the white man had rights which were entitled to respect, but still there was a line of demarcation, beyond which the white man should not trespass.

The principal speaker of the evening spoke substantially as follows;

Ladies and Gentlemen: We have come together this evening to congratulate each other upon the success of our cause. The horizon is aglow with victory from Maine to Oregon (ap-

* Located in Brooklyn, New York.

plause). We have advanced step by step, until victory is ours, and we have but to publish the glad tidings: "the bondman is freed." (Loud applause.) WE will soon extend the right hand of fellowship, without let or hindrance, to our brothers of African descent! (Tremendous and prolonged applause.) The time has come when our brothers of dark complexion and curly hair are to have their rights, and when restrictions will be no longer placed upon the development of their talents! (Tremendous cheering.) The day is dawning in which the colored man will take his proper position in life—in which he will take a foremost stand in society. (Deafening and prolonged applause.) The day is not far distant when our oppressed brothers of dark skins will have their just deserts—when, instead of being enslaved they will be honored and respected throughout the world. (Cheers, after which an enthusiastic old gentleman sprang up and shouted at the top of his voice, "Three cheers for Fred. Douglass." Three times three was given for Fred., followed by the inevitable "tiger!") My friends, this is an age of progress; men are growing wiser every day; those who, a few years ago, would not recognize the colored man as their equal, now begin to see that he is, in some instances possessed of superior qualities. (Tremendous applause.) So much for the age in which we live! We have no patience with that stupid and despicable class of men, who, from ignorance or prejudice, still fail to recognize in the colored man his superior mental endowments. (Cheers.) The speaker then entered into an eleborate discourse to prove the admirable qualities of the negro race, and to show that it did not descend from Ham, but from Ham's brother Abel, whom wicked Ham slew. After which the meeting adjourned, with cheers for some contrabands present, for Fred. Douglass, and for Vice President Hamlin.

THE SABLE NOBILITY

Since the re-election of Mr. Lincoln, the Blood Royal of Africa—the *creme de la creme* of colored society have been extremely jubilent. Soirees d'Afrique are being had throughout the country. Boston, Philadelphia, Cincinnati and New York, have all been favored with their jubilent demonstrations.

The late emancipation proclamations, the re-election of Mr.
Lincoln, together with the recent decision of the people of
Maryland to discard Slavery, has given our colored Brudders
a good opinion of themselves, and they have become, the aristocracy, proper, of the country. Codfish, Shoddy, and Fifth
avenue, are nowhere. The colored aristocracy is believed to
be more sensible in their dress and general deportment. They
are not considered bigoted or egotistical. They do not treat the
poor white trash with that contempt and disdain which is characteristic of the shoddy and codfish aristocracy. They have been
known to condescend to speak to, and, in some instances, even
to associate with the middle or lower classes of white society.
This, surely, is a commendable trait. The ebony bon ton however, are outstripping their neighbors in Fifth avenue, in regard
to dress and fashionable entertainments. There is a sound of
revelry every night, and Africa's sons and daughters (her
beauty and her chivalry) trip the fantastic toe; gorgeous lamps
shine o'er fair women and brave men; a thousand hearts beat
happily: and when music rises with its voluptuous swell shiny
eyes look love to eyes which speak again, and all goes merry
as a marriage bell.

A Journal of Racism: *The Old Guard*
and the Fear of "Mongrelization"

*The Old Guard, a Monthly Journal, Devoted to the Principles
of 1776 and 1787* first appeared in June 1862. Subsequently,
it became the leading vehicle of organized racism in the United
States. Published in New York City by Van Evrie, Horton and
Company, and under the editorial supervision of the outspoken
bigot C. Chauncey Burr, the magazine repeatedly affirmed its
commitment to white supremacy and Anglo-Saxon superiority.
For the decade of the 1860's, in tune with its frantic doctrinaire

Source: [4] "White Supremacy and Negro Subordination," *The Old
Guard*, III (May, 1865), pp. 193–199.

style, the periodical served as a major literary outlet for the nation's racist fanatics.

In a representative article, the journal decried the proposed Thirteenth Amendment to abolish slavery as a "subversion," not intended "to amend, but destroy *the Constitution."*

The supremacy of the white race, and the consequent subordination of the inferior or negro race, was one of the prominent ideas on which the Federal Union was established. It is an idea which has been faithfully adhered to, especially by the Democratic party, from the foundation of the Union down to 1861. Since 1861, a portion of the party has been supporting a war designed to overthrow this grand idea of white supremacy, by attempting to bring the negro into an equality with the white race, in the sovereignty of the country.

It is proper to say that the Democracy has not adhered so tenaciously to this idea of white supremacy with any spirit of intolerance towards the inferior race, but only as a means of preserving our own race from the deplorable consequences of *hybridism,* and of saving our country from that *mongrelism* which has destroyed some flourishing republics, which now live only in history. But the fundamental thought which has guided the Democracy in this matter is the wish to preserve this Government as it was formed by the great and wise men of the Revolution. This was a *white man's government,* nor did any one dream, at the time of its foundation, that the negro race would be admitted to an equality of citizenship in the Federal Union. Had such a thing been imagined as lying within the bounds of possibility in the future, the Union would never have been formed. The *"sovereignty,"* the governing power, of these States, was in the white race; and never in a single instance, did the word "sovereignty," or the phrase, "the people of the United States," include negroes. *Sovereignty* always meant *white* sovereignty, never *negro* sovereignty. At the time of the adoption of the Constitution, in no State were negroes regarded as a part of the civil community, or embraced in the general term of *"citizen."* In the Dred Scott decision [1857] of the Supreme Court, Chief Justice Taney clearly stated the facts in the following language:

The words "people of the United States" and "citizens," are synonymous terms, and mean the same thing. They both describe the political body who, according to our republican institutions, form the sovereignty, and who hold the power and conduct the Government through their representatives. They are what we familiarly call the "sovereign people," and every citizen is one of this people and a constituent member of this sovereignty. The question before us is, whether the class of persons described in the plea in abatement compose a portion of this people, and are constituent members of this sovereignty? We think they are not, and that they are not included, under the word "citizens" in the Constitution, and can therefore claim none of the rights and privileges which that instrument provides for and secures to citizens of the United States. On the contrary, they were at that time considered as a subordinate and inferior class of beings, who had been subjugated by the dominant race, and whether emancipated or not, yet remained subject to their authority, and had no rights or privileges but such as those who held the power and the Government might choose to grant them.

This decision caused a universal howl from the advocates of negro equality, which was, however, as senseless as it was noisy. It was easy enough to rave against it, but no one attempted to answer it. It was, and is, unanswerable. In his debates with Judge Douglas, Mr. Lincoln went so far as to counsel the people to totally disregard and set at naught this decision of the Supreme Court. The only reason he attempted to give for this counsel to insurrection and revolution was that the Declaration of Independence declared that all men are created free and equal. In reply, Judge Douglas showed that the word "equal" did not embrace *negroes,* but only the *white race,* which was declaring its independence of Great Britain. His language was:

I hold that the negro is not, and never ought to be, a citizen of the United States. I hold that this government was made on the white basis, by white men, for the benefit of white men and their posterity forever, and should be administered by white men and none others. I do not believe that the Almighty made the negro capable of self-government. I am aware that all the abolition lecturers that you find traveling about through the country are in the habit of reading the Declaration of Independence to prove that all men were created equal, and endowed by their Creator with certain inalienable rights, among which are life, liberty, and the pursuit of happiness. Mr. Lincoln is very much in the habit of following in the track of Lovejoy in this particular, by reading that part of the Declaration of Independence to prove that the negro was endowed by the Almighty with the inalienable right of equality with white men. Now, I say to you, my fellow-citizens, that in my opinion, the signers of the Declaration had no reference to the negro whatever, when they declared all men to be created equal. They desired to express by that phrase white men, men of European birth and European descent, and had no reference either to the negro, the savage Indians, the Fejee, the Malay, or any other inferior and degraded race, when they spoke of the equality of men. One great evidence that such was their understanding, is to be found in the fact that at that time every one of the thirteen colonies was a slaveholding colony, every signer of the Declaration represented a slaveholding constituency, and we know that no one of them emancipated his slaves, much less offered citizenship to them when they signed the Declaration; and yet, if they intended to declare that the negro was the equal to the white man, and entitled by divine right to an equality with him, they were bound, as honest men, that day and hour to have put their negroes on an equality with themselves. Instead of doing so, with uplifted eyes to heaven they implored the divine blessing upon them, during the seven years' bloody war they had to fight to maintain that Declaration, never dreaming that they were violating divine law by still holding the negroes in bondage and depriving them of equality.

The only reply Mr. Lincoln could make to this conclusive answer was to exclaim that if the Declaration of Independence does not include negroes, *"let us get the statute-book where we find it and tear it out. If it is not true, let us tear it out."* That is, if the Declaration of Independence does not include negroes, does not teach negro equality with the white race, let us tear it to pieces. That was Mr. Lincoln's feeling in 1858, and no one can say that he has not faithfully adhered to it, in his grotesque administration of the Government. In his crusade after negro equality, he has torn not only the Declaration of Independence to pieces, but he has torn the Constitution to pieces, and he has torn his country to pieces. This is the heart of the whole conflict. If he, and his mob of vicious fanatics in Congress were to give up the pursuit of *negro-equality* to-day, they would disband their armies tomorrow. There is neither sap nor marrow in the war, stript of this idea of *negro equality*. This is the *summum bonum* of the whole thing. It is an infidel, murderous revolution, undertaken for the purpose of making negroes what neither God nor the Constitution ever designed they should be, *the equal of the white race.* For the sake of deluding the people, the cunning supporters of this revolution sometimes say that they mean *"negro equality before the laws."* But that is just what the negro is not, before the fundamental laws of our country. The Constitution and laws deny him his equality, and there is no way of giving it to him but by revolutionizing and overthrowing the Federal Government. This is the point which we have repeatedly offered to discuss with the leaders of this bloody revolution; but it is precisely the point which they fly from, and which they dare not discuss.

In relation to the Declaration of Independence, Chief Justice Taney says:

"But it is too clear for dispute that the enslaved African race were not intended to be included, and formed no part of the people who framed and adopted this declaration; for if the language, as understood in that day, would embrace them, the conduct of the distinguished men who framed the Declaration of Independence would have been utterly and flagrantly inconsistent with the principles they asserted; and instead of the sympathy of mankind, to which they so confidently appealed, they would have deserved and received universal rebuke and reprobation."

If the conduct of the men who made the Declaration of Independence was incompatible with the idea of negro equality *before the laws,* how much more so was the conduct of those who adopted the Constitution? The Preamble to the Constitution sets forth *by* whom and *for* whom it was formed. It was

formed by "We the people of the United States," to "secure the blessings of liberty to *ourselves* and *our posterity.*" Now the instrument itself shows that "we the people," &c., did not include negroes. They were not a constituent part of the body politic; and none of "the blessings of liberty" which it sought to secure were intended for the "posterity" of negroes. It was formed by white men, for the posterity of white men. The Constitution, in several places, recognizes negroes as a separate and inferior class of beings. It reserved to every one of the original States the right to import negroes, and provided for the raising of a federal revenue from that negro importation. Again, it protects the owners of negro labor in their rights, just as it does any other species of property, and promises to maintain those rights as long as the government shall endure.
. . . From the foundation of the Confederacy, down to the election of Lincoln, there was never a respectable body of men in our country to dispute the soundness of this position. The Democratic party, especially, has, through a history of more than seventy years, been a tenacious advocate of the strictest adherence to the letter and spirit of this Constitutional doctrine of *white sovereignty* and of *negro subordination.* It has always held that any attempt to incorporate negro sovereignty with federal legislation, was revolutionary in its character, and must result in dissolving the constituent elements of the *Federal agency.* In a word, dissolving the Union. There the Democratic party has stood all through, a proud, a triumphant history; and there it must stand for the future, or lose its identity, and break like a bubble into this black and sluggish pool of miscegenated Republicanism.

Some men, calling themselves Democrats, whether from ignorance or treachery we shall not stop to inquire, tell us that "It is sound policy to ignore the negro question altogether." The answer is short and conclusive—that the question of negro sovereignty was never raised by the Democratic party; but being raised, it is the business of the Democracy to lay it. It is the mission of Democracy to preserve this Government *intact* upon its original foundations of *white sovereignty;* and whenever an effort is made to drag it off from this basis, on to that of a black, a mixed, or mongrel sovereignty, the party cannot, without eternal shame, surrender to this new and degrading African element.

. . . And this is our position none the less, since the so-called amendment [13th] to the Constitution by resolution of Congress. No matter how many State Legislators may confirm it, it is still no amendment to the Constitution, for the simple reason that the subject matter of the resolution was never in the Constitution. It never belonged to the Constitution.

. . . This is not an *amendment*, it is a *subversion*. If under the title of an amendment to the Constitution three quarters of the States may take away the property of the other quarter, they may just as easily take away the wives and daughters, nay, even the lives of all the inhabitants of the remaining States. Had we a father or a brother, who believed that this impudent Abolition dodge was really an amendment to the Constitution, and we were sure that he was neither a fool nor a rascal, we would send him to the insane asylum as a lunatic! There are but two classes of persons who will claim that this late farce is an amendment to the Constitution—one of these deserves to be *cured*, and the other to be *flogged!*

But, regardless of all this stupendous folly, the true Democracy will still cling to the glorious old Constitution, with a heart ever hopeful of being able to reinstate it as the bond of Union between all these States. But there are no just grounds for such hope except in a firm adherence to the original idea of white supremacy and negro subordination. If the Union stands at all, it must be upon its original basis. If it stands at all, the negro must be left where God and the Constitution placed him. To make him a constituent element of the Federal government, is to overthrow and destroy the character of citizenship under the Constitution—is not to *amend*, but to *destroy*, the Constitution. When the Federal administration undertakes to say what shall be the status of the negro in the States, especially when it pretends to alter the status of the negro, in violation of the Constitution of the States, and of the United States, it is time for every State to put, and to keep itself, in a defensive attitude. The Federal administration has no more right to force the people of the States to free their negroes than it has to compel them to marry negroes.

PART 5
The Racism of
Reconstruction, 1865-1880

INTRODUCTION

The Reconstruction Period represented a pivotal decade for the Negro. During these years, the government abolished slavery, granted citizenship to all blacks, and constitutionally guaranteed them the right to vote. Reconstruction afforded white America an opportunity to rectify the two hundred and fifty years of inhuman treatment of blacks and even more essentially, an opportunity to purge the nation of its distorted racial ideology.

Although the elimination of racism and the full acceptance of the black minority by white America were considered "unrealistic" goals, attempts were made to fulfill the promises of 1776 and 1789. Some leaders, particularly Radical Republicans such as Charles Sumner, were determined to guarantee to blacks the social and political gains which were their due. Because they recognized that anti-black activities were only temporarily suspended in the ex-Confederate states due to the presence of federal troops, Congress enacted several civil rights acts and constitutional provisions designed for the permanent protection of the Freedmen. With the passage of the Thirteenth, Fourteenth and Fifteenth Amendments, racism suffered a crucial setback, while blacks were provided with their greatest opportunity yet to participate in American society.

Unfortunately, with the withdrawal of federal troops from the South, the hope that derived from the theoretical, economic and social advancements for blacks was soon dispelled. The era which began with such promise ended in tragic failure in the mid-1870's.

The signal for the termination of Reconstruction was the restoration of ex-Confederates to political leadership in both the federal and state governments. Through legislation, white supremacists intensified their efforts to eliminate the gains the blacks had made in the 1860's. In addition to the "Black Codes," they sought to deprive the Freedmen of the progress they had made through the extralegal methods of night-riding terrorists, intimidation and violence. Eventually, with the political, economic and social future of blacks controlled by white racists, the opportunity for a racially harmonious coexistence was lost.

The Negro, who had savored only a modicum of the democracy guaranteed to white Americans, was once again confronted with a situation which paralleled his pre-1865 subordinate status. With the revitalization of racism in the South, the indifference of an anti-black North, and the support of racial extremists throughout the nation, black America experienced the birth of the modern "Jim Crow." Once again, the hypocrisy of Amercia's proclamations of justice and equality were exposed to the world.

The Mississippi Black Codes

The Black Codes, passed by southern legislatures under the control of ex-Confederates during the initial stages of Presidential Reconstruction (1865–1866), were an attempt to deal with the emancipated slave. The laws, which varied from Georgia's lenient enactments to Mississippi's harsher legislation, limited the civil rights of Freedmen, substituted apprenticeship and vagrancy for slavery, and restrained social mobility through the penal system.

Viewing these laws as an attempt to negate the results of the Civil War, the Radical Republicans seized control of Reconstruction from the "racially conservative" Andrew Johnson and substituted a program of their own. Thus, with the inception of Congressional Reconstruction, the Black Codes were

Source: [1] *Law of the State of Mississippi; Passed at a Regular Session of the Mississippi Legislature Held in the City of Jackson, October, November and December, 1865* (1866), pp. 82–93, 164–167, 194–195.

declared void; and realizing that permanent protection for blacks was needed, Congress proposed and passed the Fourteenth and Fifteenth Amendments.

AN ACT *to confer Civil Rights on Freedmen, and for other purposes.*

Sec. 3. Be it . . . enacted, That all freedmen, free negroes and mulattoes, who do now and have heretofore lived and cohabitated together as husband and wife shall be taken and held as legitimate for all purposes. That it shall not be lawful for any freedman, free negro or mulatto to intermarry with any white person; nor for any white person to intermarry with any freedman, free negro or mulatto; and any person who shall so intermarry shall be deemed guilty of felony, and on conviction thereof, shall be confined in the State Penitentiary for life; and those shall be deemed freedmen, free negroes and mulattoes who are of pure negro blood, and those descended from a negro to the third generation inclusive, though one ancestor of each generation may have been a white person.

Sec. 7. Be it . . . enacted, That every civil officer shall, and every person may arrest and carry back to his or her legal employer any freeman, free negro or mulatto, who shall have quit the service of his or her employer before the expiration of his or her term of service without good cause, and said officer and person shall be entitled to receive for arresting and carrying back every deserting employee aforesaid, the sum of five dollars, and ten cents per mile from the place of arrest to the place of delivery, and the same shall be paid by the employer, and held as a set-off for so much against the wages of said deserting employee.

Sec. 9. Be it . . . enacted, That if any person shall persuade or attempt to persuade, entice or cause any freedman, free negro or mulatto, to desert from the legal employment of any person, before the expiration of his or her term of service, or shall knowingly employ any such deserting freedman, free negro or mulatto, or shall knowingly give or sell to any such deserting freedman, free negro or mulatto, any food, rayment or other thing, he or she shall be guilty of a misdemeanor, and upon conviction, shall be fined not less than twenty-five dollars and not more than two hundred dollars and the costs, and if said fine and costs shall not be immediately paid, the court shall sentence said convict to not exceeding two months imprisonment in the county jail, and he or she shall moreover be liable to the party injured in damages: Provided, if any person shall, or shall attempt to persuade, entice, or cause any freedman, free negro or mulatto, to desert from any legal employment of any person, with the view to employ said freedman, free negro or mulatto, without the limits of this State, such person, on conviction, shall be fined not less than fifty dollars and not more than five hundred dollars and costs, and if said fine and costs shall not be immediately paid, the court shall sentence said convict to not exceeding six months imprisonment in the county jail.

AN ACT *to be entitled "An act to regulate the relationship of Master and Apprentice, as relates to Freedmen, Free Negroes, and Mulattoes."*

Sec. 4. Be it . . . enacted, That if any apprentice shall leave the employment of his or her master or mistress, without his or her consent, said master or mistress may pursue and recapture said apprentice, and bring him or her before any justice of the peace of the county, whose duty it shall be to remand said apprentice to the service of his or her master or mistress; and in the event of a refusal on the part of said apprentice so to return, then said justice shall commit said apprentice to the jail of said county, on failure to give bond, until the next term of the county court; and it shall be the duty of said court, at the first term thereafter, to investigate said case, and if the court shall be of opinion that said apprentice left the employment of his or her master or mistress without good cause, to order him or her to be punished, as provided for the punishment of hired freedmen, as may be from time to time provided for by law, for desertion, until he or she shall agree to return to his or her master or mistress . . .

AN ACT *to amend the Vagrant Laws of the State.*

Sec. 5. Be it . . . enacted, That . . . in case any freedman, free negro or mulatto, shall fail for five days after the

imposition of any fine or forfeiture upon him or her for violation of any of the provisions of this act, to pay the same, that
it shall be, and is hereby made the duty of the sheriff . . . to
hire out said freedman, free negro or mulatto, to any person
who will, for the shortest period of service, pay said fine or
forfeiture and all costs: Provided, a preference shall be given
to the employer, if there be one, in which case the employer
shall be entitled to deduct and retain the amount so paid from
the wages of such freeman, free negro or mulatto, then due or
to become due; and in case such freedman, free negro or mulatto cannot be hired out he or she may be delt with as a
pauper.

Sec. 7. Be it . . . enacted, That if any freedman, free
negro or mulatto shall fail, or refuse to pay any tax . . . it
shall be *prima facie* evidence of vagrancy, and it shall be the
duty of the sheriff to arrest such freedman, free negro or mulatto, or such person refusing or neglecting to pay such tax,
and proceed at once to hire, for the shortest time, such de-
linquent tax payer to any one who will pay the said tax, with
accruing costs, giving preference to the employer, if there be
one.

Sec. 2. Be it . . . enacted, That all freedmen, free negroes
and mulattoes in this State, over the age of eighteen years,
found on the second Monday in January, 1866, or thereafter,
with no lawful employment or business, or found unlawfully
assembling themselves together either in the day or night time,
and all white persons so assembling with freedmen, free negroes or mulattoes, or usually associating with freedmen, free
negroes or mulattoes on terms of equality, or living in adultery
or fornication with a freedwoman, free negro or mulatto, shall
be deemed vagrants, and on conviction thereof, shall be fined
in the sum of not exceeding, in the case of a freedman, free
negro or mulatto, fifty dollars, and a white man two hundred
dollars, and imprisoned at the discretion of the court . . .

AN ACT *to punish certain offences therein named, and for
other purposes.*

Sec. 1. Be it enacted . . . That no freedman, free negro
or mulatto, not in the military service of the United States

Government, and not licensed so to do by the board of police of his or her county, shall keep or carry fire-arms of any kind, or any ammunition, dirk or bowie knife, and on conviction thereof, in the county court, shall be punished by fine, not exceeding ten dollars, and pay the costs of such proceedings, and all such arms nor ammunition shall be forfeited to the informer, and it shall be the duty of every civil and military officer to arrest any freedman, free negro or mulatto found with any such arms or ammunition, and cause him or her to be committed for trial in default of bail . . .

Sec. 2. Be it . . . enacted, That any freedman, free negro or mulatto, committing riots, routs, affrays, trespasses, malicious mischief, cruel treatment to animals, seditious speeches, insulting gestures, language or acts, or assaults on any person, disturbance of the peace, exercising the function of a minister of the Gospel, without a license from some regularly organized church, vending spirituous or intoxicating liquors, or committing any other misdemeanor, the punishment of which is not specifically provided for by law, shall, upon conviction thereof . . . be fined, not exceeding fifty dollars and may be imprisoned, at the discretion of the court . . .

An Act *supplemental to an "Act to confer Civil Rights upon Freedmen," and for other purposes.*

Sec. 1. Be it enacted . . . That in every case where any white person has been arrested and brought to trial, by virtue of the provisions . . . of the above cited act, upon sufficient proof being made . . . that any freedman, free negro or mulatto has falsely and maliciously caused the arrest and trial of said white person or persons, the court shall render up a judgement against said freedman, free negro or mulatto for all costs of the case and impose a fine not to exceed fifty dollars and imprisonment in the county jail not to exceed twenty days; and for a failure of said freedman, free negro or mulatto to pay, or cause to be paid, all costs, fines and jail fees, and the sheriff . . . is . . . authorized and required, after giving ten days public notice, to proceed to hire out, at public outcry . . . said freedman, free negro or mulatto, for the shortest time, to raise the amount necessary to discharge said freedman, free negro or mulatto from all costs, fines and jail fees aforesaid.

The Ritual of the Knights of the White Camelia

During the years 1868–1871, the nation witnessed the activities of terrorists oppressing the South's black population. With the protective barrier of slavery eliminated, secret societies were organized and pledged "to do everything in [their] power in order to maintain . . . the supremacy of the Caucasian race, and restrain the black or African race to that condition of social and political inferiority for which God [had] destined it." Thus, a new phase of anti-black turmoil had begun.

The actions of such organizations as the Ku Klux Klan, the Knights of the White Camelia, the '76 Association, and the White Brotherhood, sprang from the avowed intention to protect the Constitution, relieve the white race from its humiliating condition (federal occupation of the South), and maintain the sanctified myth of white womanhood. And intimidation, kidnapping and murder were among the means to their ends.

Of the numerous societies created, the most powerful and well-known were the Ku Klux Klan and the Knights of the White Camelia. Despite their open and illegal assaults upon blacks and their white sympathizers, the Congress failed to take positive action against these racist organizations until the passage of the Ku Klux Klan Acts of May 1870 and April 1871. Thus, for four years these terrorist groups were free to control the political, social, and economic ambitions of five million Americans.

[Questions For Prospective Members]

1. Do you belong to the white race?

2. Did you ever marry any woman who did not, or does not, belong to the white race?

Source: [2] *Constitutional and Ritual of the Knights of the White Camelia,* 1869.

3. Do you promise never to marry any woman but one who belongs to the white race?

4. Do you believe in the superiority of your race?

5. Will you promise never to vote for any one for any office of honor, profit or trust, who does not belong to your race?

6. Will you take a solemn oath never to abstain from casting your vote at any election in which a candidate of the negro race shall be opposed to a white man attached to your principles, unless or prevented by severe illness or any other physical disability?

7. Are you opposed to allowing the control of the political affairs of this country to go in whole or in part, into the hands of the African race, and will you do everything in your power to prevent it?

8. Will you devote your intelligence, energy and influence to the furtherance and propagation of the principles of our Order?

9. Will you, under all circumstances, defend and protect persons of the white race in their lives, rights and property, against all encroachments or invasions from any inferior race, and especially the African?

10. Are you willing to take an oath forever to cherish these grand principles, and to unite yourself with others who, like you, believing in their truth, have firmly bound themselves to stand by and defend them against all?

The Commander shall then say: If you consent to join our Association, raise your right hand and I will administer to you the oath we have all taken:

[Charge to those who have been accepted]

Brothers: You have been initiated into one of the most important Orders, which have been established on this continent: an Order, which, if its principles are faithfully observed and its objects diligently carried out, is destined to regenerate our unfortunate country and to relieve the White Race from the humiliating condition to which it has lately been reduced in this Republic. It is necessary, therefore, that before taking part in the labors of this Association, you should understand fully its principles and objects and the duties which devolve upon you as one of its members.

As you may have already gathered from the questions which propounded to you, and which you have answered so satisfactorily, and from the clauses of the Oath which you have taken, our main and fundamental object is the MAINTENANCE OF THE SUPREMACY OF THE WHITE RACE in this Republic. History and physiology teach us that we belong to a race which nature has endowed with an evident superiority over all other races, and that the Maker, in thus elevating us above the common standard of human creation, has intended to give us over inferior races, a dominion from which no human laws can permanently derogate. The experience of ages demonstrates that, from the origin of the world, this dominion has always remained in the hands of the Caucasian race; whilst all the other races have constantly occupied a subordinate and secondary position; a fact which triumphantly confirms this great law of nature. Powerful nations have succeeded each other on the face of the world, and have marked their passage by glorious and memorable deeds: and among those who have thus left on this globe indelible traces of their splendor and greatness, we find none but descended from the Caucasian stock. We see, on the contrary, that most of the countries inhabited by other races have remained in a state of complete barbarity; whilst the small number of those who have advanced beyond this savage existence, have, for centuries, stagnated in a semi-barbarous condition of which there can be no progress or improvement. And it is a remarkable fact that as a race of men is more remote from the Caucasian and approaches nearer to the black African the more fatally that stamp of inferiority is affixed to its sons, and irrevocably dooms them to eternal imperfectability and degradation.

Convinced that we are of these elements of natural ethics, we know, besides, that the government of our Republic was established by white men, for white men alone, and that it never was in the contemplation of its founders that it should fall into the hands of an inferior and degraded race. We hold, therefore, that any attempt to wrest from the white race the management of its affairs in order to transfer it to control of the black population, is an invasion of the sacred prerogatives vouchsafed to us by the Constitution, and a violation of the laws established by God himself; that such encroachments are subversive of the established institutions of our Republic, and that no individual of the white race can submit to them without humiliation and shame.

It, then, becomes our solemn duty, as white men, to resist strenuously and persistently those attempts against our natural and constitutional rights, and to do everything in our power in order to maintain, in this Republic, the supremacy of the Caucasian race, and restrain the black or African race to that condition of social and political inferiority for which God has destined it. This is the object for which our Order was instituted; and, in carrying it out, we intend to infringe no laws, to violate no rights, and to resort to no forcible means, except for purposes of legitimate and necessary defense.

As an essential condition of success, this Order proscribes absolutely all social equality between the races. If we were to admit persons of African race on the same level with ourselves, a state of personal relations would follow which would unavoidably lead to political equality; for it would be a virtual recognition of *status,* after which we could not consistently deny them an equal share in the administration of our public affairs. The man who is good enough to be our familiar companion, is good enough also to participate in our political government; and if we were to grant the one, there could be no good reason for us not to concede the other of these two privileges.

There is another reason, Brothers, for which we condemn this social equality. Its toleration would soon be a fruitful source of intermarriages between individuals of the two races; and the result of this *miscegenation* would be gradual amalgamation and the production of a degenerate and bastard offspring, which would soon populate these States with a degraded and ignoble population, incapable of moral and intellectual development and unfitted to support a great and powerful country. We must maintain the purity of the white blood, if we would preserve for it that natural superiority with which God has ennobled it.

To avoid these evils, therefore, we take the obligation TO OBSERVE A MARKED DISTINCTION BETWEEN THE TWO RACES, not only in the relations of public affairs, but also in the more intimate dealings and intercourse of private life which, by the frequency of their occurrence, are more apt to have an influence on the attainment of the purposes of the Order.

Now that I have laid before you the objects of this Association, let me charge you specially in relation to one of your most important duties as one of its members. Our statutes make us bound to respect sedulously the rights of the colored inhabitants of this Republic, and in every instance, to give to them whatever lawfully belongs to them. It is an act of simple justice not to deny them any of the privileges to which they are legitimately entitled; and we cannot better show the inherent superiority of our race than by dealing with them in that spirit of firmness, liberality and impartiality which characterizes all superior organizations. Besides, it would be ungenerous for us to undertake to restrict them to the narrowest limits as to the exercise of certain rights, without conceding to them, at the same time, the fullest measure of those which we recognize as theirs; and a fair construction of a white man's duty towards them would be, not only to respect and observe their acknowledged rights, but also to see that these are respected and observed by others.

From the brief explanation which I have just given you, you must have satisfied yourselves that our Association is not a political party, and has no connection with any of the organized parties of the day. Nor will it lend itself to the personal advancement of individuals, or listen to the cravings of any partisan spirit. It was organized in order to carry out certain great principles, from which it must never swerve by favoring private ambitions and political aspirations. These, as well as all sentiments of private enmity, animosity and other personal feelings, we must leave at the door before we enter this Council. You may meet here, congregated together, men who belong to all the political organizations which now divide, or may divide, this country; you see some whom embittered feuds and irreconcilable hatred have long and widely separated; they have

cast away these rankling feelings to unite cordially and zealously in the labors of our great undertaking. Let their example
be to you a useful lesson of the disinterestedness and devoted-
ness which should characterize our efforts for the success of
our cause!

A Racist Description of
the South Carolina Legislature

*James S. Pike, a journalist for the New York Tribune, wit-
nessed the activities of the allegedly black-dominated South
Carolina legislature in 1873. Upon his return to New York,
in an effort to air his racist views, he wrote a highly inaccurate
account * of the proceedings. With the publication of* The
Prostrate State, *in which black legislators were portrayed as
buffoons, he helped instill in the minds of his northern readers
the notion that a "racial crisis" confronted their southern
brethren.*

*In the preface to his book, Pike admitted that he had favored
the enfranchisement of blacks at the conclusion of the war, but
after viewing the "spectacle" of Radical Reconstruction, he
decided to "combat this sentiment as regards South Carolina."
Moreover, he demanded the termination of the "Africanization" of that state. And, he concluded, it was not only a matter
of concern for the South, but "the people of the other states,
and it [was to] their attention that [he] invoke[d] the following exposition."*

Yesterday, about 4 P.M., the assembled wisdom of the State,
whose achievements are illustrated on that theatre, issued forth
from the State-House. About three-quarters of the crowd belonged to the African race. They were of every hue, from the

Source: [3] James S. Pike, *The Prostrate State: South Carolina Under
Negro Government* (New York, 1874), pp. 10, 15–22.

* Although Pike's description was deliberately inaccurate, it remained
an accepted historical account of one aspect of the Reconstruction
Period well into the twentieth century. (Ed.)

light octoroon to the deep black. They were such a looking body of men as might pour out of a market-house or a court-house at random in any Southern State. Every negro type and physiognomy was here to be seen, from the genteel serving-man to the rough-hewn customer from the rice or cotton field.

As things stand, the body is almost literally a Black Parliament, and it is the only one on the face of the earth which is the representative of a white constituency and the professed exponent of an advanced type of modern civilization. But the reader will find almost any portraiture inadequate to give a vivid idea of the body, and enable him to comprehend the complete metamorphosis of the South Carolina Legislature, without observing its details. The Speaker is black, the Clerk is black, the door-keepers are black, the little pages are black, the chairman of the Ways and Means is black, and the chaplain is coal-black. At some of the desks sit colored men whose types it would be hard to find outside of Congo; whose costume, visages, attitudes, and expression, only befit the forecastle of a buccaneer. It must be remembered, also, that these men, with not more than half a dozen exceptions, have been themselves slaves, and that their ancestors were slaves for generations.

. . . One of the things that first strike a casual observer in this negro assembly is the fluency of debate, if the endless chatter that goes on there can be dignified with this term. The leading topics of discussion are all well understood by the members, as they are of a practical character, and appeal directly to the personal interests of every legislator, as well as to those of his constituents. When an appropriation bill is up to raise money to catch and punish the Ku-klux, they know exactly what it means. They feel it in their bones. So, too, with educational measures. The free school comes right home to them; then the business of arming and drilling the black militia. They are eager on this point. Sambo can talk on these topics and those of a kindred character, and their endless ramifications, day in and day out. There is no end to his gush and babble. The intellectual level is that of a bevy of fresh converts at a negro camp-meeting. Of course this kind of talk can be extended indefinitely. It is the doggerel of debate, and not beyond the reach of the lowest parts. Then the negro is imitative in the extreme. He can copy like a parrot or a monkey, and he is always ready for a trial of his skill. He believes he can do anything, and never loses a chance to try, and is just as ready to be laughed at for his failure as applauded for his success. He is more vivacious than the white, and, being more volatile and good-natured, he is correspondingly more irrepressible. His misuse of language in his imitations is at times ludicrous beyond measure. He notoriously loves a joke or an anecdote, and will burst into a broad guffaw on the smallest provocation. He breaks out into an incoherent harangue on the floor just as easily, and being without practice, discipline, or experience, and wholly oblivious of Lindley Murray, or any other restraint on composition, he will go on repeating himself, dancing as it were to the music of his own voice, forever. He will speak half a dozen times on one question, and every time say the same things without knowing it. He answers completely to the description of a stupid speaker in Parliament, given by Lord Derby on one occasion. It was said of him that he did not know what he was going to say when he got up; he did not know what he was saying while he was speaking, and he did not know what he had said when he sat down.

But the old stagers admit that the colored brethren have a wonderful aptness at legislative proceedings. They are "quick as lightning" at detecting points of order, and they certainly make incessant and extraordinary use of their knowledge. No one is allowed to talk five minutes without interruption, and one interruption is the signal for another and another, until the original speaker is smothered under an avalanche of them. Forty questions of privilege will be raised in a day. At times, nothing goes on but alternating questions of order and of privilege. The inefficient colored friend who sits in the Speaker's chair cannot suppress this extraordinary element of the debate. Some of the blackest members exhibit a pertinacity of intrusion in raising these points of order and questions of privilege that few white men can equal. Their struggles to get the floor, their bellowings and physical contortions, baffle decription. The Speaker's hammer plays a perpetual tattoo all to no purpose. The talking and the interruptions from all quarters go on with the utmost license. Every one esteems himself as good as his neighbor, and puts in his oar, apparently as often for love of riot and confusion as for any thing else. It is easy to imagine what are his ideas of propriety among a crowd of his own color, and these are illustrated without reserve. The Speaker orders a member whom he has discovered to be particularly unruly to take his seat. The member obeys, and with the same motion that he sits down, throws his feet on to his desk, hiding himself from the Speaker by the soles of his boots. In an instant he appears again on the floor. After a few experiences of this sort, the Speaker threatens, in a laugh, to call "the gemman" to order. This is considered a capital joke, and a guffaw follows. The laugh goes round, and then the peanuts are cracked and munched faster than ever; one hand being employed in fortifying the inner man with this nutriment of universal use, while the other enforces the views of the orator. This laughing propensity of the sable crowd is a great cause of disorder. They laugh as hens cackle—one begins and all follow.

But underneath all this shocking burlesque upon legislative proceedings, we must not forget that there is something very real to this uncouth and untutored multitude. It is not all sham, nor all burlesque. They have a genuine interest and a genuine earnestness in the business of the assembly which we are bound to recognize and respect, unless we would be accounted shallow critics. They have an earnest purpose, born of a conviction that their position and condition are not fully assured, which lends a sort of dignity to their proceedings. The barbarous, animated jargon in which they so often indulge is on occasion seen to be so transparently sincere and weighty in their own minds that sympathy supplants disgust. The whole thing is a wonderful novelty to them as well as to observers. Seven years ago these men were raising corn and cotton under the whip of the overseer. To-day they are raising points of order and questions of privilege. They find they can raise one as well as the other. They prefer the latter. It is easier, and better paid. Then, it is the evidence of an accomplished result. It means escape and defense from old oppressors. It means liberty. It means the destruction of prison-walls only too real to them. It is the sunshine of their lives. It is their day of jubilee. It is their long-promised vision of the Lord God Almighty.

Shall we, then, be too critical over the spectacle? Perhaps we might more wisely wonder that they can do so well in so short a time. The barbarians overran Rome. The dark ages followed. But then the day finally broke, and civilization followed. The days were long and weary; but they came to an end at last. Now we have the printing-press, the railroad, the telegraph; and these denote an utter revolution in the affairs of mankind. Years may now accomplish what it formerly took ages to achieve. Under the new lights and influences shall not the black man speedily emerge? Who knows? We may fear, but we may hope. Nothing in our day is impossible. Take the contested supposition that South Carolina is to be Africanized. We have a Federal Union of great and growing States. It is incontestably white at the centre. We know it to possess vital powers. It is well abreast of all modern progress in ideas and improvements. Its influence is all-pervading. How can a State of the Union escape it? South Carolina alone, if left to herself, might fall into midnight darkness. Can she do it while she remains an integral part of the nation?

But will South Carolina be Africanized? That depends. Let us hear the judgment of an intelligent foreigner who has long lived in the South, and who was here when the war began. He does not believe it. White people from abroad are drifting in, bad as things are. Under freedom the blacks do not multiply as in slavery. The pickaninnies die off from want of care. Some blacks are coming in from North Carolina and Virginia, but others are going off farther South. The white young men who were growing into manhood did not seem inclined to leave their homes and migrate to foreign parts. There was an exodus after the war, but it has stopped, and many have come back. The old slave-holders still hold their lands. The negroes were poor and unable to buy, even if the land-owners would sell. This was a powerful impediment to the development of the negro into a controlling force in the State. His whole power was in his numbers. The present disproportion of four blacks to three whites in the State he believed was already decreasing.

The whites seemed likely to more than hold their own, while the blacks would fall off. Cumulative voting would encourage the growth and add to the political power of the whites in the Legislature, where they were at present overslaughed.

PART 6

The Triumph of American Racism, 1880-1930

INTRODUCTION

The years following 1880 ushered in a new phase of American racism. After the Compromise of 1877, it had become abundantly clear that another opportunity to include blacks in the mainstream of American life had been fruitless. Through terrorism and local legislation, the white supremacists had doomed Radical Reconstruction. Recognizing the fact that the Thirteenth, Fourteenth, and Fifteenth Amendments were permanent parts of the Federal Constitution, racists resorted to more sophisticated forms of discrimination than those which had been employed in the very early days of Reconstruction.

After 1880, southern leaders, aided by favorable court decisions, institutionalized white supremacy by adopting discriminative social customs and restrictive legislation. The major attack was directed against the Negro's right to vote. In addition to the tried and true methods of terror, ballot-box stuffing, and vote-repeating, the supremacists also located the polling places so that they were far removed from black communities, and complicated the voting procedures in order to discourage Negro participation. Moreover, "Jim Crow" was given legal sanction by the United States Supreme Court; in 1883, the Court declared unconstitutional the Civil Rights Law of 1875 which had sought to render discrimination in public places illegal.

Yet white supremacy was not "inevitable"; in the 1880's and early 1890's, there was a glimmer of hope for racial equality in the South. The agricultural depression of the post-Civil War era continued to plague the small farmers of the South, black and white alike. Some of the farmers believed that the traditional Democratic party did not function to their advantage. Consequently, many black and white farmers became active in the granges and farmers' alliances of this period. At the

start of the Populist movement, leaders like Tom Watson of
Georgia urged black and white solidarity for the purpose of
presenting a united front against the railroads and corporate
interests. But when the Populists realized that they could not
control the black vote, they embraced the racist ideas of Populist leaders like "Pitchfork" Ben Tillman.

After the decline of the Populist movement in the South, a
broad, frontal attack upon Negro rights and status was re-
sumed. By state legislation and constitutional revision, the
speediest and most complete disenfranchisement of a minority
group in American history was effected. Through poll taxes,
literacy requirements, and "grandfather clauses," vast numbers of Negroes lost the right to vote. In Louisiana, in 1896,
there had been 130,344 registered black voters. Four years
later, under a new constitution, there were only 5,320 Negro
voters in the state.

Gaining a stranglehold on local governments, the racists
completed their program of Jim Crow laws with enactments
that barred interracial marriages and the mixed use of public
facilities. In 1896, the Supreme Court in the *Plessy v. Ferguson* decision gave legal sanction to the "separate but equal"
approach to the use of public accommodations and facilities.

Although the nation's intellectuals appeared to be uncon-
cerned with the political implications of white supremacy, they
were actually providing racists with their rationale. From the
pseudoscientific findings of Europeans, such as the Comte de
Gobineau and Houston Chamberlain, and the pioneering
efforts of Sir Francis Galton in the field of heredity, American
scholars, notably Madison Grant and Lothrop Stoddard, syn-
thesized racist theories for American intellectuals. While Grant
and Stoddard regarded the Negro as a "congenital barbarian,"
their main interest was propounding the Nordic or Teutonic
supremacy theory as a major argument against a free immigration policy. In the hands of southern intellectuals, the black
man became the central figure in racial theorizing. The American historians, James Ford Rhodes, William Dunning, and
Walter Fleming, subscribed to the concept of Negro inferiority
and applied it to their interpretation of Reconstruction. More
significant than the intellectuals, however, were the writers for

magazines and periodicals, and the novelists, all of whom helped to popularize racism. The works of literary figures like Thomas Nelson Page and Thomas Dixon defended the southern point of view, insisted upon black inferiority, and perpetuated the common Negro stereotypes.

Not all Negroes, however, submitted meekly to the rising tide of racism and discrimination. A new generation of black scholars, most notably, William E. B. Du Bois, refused to accept the Booker T. Washington policy of accommodation. The Niagara Movement and the formation of the N.A.A.C.P. in the early 1900's embodied the desire of many blacks to fight segregation and Jim Crow. Negroes were outraged by the growing number of lynchings, and believed that their contribution to the nation's effort in World War I was not sufficiently appreciated.

Moreover, the tens of thousands of blacks who had left the South for the northern industrial areas faced new and subtle forms of discrimination. When violence threatened them in the northern cities they took to the streets. The years during, and immediately after World War I, were marked by serious race riots in the North. In the summer of 1919, thirty-nine persons, including twenty-three blacks, were killed in Chicago alone. Conditions appeared so desperate that Marcus Garvey, an advocate of separatism and the return to Africa, was able to assemble around him the largest mass movement of blacks in American history. And protest was the central theme of the black literary movement that came to be known as the Harlem Renaissance.

Despite the depth of anti-black feeling in the United States, most racist literature in the late nineteenth and early twentieth centuries was directed against the new immigrants—those who came from southern and eastern Europe. The scientific racists held that the Nordic (or Anglo-Saxon, or Teutonic, or Aryan) race was superior to all others, and that it was the foundation of America's early greatness. Social Darwinists and eugenicists provided additional arguments for the racist theoreticians. They held that there were immutable laws of heredity with which men should not interfere, and that heredity was a far more crucial factor in shaping individuals and society than environment. Races were thought to represent different stages of "the evolutionary scale with the white" race at the top. To nativists, these "findings" were proof that our immigration laws should favor immigrants from northern and western European countries; it was claimed that these newcomers were closer to the Nordic or Anglo-Saxon stock that first settled this nation than those who migrated from southern and eastern European countries.

Moreover, nativists believed that if these arguments had merit with regard to Europeans, they had an even greater validity in the case of Orientals. Anti-Oriental feeling first appeared on the West Coast as an anti-Chinese movement. California nativists reacted violently to the rising number of Chinese who settled there in the 1850's and 1860's. They charged that Orientals were barbarians and presented an unfair source of labor competition for white workers. They demanded and eventually obtained the passage of a federal Chinese Exclusion Act in 1882.

After 1882, the anti-Oriental movement became directed primarily against the Japanese. In opposing Japanese immigration, the nativists reiterated with slight modifications most of the anti-Chinese arguments. The rise of modern Japan, particularly after the Russo-Japanese War, provoked nativists to invoke the "Yellow Peril" scare. Employing the racial theories that came into vogue at the turn of the century, the advocates of the Yellow Peril thesis maintained that Japanese expansionism represented the modern Asiatic threat to Western civilization, especially to its Anglo-Saxon leadership, and that the Japanese in the United States comprised a potential Trojan Horse.

While nativists were using racial theories to oppose free immigration, the advocates of American colonialism were adopting racial arguments to support their program of imperialism. Politicians and intellectuals claimed that since the Anglo-Saxons had brought Western civilization to its zenith, it was their mission to bring the benefits of civilization to the less fortunate peoples of the world. Thus, Americans had their own version of the "White Man's Burden."

FREEDOM LOST: THE SEPARATE AND UNEQUAL STATUS OF THE BLACK

Benjamin Tillman and the Inception of Segregation

In the 1870's and 1880's, the influence of the Republican Party in the South depended upon the black vote. To destroy both Republican power and the black voting majority, the theme of white supremacy became the principal tactical weapon of the southern racists.

Senator Benjamin R. Tillman, the class-conscious spokesman for the "poor white" segment of South Carolina society, attained prominence as a result of his rhetorical assaults on the political and social gains of the Negro. He recognized both the political value and "social desirability" of the racist appeal for his constituents. The success of this mode of politics, in the tremendous drawing power it had for the "red-neck" vote, led white supremacy candidates to imitate the Tillman style.

Tillman, in his landmark speech at the South Carolina Constitutional Convention of 1895, signaled the death-knell of black political participation. The speech, which contained a prescription for the total disfranchisement of South Carolina blacks, eventually served as the model for the entire South.

. . . There is no man on this floor living in the country who dared during that dark period [Reconstruction] to leave his fireside without dread that when he returned he would find some harm to his family; and he dared not go forth without being armed, fearful of robbery. The sky was lit almost every

Source: [1] *Speech of Hon. B. R. Tillman in the Constitutional Convention of South Carolina, Thursday, October 31st, 1895.* Suffrage (1895), pp. 22–24.

night by the glare of burning dwellings and gin houses. Our
Courts of justice were filled with bribe-takers, and the Judges
themselves were not free from bribery. How did it come about,
and who must bear the blame? We are told the negroes didn't
do it. "Oh, we didn't do it," they say. [Addressing the negro
delegates.] You blindly followed and obeyed the orders of the
Freedman's Bureau and the Union League and ignored the
appeals of your former masters, who treated you with kindness
and furnished you with your daily bread. I myself can testify
that appeal after appeal was made by me, and by almost every
white man in this State, with the negroes with whom he came
in contact on his plantation: "Stop! come back! help us free
ourselves from this burden!" But every one of you, almost up
to 1876, blindly followed wherever these white thieves ordered.
Was it negro government? The negroes furnished the ballots,
and that is what we are dealing with. The negroes put the little
pieces of paper in the box that gave the commission to these
white scoundrels who were their leaders and the men who debauched them; and this must be our justification, our vindication and our excuse to the world that we are met in Convention
openly, boldly, without any pretense of secrecy, to announce
that it is our purpose, as far as we may, without coming in conflict with the United States Constitution, to put such safeguards
around this ballot in future, to so restrict the suffrage and cir-
cumscribe it, that this infamy can never come about again.

The negroes were the tools of designing white men, I ac-
knowledge—participators and willing tools. The poor, ignorant
cotton field hands, who never reaped any advantage, nor saw
anything except a pistol, blindly followed like sheep where-
ever their black and white leaders told them to go, voted unanimously every time for the Republican ticket during that dark
period, and these results were achieved solely and wholly by
reason of the ballot being in the hands of such cattle. Is the
danger gone? No. How did we recover our liberty? By fraud
and violence. We tried to overcome the thirty thousand majority by honest methods, which was a mathematical impossibility.
After we had borne these indignities for eight years life became
worthless under such conditions.

. . . How did we bring it about? Every white man sunk

his personal feelings and ambitions. The white people of the State, illustrating our glorious motto, "Ready with their lives and fortunes," came together as one. By fraud and violence, if you please, we threw it off. In 1878 we had to resort to more fraud and violence, and so again in 1880. Then the Registration Law and eight-box system was evolved from the superior intelligence of the white man to check and control this surging, muddy stream of ignorance and to tell it to back, and since then we have carried our elections without resort to any illegal methods, simply because the whites were united. If we were to remain united it would still be desirable that we should guard against the possibility of this flood, which is now dammed up, breaking loose; or, like the viper that is asleep, only to be warmed into life again and sting us whenever some more white rascals, native or foreign, come here and mobilize the ignorant blacks. Therefore, the only thing we can do as patriots and as statesmen is to take from them every ballot that we can under the laws of our national government.

I read a moment ago from the report of the Committee that good government can only rest on intelligence and good morals. I will go further and say that good government and the very life of republics rest on virtue, patriotism and intelligence. The chief amongst the three is intelligence. It has been said, and it must be apparent to any one who thinks, that even if we restrict the suffrage as we propose, that with 40,000 Conservatives and 40,000 Reformers, divided and striving for mastery, and 15,000 illiterate white men disfranchised, that the negroes are still here in sufficient numbers to control us. Are we so besotted, so forgetful and oblivious of the record which I have just read to you? Have our memories grown so callous that we as a white race—kinsmen, brothers, common inheritors of the glorious past and of the freedom transmitted to us by our forefathers—have we got to the point where we cannot unite as brothers, throwing aside the petty bickerings and animosities that have been engendered in the last five years, and, without regard to personal ambition or partisan advantage to anybody, can we not provide so that we will not have to appeal to these people as arbitrators of our fate? Can we not rise to the necessities of the occasion and put into this Constitution such an Article in reference to suffrage as will guarantee, as far as the law can guarantee, to future generations that they shall have the blessings of Anglo-Saxon civilization and liberty in this State? How pitiable, how puerile, how ineffably, unutterably contemptible appear the personal ambitions and petty spites of men alongside of this grand and glorious purpose!

Booker T. Washington and the Negro: A Critique by Thomas Dixon

Thomas Dixon, Jr. was a widely read and esteemed literary figure at the turn of the century. In his two most popular books, The Leopard's Spots *(1902) and* The Clansman *(1905), he reminded the American people of the danger of an alien Negro population.*

In his typical style, Dixon, writing in the popular and highly regarded Saturday Evening Post, *exposed the "dangerous" work being conducted by Booker T. Washington at Tuskegee Institute. The education offered at this institution, he asserted, formed the basis for a grand plot to prepare the United States for amalgamation. And equally sinister was Washington's leadership in "attempting to build a nation inside a nation of two hostile races."*

Dixon charged that the instruction at Tuskegee was clearly a threat because Negroes were not being trained "to take their places in any industrial system of the South in which the white man [could] direct or control him. [Washington] was not training his students to be servants and come at the beck and call of any man. He [was] training them all *to be masters of men, to be independent . . . [and was] destroying the last vestige of dependence on the white man for anything."*

Although all his numerous writings were variations on the above-mentioned theme, Dixon claimed that he had only "pity and sympathy" for the Negro race, and that it was a mistake

Source: [2] Thomas Dixon, Jr., "Booker T. Washington and the Negro," *The Saturday Evening Post,* CLXXVIII (August 19, 1905), pp. 1–3.

for black leaders to consider his writings to be "caricatures and libels on their people."

In the selection presented below, Dixon concluded that the revival of the African colonization plan was the only rational basis for a solution to the American race problem.

SOME DANGEROUS ASPECTS OF
THE WORKS OF TUSKEGEE

For Mr. Booker T. Washington as a man and leader of his race I have always had the warmest admiration. His life is a romance which appeals to the heart of universal humanity. The story of a little ragged, bare-footed piccaninny who lifted his eyes from a cabin in the hills of Virginia, saw a vision and followed it, until at last he presides over the richest and most powerful institution of learning in the South, and sits down with crowned heads and Presidents, has no parallel even in the *Tales of the Arabian Nights.*

The spirit of the man, too, has always impressed me with its breadth, generosity and wisdom. The aim of his work is noble and inspiring. As I understand it from his own words, it is "to make Negroes producers, lovers of labor, honest, independent, good." His plan for doing this is to lead the Negro to the goal through the development of solid character, intelligent industry and material acquisition.

Only a fool or a knave can find fault with such an ideal. It rests squarely on the eternal verities. And yet it will not solve the Negro problem nor bring us within sight of its solution. Upon the other hand, it will only intensify that problem's dangerous features, complicate and make more difficult its ultimate settlement.

It is this tragic fact to which I am trying to call the attention of the nation.

I have for the Negro race only pity and sympathy, though every large convention of Negroes since the appearance of my first historical novel on the race problem has gone out of its way to denounce me and declare my books caricatures and libels on their people. Their mistake is a natural one. My books are hard reading for a Negro, and yet the Negroes, in denouncing them, are unwittingly denouncing one of their best friends.

I have been intimately associated with Negroes since the morning of my birth during the Civil War. My household servants are all Negroes. I took them to Boston with me, moved them to New York, and they now have entire charge of my Virginia home. The first row I ever had on the Negro problem was when I moved to Boston from the South to take charge of a fashionable church at the Hub. I attempted to import my baby's Negro nurse into a Boston hotel. The proprietor informed me that no "coon" could occupy a room in his house in any capacity, either as a guest or servant. I gave him a piece of my mind and left within an hour.

As a friend of the Negro race I claim that he should have the opportunity for the highest, noblest and freest development of his full, rounded manhood. He has never had this opportunity in America, either North or South, and he never can have it. The forces against him are overwhelming.

My books are simply merciless records of conditions as they exist, conditions, that can have but one ending if they are not honestly and fearlessly faced. The Civil War abolished chattel slavery. It did not settle the Negro problem. It settled the Union question and created the Negro problem. Frederick Harrison, the English philosopher, declared that the one great shadow which clouds the future of the American Republic is the approaching tragedy of the irreconcilable conflict between the Negro and the White Man in the development of our Society. Mr. James Bryce recently made a similar statement.

The Argument of the Ostrich Man

If allowed to remain here the Negro race in the United States will number 60,000,000 at the end of this century by their present rate of increase. Think of what this means for a moment and you face the gravest problem which ever puzzled the brain of statesman or philosopher. No such problem ever before confronted the white man in his recorded history. It cannot be whistled down by opportunists, politicians, weak-minded optimists or female men. It must be squarely met and fought to a finish.

Several classes of people at present obstruct any serious consideration of this question—the pot-house politician, the ostrich man, the pooh-pooh man, and the benevolent old maid. The politician is still busy over the black man's vote in doubtful States. The pooh-pooh man needs no definition—he was born a fool. The benevolent old maid contributes every time the hat is passed and is pretty sure to do as much harm as good in the long run to any cause. The ostrich man is the funniest of all this group of obstructionists, for he is a man of brains and capacity.

I have a friend of this kind in New York. He got after me the other day somewhat in this fashion:

"What do you want to keep agitating this infernal question for? There's no danger in it unless you stir it. Let it alone. I grant you that the Negro race is a poor, worthless, parasite, whose criminal and animal instincts threaten society. But the Negro is here to stay. We must train him. It is the only thing we can do. So what's the use to waste your breath?"

"But what about the future when you have educated the Negro?" I asked timidly.

"Let the future take care of itself!" the ostrich man snorted. "We live in the present. What's the use to worry about Hell? If I can scramble through this world successfully I'll take my chances with the Hell problem!"

My friend forgets that this was precisely the line of arguments of our fathers over the question of Negro slavery. When the constructive statesmen of Virginia (called pessimists and infidels in their day) foresaw the coming baptism of fire and blood ('61 to '65) over the Negro slave, they attempted to destroy the slave trade and abolish slavery. My friend can find his very words in the answers of their opponents. "Let the future take care of itself! The slaves are here and here to stay. Greater evils await their freedom. We need their labor. Let the question alone. There is no danger in it unless you stir it."

The truth which is gradually forcing itself upon thoughtful students of our national life is that no scheme of education or religion can solve the race problem, and that Mr. Booker T. Washington's plan, however high and noble, can only intensify its difficulties.

This conviction is based on a few big fundamental facts, which no pooh-poohing, ostrich-dodging, weak-minded philanthropy or political rant can obscure.

The first one is that no amount of education of any kind, industrial, classical or religious, can make a Negro a white man or bridge the chasm of the centuries which separate him from the white man in the evolution of human civilization.

Expressed even in the most brutal terms of Anglo-Saxon superiority, there is here an irreducible fact. It is possibly true, as the Negro, Professor Kelly Miller, claims, that the Anglo-Saxon is "the most arrogant and rapacious, the most exclusive and intolerant race in history." Even so, what answer can be given to his cold-blooded proposition: "Can you change the color of the Negro's skin, the kink of his hair, the bulge of his lip or the beat of his heart with a spelling-book or a machine?"

What Abraham Lincoln Said

No Man has expressed this idea more clearly than Abraham Lincoln when he said: *"There is a physical difference between the white and black races which, I believe, will forever forbid them living together on terms of social and political equality."*

Whence this physical difference? Its secret lies in the gulf of thousands of years of inherited progress which separates the child of the Aryan from the child of the African.

Buckle in his *History of Civilization* says: "The actions of bad men produce only temporary evil, the actions of good men only temporary good. The discoveries of genius alone remain: it is to them we owe all that we now have; they are for all ages and for all times; never young, and never old, they bear the seeds of their own lives; they are essentially cumulative."

Judged by this supreme test, what contribution to human progress have the millions of Africans who inhabit this planet made during the past four thousand years? Absolutely nothing. And yet, Mr. Booker T. Washington in a recent burst of eloquence over his educational work boldly declares:

"The Negro race has developed more rapidly in the thirty years of its freedom than the Latin race has in one thousand years of freedom."

Think for a moment of the pitiful puerility of this statement falling from the lips of the greatest and wisest leader the Negro race has yet produced!

Italy is the mother of genius, the inspiration of the ages, the creator of architecture, agriculture, manufacture, commerce, law, science, philosophy, finance, church organization, sculpture, music, painting and literature, and yet the American Negro in thirty years has outstripped her thousands of years of priceless achievement!

Education is the development of that which *is*. The Negro has held the Continent of Africa since the dawn of history, crunching acres of diamonds beneath his feet. Yet he never picked one up from the dust until a white man showed to him its light. His land swarmed with powerful and docile animals, yet he never built a harness, cart or sled. A hunter by necessity, he never made an ax, spear or arrowhead worth preserving beyond the moment of its use. In a land of stone and timber, he never carved a block, sawed a foot of lumber or built a house save of broken sticks and mud, and for four thousand years he gazed upon the sea yet never dreamed a sail.

Who is the greatest Negro that ever lived according to Mr. Booker T. Washington? Through all his books he speaks this man's name with bated breath and uncovered head—"Frederick Douglass of sainted memory!" And what did Saint Frederick do? Spent a life in bombastic vituperation of the men whose genius created the American Republic, wore himself out finally drawing his salary as a Federal office-holder, and at last achieved the climax of Negro sainthood by marrying a white woman!

What Education Cannot Do

Says the author of *Napoleon*, Honorable Thomas E. Watson: "Education is a good thing, but it never did and never will alter the essential character of any man or race of men."

I repeat, education is the development of that which *is*. Behold the man whom the rags of slavery once concealed—nine millions strong! This creature, with a racial record of four thousand years of incapacity, half-child, half-animal, the sport of impulse, whim and conceit, pleased with a rattle, tickled with a straw, a being who, left to his will, roams at night and sleeps in the day, whose native tongue has framed no word of love, whose passions once aroused are as the tiger's—equality is the law of our life!—when he is educated and ceases to fill his useful sphere as servant and peasant, what are you going to do with him?

The second big fact which confronts the thoughtful, patriotic American is that the greatest calamity which could possibly befall this Republic would be the corruption of our national character by the assimiliation of the Negro race. I have never seen a white man of any brains who disputes this fact. I have never seen a Negro of any capacity who did not deny it.

One thought I would burn into the soul of every young American (and who thinks of a Negro when he says "American?")—this: Our Republic is great not by reason of the amount of dirt we possess, or the size of our census rolls, but because of the genius of the race of pioneer white freemen who settled this continent, dared the might of kings, and blazed the way through our wilderness for the trembling feet of liberty.

A distinguished Negro college professor recently expressed himself as to the future American in one of our great periodicals as follows:

"All race prejudice will be eradicated. Physically, the new race will be much the stronger. It will be endowed with a higher intelligence and clearer conception of God than the whites of the West have ever had. It will be much less material than the American white of to-day. It will be especially concerned with the things of the mind, and moral excellence will become the dominant factor in the life of the new nation. The new race is to gain more from the Black element than from the White."

We have here an accurate statement of the passionate faith of ninety-nine Negroes out of every hundred. Professor Du-Bois, author of *The Souls of Black Folk,* undoubtedly believes this. His book is a remarkable contribution to the literature of our race problem. In it for the first time we see the naked soul of a Negro beating itself to death against the bars in which Aryan society has caged him! No white man with a soul can read this book without a tear. Mr. Charles W. Chestnutt, the

Negro novelist, believes in amalgamation, for he told me so.
Professor Kelly Miller, the distinguished Negro teacher of
Washington, believes it. In a recent article he declares:

"It is, of course, impossible to conceive of two races occupying the same area, speaking the same language, worshipping
according to the same ritual, and endowed with the same political and civil privileges without ultimately fusing. Social
equality is not an individual matter, as many contend, but is
rigourously under control of public sentiment."

I commend the solid logic of these sentences from a thoughtful Negro to the illustrious Society of Pooh-Poohs.

What is the attitude of Mr. Booker T. Washington on this
vital issue? You will search his books and listen to his lectures
in vain for any direct answer. Why? Because, if he dared to
say what he really in his soul of souls believes, it would end his
great career, both North and South. In no other way has he
shown his talent as an organizer and leader of his people with
such consummate skill as in the dexterity with which he has
for twenty years dodged this issue, holding steadily the good-
will of the Southern white man and the Northern philanthro-
pist. He is the greatest diplomat his race has ever produced.

Yet he who reads between the lines of his written and spoken
words will find the same purpose and the same faith which his
more blunt and fearless brethren have honestly and boldly proclaimed. He shows this in his worship of Frederick Douglass.
In his book, *The Future of the American Negro,* we find this
careful sentence:

"To state in detail just what place the black man will occupy
in the South as a citizen when he has developed in the direction
named is beyond the wisdom of any one."

Yet on page 69 he says:

"The surest way for the Negro to reach the highest positions
is to prepare himself to fill well at the present the basic occupations"—independent industries, of course—for you, mark you.
"Tuskegee Institute is not a servant-training school!"

Again on pages 83 and 85 we are told: "There is an un-
mistakable influence that comes over a white man when he
sees a black man living in a two-story brick house that has been

paid for. I need not stop to explain. Just in so far as we can place rich Negroes in the South who can loan money to white men, this race question will disappear."

Why?

The conclusion is obvious: The Negro who holds a mortgage on a white man's house will ultimately demand and receive social recognition from him.

On page 66 of his *Future of the American Negro* he says: "The Jew, who was once in about the same position as the Negro is to-day, has now recognition because he has entwined himself about America in a business and industrial way."

Again his conclusion is obvious. The absurdity of the comparison, however, is the important point in this sentence, not only for the pathetic ignorance of history it displays but for the revelation of the writer's secret hopes and dreams.

The Jew has not been assimilated into our civil and social life because of his money—but for a very different reason. The Jew belongs to our race, the same great division of humanity. The Semitic group of the white race is, all in all, the greatest evolved in history. Their children have ever led the vanguard of human progress and achievements. A great historian and philosopher once said, "Show me a man of transcendent genius at any period of the world's history and I'll show you a man with Hebrew blood in his veins." Our prejudice against the Jew is not because of his inferiority, but because of his genius. We are afraid of him, we Gentiles who meet him in the arena of life, get licked and then make faces at him. The truth is the Jew had achieved a noble civilization —had his poets, prophets, priests and kings—when our Germanic ancestors were still in the woods cracking cocoanuts and hickory-nuts with monkeys. We have assimilated the Jew because his daughter is beautiful and his son strong in mind and body!

The Danger of a Nation Within a Nation

The trouble with Mr. Booker T. Washington's work is that he is silently preparing us for the future heaven of Amalgamation—*or he is doing something equally dangerous,* namely, he is attempting to build a nation inside a nation of two hostile races. In this event he is storing dynamite beneath the pathway of our children—the end at last can only be in bloodshed.

Mr. Washington is not training Negroes to take their place in any industrial system of the South in which the white man can direct or control him. He is not training his students to be servants and come at the beck and call of any man. He is training them *all* to be masters of men, to be independent, to own and operate their own industries, plant their own fields, buy and sell their own goods, and in every shape and form destroy the last vestige of dependence on the white man for anything.

I do not say this is not laudable—I do not say that it is not noble. I only ask what will be its end for the Negro when the work is perfect? Every pupil who passes through Mr. Washington's hands ceases forever to work under a white man. Not only so, but he goes forth trained as an evangelist to preach the doctrine of separation and independence.

The Negro remains on this Continent for one reason only. The Southern white man has needed his labor, and therefore has fought every suggestion of his removal. But when he refuses longer to work for the white man, then what? Mr. Booker T. Washington says on page 65 of his book: "The Negro must live for all time beside the Southern white man."

On what sort of terms are they to live together? As banker and borrower? Hardly, if the Negro is the banker. Even now, with the white man still hugging the hoary delusion that he can't get along with the Negro, he is being forced to look to the Old World for labor. The simple truth is, the South will lag behind the world industrially in just so far as she depends on Negro labor. The idea that a white man cannot work in the fields of the South is exploded. Only one-third of the cotton crop is to-day raised by Negro labor. Even now the relations of the races, with the Negro an integral part of the white man's industrial scheme, become more and more difficult.

A Gulf that Grows Wide

Professor Kelly Miller says: "It is a matter of common observation that the races are growing further and further apart."

Mr. Washington says on this point: "For the sake of the Negro and the Southern white man there are many things in

the relations of the two races that must soon be changed"
(page 65). The point I raise is that education necessarily
drives the races further and further apart, and Mr. Washington's brand of education makes the gulf between them if anything a little deeper. If there is one thing a Southern white man
cannot endure it is an educated Negro. What's to be the end of
it if the two races are to live forever side by side in the South?

Mr. Washington says: "Give the black man so much skill
and brains that he can cut oats like the white man—then he
can compete with him."

And then the real tragedy will begin. Does any sane man
believe that when the Negro ceases to work under the direction
of the Southern white man, this "arrogant," "rapacious" and
"intolerant" race will allow the Negro to master his industrial
system, take the bread from his mouth, crowd him to the wall
and place a mortgage on his house? Competition is war—the
most fierce and brutal of all its forms. Could fatuity reach a
sublimer height than the idea that the white man will stand
idly by and see this performance? What will he do when put to
the test? He will do exactly what his white neighbor in the
North does when the Negro threatens his bread—kill him.

Abraham Lincoln foresaw this tragedy when he wrote his
Emancipation Proclamation, and he asked Congress for an
appropriation of a billion dollars to colonize the whole Negro
race. He never believed it possible to assimilate the Negro into
our national life. This nation will yet come back to Lincoln's
plan, still so eloquently advocated by the Negro Bishop, Henry
M. Turner.

It is curious how the baldheaded assertion of a lie can be
repeated and repeated until millions of sane people will accept
the bare assertion as an established fact. At the close of the
War, Mr. Lincoln, brooding over the insoluble problem of the
Negro's future which his proclamation had created, asked General Benjamin F. Butler to devise and report to him immediately a plan to colonize the Negroes. General Butler, naturally
hostile to the idea, made at once his famous, false, and face-
tious report," that ships could not be found to carry the Negro
babies to Africa as fast as they are born!" The President was
assassinated a few days later. This lie is now forty odd years

old, and Mr. Booker T. Washington actually repeats is as a verbal inspiration though entirely unconscious of its historic origin.

We have spent about $800,000,000 on Negro education since the War. One-half of this sum would have been sufficient to have made Liberia a rich and powerful Negro state. Liberia is capable of supporting every Negro in America. Why not face this question squarely? We are temporizing and playing with it. All our educational schemes are compromises and temporary makeshifts. Mr. Booker T. Washington's work is one of noble aims. A branch of it should be immediately established in Monrovia, the capital of Liberia. A gift of ten millions would do this, and establish a colony of half a million Negroes within two years. They could lay the foundation of a free black republic which within twenty-five years would solve our race problem on the only rational basis within human power. Colonization is not a failure. It has never been tried.

We owe this to the Negro. At present we are deceiving him and allowing him to deceive himself. He hopes and dreams of amalgamation, forgetting that self-preservation is the first law of Nature. Our present attitude of hypocrisy is unhuman toward a weaker race brought to our shores by the sins of our fathers. We owe him a square deal, and we will never give it to him on this Continent.

A Twentieth-Century View of Intermarriage

One of the prime targets of all segregationists, whether moderate or extreme, northern or southern, was intermarriage. The reaction to marital relationships between blacks and whites displayed itself in what can only be described as a manic concern.

Senator J. Thomas Heflin, Alabama's extreme segregationist, reflected the psychotic attitudes that prevailed among his

Source: [3] *United States Congressional Record,* Vol. 72, Part 3, 71st Cong., 2nd Sess., pp. 3234–3239.

*racist colleagues. The letter reprinted below, which Heflin
wrote in response to a communication from a Philadelphia
news service, contains a vivid description of the views of "Black
Belt" Congressmen on the subject of intermarriage.*

Letters Regarding the Marriage of Negro and Nordic!

Mr. Heflin, Mr. President, I wish to have printed in the
Record a letter addressed to me by Sam H. Reading, broad-
casting a national news service, and my reply, regarding the
marriage of a negro and a Nordic.

There being no objection, the letters were ordered to be
printed in the Record, as follows:

Philadelphia, October 8, 1929.

Hon. Thomas J. Heflin,
    United States Senator from Alabama, Washington, D. C.
Sir: In view of your generally expressed opinions on such subjects, the writer will be interested to know your opinion of the
within-mentioned marriage of Phil Edwards, the negro captain
of New York University, to a pure Nordic woman (white
woman).
Your expression in this matter will be much appreciated by
the readers of the country who often base their opinions on
your expressions in such matters.

Thanking you in advance for your expression, believe me,

Very respectfully yours,

Sam H. Reading.

Washington, D.C.,
October 15, 1929.

Mr. Sam H. Reading,
            National News Service,
                24 North Fifty-ninth Street,
                    Philadelphia, Pa.
My Dear Sir: In reply to your request I will say that I have
read with a feeling of sadness and indignation the newspaper
account of the humiliated and grief-striken white father and
mother in New York City who could get no assistance from
either Governor Roosevelt or Mayor Walker or anyone else

in authority in their effort to prevent the marriage of their daughter to a negro. The press reports tell us that the white father and mother wept freely when interviewed by the newspaper men and made no attempt to hide their tears and humiliation when New York officials issued a marriage license to a negro to marry their daughter. And this terrible thing has happened here in what we used to call the land of Anglo-Saxon rule and white supremacy. Shame on those in authority who will permit such a humiliating, disgraceful, and dangerous thing to happen in the United States. Where are the white men of self-respect, of race pride, and love of the white man's country in America whose brave forebears long ago decreed that there should be no pollution of the blood of the white race by permitting marriage between whites and negroes? What has become of the brave knights of the white race who once boasted of their proud Caucasian lineage? For many generations they stood guard on the dividing line between the Caucasian race and the Negro race.

The far-reaching harm and danger of marriage between whites and negroes to the great white race that God intended should rule the world is apparent to all intelligent students of history; such mixtures have always resulted in weakening, degrading and dragging down the superior to the level of the inferior race. God had a purpose in making four separate and distinct races. The white, the red, the yellow and the black. God intended that each of the four races should preserve its blood free from mixture with other races and preserve race integrity and prove itself true to the purpose that God had in mind for each of them when He brought them into being. The great white race is the climax and crowning glory of God's creation. God in His infinite wisdom has clothed the white man with the elements and the fitness of dominion and rulership, and the history of the human race shows that wherever he has planted his foot and unfurled the flag of his authority he has continued to rule. No true member of the great white race in America is going to approve or permit, if he can prevent it, the marriage between whites and negroes.

This desire and purpose on the part of the great white race in America to keep its blood strain pure and to prevent mar-

208 THE POISONED TONGUE

riage between whites and negroes can better be designed as the "call of the blood." It has come down to us through the centuries. White women, rather than become the wives of the black man, whenever the issue was presented, fought and died, if necessary, to remain true to the "call of the blood." But it seems that in New York, under alien influence, that the line of demarcation between the great white race and the Negro race, the "great divide," that once constituted the "dead line" in America on questions of social equality and marriage between whites and negroes, have been repudiated by those of the Roman-Tammany regime now in charge of New York City and New York State. These officials owe it to the great white race in the State of New York and in the whole United States to protect, safeguard, and preserve in their integrity these principles and ideals so dear to the great white race in America.

The time has come for all true Americans of the Caucasian race to wake up to the dangers that threaten us. There can be no yielding on this great question in order to serve the program and purpose of the Roman-Tammany political machine. We must stand steadfast, and we will stand steadfast, in our purpose and determination to preserve in its integrity race pride and purity and white man's government in the United States. I regret to say that the present disgusting and deplorable situation in New York State, which permitted a white father and mother to be subjected to the humiliating and shameful ordeal of having to submit to the marriage of their daughter to a negro, is not new under the modern Roman-Tammany system in New York City and State. Scores of negroes in Harlem, New York, members of the so-called Democratic Tammany organization, have been permitted to marry white wives with license granted by and with the hearty approval of the State and city government presided over by Governor Smith and Jimmie Walker and now by Gov. Franklin Roosevelt and Jimmy Walker. These things are shocking, disgusting, and sickening not only to the Democrats but to the true representatives of the great white race in all parties the country over.

Very truly,

J. Thos. Heflin

THE "YELLOW PERIL":
CAMPAIGN AGAINST THE CHINESE

Until 1868, the eastern part of the United States harbored little concern over the "Chinese problem." That year the attempt of a labor contractor, C. Koopanschap, to introduce Chinese workers in the South, provoked a wave of anti-Chinese sentiment in the East.

Although there were fewer than two hundred Chinese living in New York City, reports of the efforts to employ Chinese workers in the South and East were sensationalized by the New York City press. The New York Sun suspiciously followed the proceedings of the 1868 Memphis convention which was convoked to discuss plans for using Chinese contract laborers. The Irish-American charged that an enterprising New England Yankee had embarked for China with funds to purchase a "full line of yellow chattels." When a Massachusetts shoe manufacturer tried to break a strike against his plant by importing seventy-five Chinese workers, and a laundry operator in nearby Belleville, New Jersey, brought in Orientals, anti-Chinese feeling in New York reached a fever pitch. In 1870 and 1871, the following headlines appeared in the city's newspapers: "How the Chinamen Live and Die," "Chinese Cheap Labor," "Chinese Scourge," "Heathen Chinee," "The Great Wave," "Coolie Revolt," and "John Chinaman's Holiday."

The documents presented below are indicative of the fear that gripped the New York City press and the city's workingmen in the late 1860's and early 1870's.

The "Coolie" Question
The Irish-American, July 31, 1869

One of the peculiarities of American society, is the avidity with which every "new idea" is caught up, and acted and com-

Sources: [4] *The Irish-American,* July 31, 1869; [5] New York *Star,* September 29, 1870.

mented on, until, as too often happens, what might be productive of good if judiciously used, is driven into the ground, whilst the worst features of what may prove to be bad or detrimental to the *morale* of the community, are exaggerated and thrust forward with a pertinacity that can only be accounted for on the ground of that judicial blindness, which is one of the certain attributes of fanaticism in every shape.

A recent "labor convention," held in Memphis, Tenn., has furnished the opportunity for one of those displays, so little creditable to American judgment or common sense. The disruption of the relations between the negroes and their former masters in the South, has left the labor system of that section in a state of chaos. Money, also, is scarce there; and these two facts, combined with the understanding that the Chinese element in California has been found a reliable source of cheap labor, suggested the idea of importing "Coolies" into the Southern States, in sufficient numbers to make the planters independent of all other sources of labor. A Chinese-Hollander, who rejoices in the appropriate name of "Koop-mans-chap," and who has been for many years the chief Coolie trader of the Indian Archipelago, was present, and offered to furnish any number of Chinamen at so much a head, "cash on delivery." The records of the Coolie trade, as brought out on investigation some years ago, by the English Parliament, shows that a large proportion of the "cargoes" which were "run" by those philanthropic labor-purveyors, were literally kidnapped from their homes while the overflow of Chinese prisons furnished no small share of the remainder—the Mandarins finding it much more profitable to dispose of the living body of a culprit, for cash, than to decapitate it and then have to bury the carcase. [*sic*] Under such circumstances, even at the moderate figure of ten dollars a head, and "expenses," Koop-mans-chap & Co., might reasonably calculate to realize a handsome profit; though whether the quality of the article they intend to furnish will meet the expectations of the purchasers, remains to be seen. That the business is regarded as a paying one, may be judged from the fact that an enterprising Yankee has already started for China with funds enough to purchase a "full line" of yellow "chattels," notwithstanding that there is a law of Congress on the statute books expressly declaring such traffic illegal. New

England, however, will find a way to get around all such troublesome enactments. A "coolie" may be a contraband article; but he becomes perfectly legitimate when you label him "Chinese emigrant." And then, though some fastidious people may regard all branches of the trade in human flesh as immoral, and hint at its similarity to the slave-commerce from which many of the "Pilgrim sons" derived the fortunes which have made their descendants the aristocracy of "the hub," still there are the facts that the Chinaman is an Asiatic, not African; that he wears his hair in a "Pig-tail," instead of the orthodox wooly kink; that his skin is yellow, and not black; and finally, if delivered, "in good condition and warranted," he represents net profit of ten dollars—all of which consideration made a vital difference in the case, according to Boston ethics.

There is another element in the calculation to which we shall refer hereafter—that is the antagonism to and jealousy of the Irish which the ventilation of the "Coolie question" has developed in many quarters, and which has found expression in the hope that the advent of the "coming (China)man" would enable the American community to substitute his services for those now rendered by Irish men and women. Of this we shall treat more freely next week. And, meanwhile, we shall venture to predict that this little speculation in "Coolie-ism" will prove a failure, like others of its kind, and those who meddle with it will burn their fingers more thoroughly than they have any idea at present.

The Chinese Puzzle

New York Star, September 29, 1870

An Indignation Meeting at Belleville Last Evening—Speeches of the Right Wing—The Coolie Evil Portrayed In Its True Light—The Great Out-door Mass Meeting to Denounce the Rat-Eaters.

A call having been issued for an anti-Chinese indignation meeting, to be held in Belleville last night, a stand was erected in the open air in front of the Mansion House, and on the opposite side of the river from that on which the residence of

Capt. Harvey, the employer of the "heathen Chinese" is located. The meeting was presided over by Mr. Robert S. Osbourne; on the other side of him was seated Phillip Rafferty, Democratic candidate for Congress in the Fourth District, and Dr. Vail, of Newark.

The chairman said the laborer and mechanic were equally interested in the object of the meeting.

Dr. Vail was called for and said he should use his every effort to sustain the interests of the laboring man. The little cloud which a few years ago was no larger than a man's hand is growing, and soon it will

BREAK LIKE A THUNDER-STORM.

He said these people (the Chinese) differed in every respect from our people and our other immigrants. We had received immigrants from all over Europe. Few opposed it. And now came the Asiatic race to take the labor of those already here, who had helped to make us one of the greatest nations on the globe. But how different is the class of people now being imported upon us. They are base idolators. (Great Cheers.) We can never associate with idolators. The cry has gone forth that we want cheaper labor and more. I have no sympathy with that cry, because I do not believe we need more labor. The curse of slavery has been removed, and labor is therefore made plenty. I believe there are plenty of laborers but no work for them. I have no sympathy for men who want cheap labor. Most men want due consideration for the labor they perform. We have now 41,000,000 of people in the country and it is rapidly increasing. Do we suffer for laborers? No. These idolators came here

UNDER TASKMASTERS AND AS SLAVES.

They came not like the Irish, the Frenchmen, the Germans. The people who hire this help are the ones who were loudest against African slavery, but they hire these idolatrous slaves. Now, in the name of common sense, is not the world wide enough for us to hire those who accept the law of Christ as their God? The Chinese race is the only people who lift the dagger to plunge into the Christian Missionaries. (Cries of good, good.) But we take them to us because they will work half price, and live upon a mouse or a rat, and call it a dainty morsel, while you and I would prefer the leg of a Shanghai chicken. Capt. Harvey may see the time

WHEN RATS ARE IN BED WITH HIM,

and a Chinese holding a mouse over his head. This immigration of idolatrous men must be stopped, or it will increase and drive other laborers from the land. The Chinese receive their pay at the end of three years, and if they shuffle off this mortal coil there is a promise that they shall be sent back to their native land. They are too good to repose on our soil. None of our traders will derive any benefit from them unless it be Gov. Marcus L. Ward, of Newark, who will sell them some grease to grease their pigtails. He closed by repeating a poem to the laboring people, and adding: "You must make a gigantic effort

TO PREVENT THE INTRODUCTION OF THESE HEATHEN

people; vote for no man who favors it; have nothing to do with any man who favors it."

Michael R. Kinney of Newark, was next introduced, and said he hoped the chairman would introduce a resolution protecting against Chinese labor. Captain Harvey is not alone responsible for this; he could not do it unless there was a sentiment in favor of it. He stated that the only remedy for that evil is to vote the Democratic ticket. He continued in this strain, and the other speakers of the evening were few and of the same opinion as those who preceded them. Colonel Rafferty, Democratic nominee in the Fourth District, was present but did not speak. There were about 900 persons present, and the meeting was quiet and orderly.

A Brutal and Causeless Butchery:
The Los Angeles Riot of 1871

Anti-Oriental sentiment, an important aspect of American nativism, emerged initially in the anti-Chinese movement of Cali-

Source: [6] New York *Daily Tribune*, November 12, 1871.

fornia's early history. In the state's formative years, Chinese arrived in California in increasing numbers. During the 1850's, the state legislature passed laws directed at preventing Chinese immigration, and limiting their ability to own property. These laws, however, were declared unconstitutional by the courts.

After the Civil War, the anti-Chinese movement became a major factor in the state's politics. The California state census of 1867 counted 478,000 whites and only 60,000 Chinese, or 11 percent of the state's total population. Many Chinese were employed in railroad construction, and the completion of the transcontinental railroad hurled thousands of Chinese laborers on the California labor market. To the earlier cultural objections to Chinese immigration the exclusionists added the claim of unfair labor competition. In the late 1860's and early 1870's, anti-Chinese sentiment reached a new peak and resulted in one of the most outrageous attacks on a minority group in American history.

In October of 1871, a Los Angeles mob brutally shot and hanged twenty Chinese. The incident stemmed from a police attempt to make peace between feuding Chinese factions. One of the groups, which had taken refuge in a store, wounded two officers and killed a well-known local citizen. After word of the "killings," and a rumor that the shop contained many valuable items had spread through the town, a huge mob marched on the refuge, overwhelmed the police, and mercilessly slaughtered many of the Chinese.

New York Daily Tribune, November 12, 1871.
THE LOS ANGELES RIOT

A BRUTAL AND CAUSELESS BUTCHERY.
NOT THE GUILTY, BUT THE INNOCENT CHINESE
HUNG BY THE MOB—DISGUSTING DETAILS OF
THE MASSACRE—PILLAGE AND TORTURE—
THE IRISH AND MEXICAN RIOTERS.

From an Occasional Correspondent Of the Tribune.

Los Angeles, Cal., Oct. 26—The damnable doings in Los Angeles, last Tuesday night, are frowned upon and disapproved by all parties, sects, races, and grades, without distinction and without equivocation. The telegraph has, of course, informed you briefly of them, but I hasten to send the details. There are two or three different companies of Chinese merchants in San Francisco, who consign, in a business way, through and to agents, the Celestial emigrants who arrive from China intrusted to their care. On Monday last, the 23d inst., the day before the tragedy, a sort of war broke out between some of the members of the two different companies, and pistols were freely used. The disturbers of the peace were at once taken in hand by the proper officers of the law and carried to a Justice of the Peace, who bound them over in $1,000 bonds to appear the next day at Court for trial. There was no end of Celestials who were anxious to become bondsmen in any sum as sureties for the combatants. The Judge questioned the responsibility of the latter parties, at which one of the Chinamen declared his ability to double, treble, or quadruple the sum named, in proof of which he agreed to demonstrate by an exhibition of his exchequer. Down to the Chinaman's den went the wealthy Celestial, his lawyer, and two constables; and lo! in a good strong box were bright stacks of $20 gold pieces, in eight $500 piles. Others, who were anxious to succor their companions, ocularly demonstrated they were "well fixed." Before dark the same day it was generally noised about, and many think by the constables and policemen themselves, that the low reeking abodes of filth inhabited by the Chinamen were stored with precious goods. Be this as it may, it was certainly the incentive of plunder, and the ultimate cause of the sacking of the hovels and the carnival of crime. But, really, the commencement of what terminated in a dance of death, was precisely the same in characters as that of the day preceding. The gold quarrel again became warm, and on Wednesday evening, about 5 o'clock, the combatants again met on the piazza, in front of Yo Hing's store, and a general and indiscriminate discharge of pistols followed. Two or three officers, however, who had been on the alert, rushed up to the scene boldly, and attempted to arrest the participants. Quick as a flash the doors and windows were barred and bolted, and all of a sudden a shot from an aperture tore away the right shoulder of officer Beldervain, who was in the discharge of his duty. Another shot took effect in the knee of a young man standing near, inflicting a serious and dangerous wound. At this juncture, a Mr. Robert Thompson, a well-known and esteemed citizen, who had been summoned by Beldervain as aid, made his appearance armed, when he was confronted by a Chinaman, with a pistol in each hand, both of which were discharged, a bullet from one piercing the right breast of Thompson, and killing him almost instantly. At once the intelligence of the murder by Chinamen of officers of the law was conveyed to all parts of the city, and following in the wake of the alarm came stretchers with the American dead and wounded. It was not to be supposed that any community in the world could have resisted, at this moment, the desire to capture the murderer or murderers, and inflict summary punishment, especially when it must be taken into consideration that the Chinese population of the neighborhood of strife were, for the most part, gamblers, thieves, brawlers, and women of dissolute habits.

It was at this juncture when the City Marshal made his appearance near the scene of conflict; he at once summoned all within the hearing of his voice to volunteer, at which the Chinamen, who had been engaged in the firing, closed their doors and windows, and improvised an apparently effectual barricade. A large number of the people of the city, agreeably to the summons of the Marshal, made their appearance armed with pistols, shot-guns, and other instruments of war. It was, in fact, an occasion when any exhibition of hesitation would have been quite the reverse of good citizenship. The Sheriff was also upon the ground with all the constables and policemen beside the volunteers. A complete cordon had been formed, and both the Sheriff and Marshal felt that they had the thing under their control. In fact, the disposition of the citizen forces was so soldier-like that the house could have been completely guarded until daylight, and the proper arrests could have been made the next morning. But, here and there, what had been angry murmurings, had grown deeper, and cries of "Hang them! Hang them!" "Burn them out!" &c., filled the air. Great crowds of desperate and vile-looking men gathered around the premises. The knights of the dead falls, short card players, drunken teamsters, thieves, robbers of drunkards, and a very large arm of indolent Mexicans and others, constituting on the whole the very scum of the city, appeared in great numbers, and in a few moments forced back the citizen guard, the greater portion of whom, as well as most of the officers, quit the ground. Then commenced the work of pillage, plunder, and murder. For a few minutes the firearms rained bullets against the doors and windows, during this time the shouts and cries of the drunken multitude, and the attempts to force an entrance through the roof and at the windows and doorways by axes, made a scene like hell itself, and one which entirely beggars description. Suffice it to say that the mob triumphed. It gained access to the premises in which were the "stacks of gold." Hats, caps, boots, shoes, clothing, jewelry, eatables, choice liquors, and $17,000 in coin were taken, and to cover up the sacking and pillage, four Celestials were shot dead, seven or eight were wounded, and seventeen were taken—most of them to the public streets—and hung. Where the murder would have ended no one can tell, had not the better portion of the people, including many of the members of the Vigilance Committee, arrested its progress by forcibly taking scores of inoffensive Chinamen from the possession of squads of the mob, which had, after the plunder, scattered in all directions, each with one or more intended victims.

This affair, which will be ever looked upon as a historical disgrace, and will place Los Angeles in the category of other cities where such tumults have occurred, must not be taken as a popular outburst, any more than the riot in New York in July, 1863 [the anti-black Draft Riots]. Los Angeles, to all intents and purposes, is as fair in fame and as free from blemish as ever. A law-abiding community must not be made to suffer in reputation for the mob-violence of the half-civilized scum.

The horrible incidents of the tragedy are of a nature to rival the most brutal in the history of riots. I will seek to give enough to show you the character of the violence, and the standing of the principal victims.

Wong Chin, a merchant, was the first victim of hanging. He was led through the streets by two lusty Irishmen, who were cheered on by a crowd of men and grown-up boys, mostly of

Irish and Mexican birth. Several times the unfortunate faltered or attempted to extricate himself free from the two brutes who were leading him, at which a half-drunken Mexican in his immediate rear would plunge the point of a large dirk-knife into his back. This would, of course, accelerate his speed, yet never a syllable fell from his mouth. Arriving at the eastern end of Tomlinson's old lumber-yard, just out of Temple-st., hasty preparations for launching the inoffensive man into eternity were followed by his being pulled up to the beam with a rope around his neck. He didn't seem to "hang right," and one of the Irishmen, who had assisted in the adjustment of the rope around his neck got upon his shoulders and jumped upon them, breaking his collar bone. What with shots and stabs, and strangulation, and other modes of civilized torture, the victim was "hitched up" for dead, and the crowd gave vent to their savage delight in demoniac yells, and a jargon which too plainly denoted their Hibernian nationality.

The next four Chinamen hung were Dr. Gene Tong, a Chinese physician of some celebrity and good standing; Chang Wang, a resident with the doctor; Leong Quai, a laundryman, and Ah Long, a cigar-maker. Gene Tong was dragged from his office, with Chang Wong. They were both hurried to the lumber-yard, and taken up on High-st., to the western gate where the Vigilance Committee hung the murderer Lachmais a few months ago. Here were found Seong Juai and Ah Long swinging in the moonlight, half-naked, dead, and alone. Gene Tong who spoke good English, upon glancing at his gibbeted countrymen, declared himself entirely innocent of the cause of, of the participation in, the disturbance, and offered the men who had him in charge, who were Irishmen and Mexicans, $4,000 in gold if they would let him go. No sooner did he make the proposition than his pockets were cut and ransacked, during which some ruffian, either for pastime, or with a determination to place him beyond the bounds of release, shot a bullet into his head, mutilating one side of his face dreadfully. In the meantime Chang Wang had been hauled up to the beam with great violence when the rope parted, and he fell heavily to the ground. A stronger rope was at once procured, and at the words "all right, pull away!" he was jerked up with a great force against the beam, and the operation was repeated until his head was smashed into a jelly. Then the demons stretched up the unfortunate physician, and with a concerted yell and a "hurra" the four pagans were left dangling between heaven and earth, and the Christians bounded down Temple-st., frantic as a bull at the spilling of innocent blood.

But if the scenes of this bloody drama recorded above make the heart sick, what can be the effect upon the temper of any Christian when the details of the revolting spectacle enacted in Los Angeles-st. are incidentally set forth? Here were the evidences of the most savage skill in the persons of seven Chinamen dangling from the tin gutter of a verandah near the corner of Commercial-st. Near by were five more unfortunates of the same class, hanging by their necks from a large transportation wagon (called "prairie schooner" in California), all dead and mangled, after a most barbarous act of slow and measured strangulation. Fong Wong, a cook, Won Foo, also a cook, and Ah Too, a young fellow who had just come from China, were all hauled up to the verandah together amid the most unearthly yells of an infuriated gang of drunken Irishmen and Mexicans, for no Americans or Germans at all participated in these revolting festivities of savage crime and cruelty. These three victims were all innocent of even the knowledge of a disturbance, having been picked up in the street while quitting their daily toil, and taken in a body to their dastardly execution. Hardly a word escaped them, except that the younger, who was only about 15 years old, said, as the murderers were placing a piece of baling rope about his neck: "Me no 'fraid to die; me velly good China boy; me no hurt no man." A few feet apart, and near this group, four others were hung. . . . During their hanging several of them were fired at, cut, and otherwise mutilated.

Ah Won and Wong Chu, both cooks in private families, were seized in the street by some wild Mexicans and hung on the front of the transportation wagon, one each side of the tongue. A shot was fired at one of them while in the throes of death, the bullet entering his mouth. Wong Chin, Tong Wang, and Ah Loo—the first one a cook in a Chinese boarding-house, the other a cigar-maker, and the third a domestic—

were all hung on the side of the wagon. All three of these boys struggled somewhat for their lives, the latter managing to get both of his hands above his head and hold of the rope, by which he temporarily kept off the strangulation. For nearly five minutes a couple of Irishmen beat his hands with clubs and pistols, and not until they had broken nearly every bone in both hands and beaten the flesh to a bloody pulp did he release his hold and drop into a hanging position; at this three ruffians blazed away at him, perforating his head with bullets.

A California Memorial Against Chinese Immigration

Before 1882, Congress was under constant pressure from Californians to pass a Chinese exclusion act. In 1877, the California senate presented a memorial to the United States Senate requesting the exclusion of Chinese immigrants. The document contained the current social, moral, and political arguments for restriction. It emphasized the popular ideas that Chinese immigrants were dirty, smelly people from the "dregs of the population," who were mostly criminals and opium addicts. Their women were alleged to be especially degraded. As for the Chinese who were not criminals, the exclusionists charged that the Orientals were the source of unfair labor competition for white workers; the Chinese, they maintained, could subsist on a living standard which no white man could endure. Moreover, the memorialists claimed that most of the Chinese workers did not spend their earnings here, but instead, sent the money home to China. The legislators rejected the environmentalists' argument that education and Christianity would bring the Chinese immigrant into the mainstream of American life. They insisted that the Chinese were "impregnable to all the influences of our Anglo-American life."

Source: [7] *Chinese Immigration. The Social, Moral and Political Effect of Chinese Immigration.* Prepared by a Committee of the Senate of California (Sacramento, 1877), pp. 4–7.

. . . The State of California has a population variously estimated at from seven hundred thousand to eight hundred thousand of which one hundred and twenty-five thousand are Chinese. The additions to this class have been very rapid since the organization of the State but have been caused almost entirely by immigration, and scarcely at all by natural increase. The evidence demonstrates beyond cavil that nearly the entire immigration consists of the lowest orders of the Chinese people, and mainly of those having no homes or occupations on the land, but living in boats on the rivers, especially those in the vicinity of Canton.

This class of the people, according to the castes into which Chinese society is divided, are virtually pariahs—the dregs of the population. None of them are admitted into any of the privileges of the orders ranking above them. And while rudimentary education is encouraged, and even enforced among the masses of the people, the fishermen and those living on the waters and harbors of China are excluded by the rigid and hoary constitution of caste from all participation in such advantages.

It would seem to be a necessary consequence, flowing from this class of immigration, that a large proportion of criminals should be found among it; and this deduction is abundantly sustained by the facts before us, for of five hundred and forty-five of the foreign criminals in our State Prison, one hundred and ninety-eight are Chinese—nearly two-fifths of the whole—while our jails and reformatories swarm with the lower grade of malefactors.

The startling fact also appears that the actual costs of keeping these one hundred and ninety-eight State prisoners alone exceeds by twelve thousand dollars per annum the entire amount of revenue collected by the State from all the property assessed to Chinese.

But the criminal element in the Chinese population is very much greater than the figures above given would indicate, for conviction for crime among this class is extremely difficult. Our ignorance of the Chinese language, the utter want of comprehension by them of the crime of perjury, their systematic bribery, and intimidation of witnesses, and other methods of baffling judicial action, all tend to weaken the authority of our laws and to paralyze the power of our Courts.

A graver difficulty still is developed in the existence among the Chinese population of secret tribunals unrecognized by our laws and in open defiance thereof, an *imperium in imperio* that undertake and actually administer punishment, not infrequently of death. These tribunals exercise the power of levying taxes, commanding masses of men, intimidating interpreters and witnesses, enforcing perjury, punishing the refractory, removing witnesses beyond the reach of process, controlling liberty of action, and preventing the return of Chinese to their homes in China. In fact, there exists amongst us tribunals and laws alien to our form of government and which practically nullify and supersede both National and State authority.

The Chinese females who immigrate to this State are, almost without exception, of the vilest and most degraded class of abandoned women. The effect of this element in our midst upon the health and morals of our youth is exhibited in the testimony. Its disgusting details cannot, for obvious reasons, be enlarged upon in this memorial. These women exist here in a state of servitude, beside which African slavery was a beneficent captivity. The contracts upon which their bodies are held under this system are fully explained and set out in the evidence, and we submit more than sustain what might otherwise be regarded as an extravagant deduction.

The male element of this population, where not criminal, comes into a painful competition with the most needy and most deserving of our people—those who are engaged, or entitled to be engaged, in industrial pursuits in our midst. The common laborer, the farm hand, the shoe-maker, the cigar-maker, the domestic male and female, and workmen of all descriptions, find their various occupations monopolized by Chinese labor, employed at a compensation upon which white labor cannot possibly exist. Amelioration of this hardship might be possible to a limited extent if the proceeds of this labor were invested in our State, distributed among our people, and made to yield a revenue to the government for the protection afforded by it to this class of our population. But the reverse is the fact, for of six hundred millions of taxable property in the State, in the last fiscal year, but one million and a half was assessed to Chinese. Thus one-sixth of the entire population pays less than one four-hundredths part of the revenue required to support the State Government.

And, in addition to this alarming fact, we find that of the one hundred and eighty millions, if not more, earned by them during their continuance here, the whole is abstracted from the State and exported to China, thus absolutely impoverishing instead of enriching the country affording them an asylum. The sharp contrast between the results of that kind of labor and of white labor with its investment in homes, its accumulation of wealth, and additions to our revenue, must be obvious even to a partial mind. Fertile lands, that scarcely require tillage to produce a harvest, are lying idle, partially because the laborer that would purchase and improve them can earn nothing above a bare support wherewith to buy, while the Chinese, who can by their habits of life practically subsist on nothing and save money, export their savings instead of here accumulating property. What the one hundred and eighty millions of solid gold shipped from California to a foreign country would produce, if retained here by white labor and invested in the soil, in the homes and firesides of our own race, requires no illustration or argument. California, instead of being a State of cities, might be a State of prosperous farms; instead of being in a condition (considering her extraordinary natural advantages) of wonderful yet healthy progress, we find her so retarded in her growth as to amount almost to retrogression.

It is a trite saying, however, that competition in labor is healthful. True—but not between free and slave labor; and the Chinese in California are substantially in a condition of servitude. Ninety-nine one-hundredths of them are imported here by large companies under contracts to repay to the importers out of their labor the cost of their transportation and large interest upon the outlay, and these contracts frequently hold their subjects for long periods. During the existence of these contracts the Chinese are, to all intents, serfs, and as such are let out to service at a miserable pittance to perform the labor that it ought to be the privilege of our own race to perform. Even were it possible for the white laborer to maintain existence upon the wages paid to the Chinese, his condition nevertheless becomes that of an abject slave, for grinding poverty is absolute slavery. The vaunted "dignity of labor" becomes a biting sarcasm when the laborer becomes a serf.

Irrespective, however, of this slavery by contract, the Chinese who inundate our shores are, by the very constitution of their nature, by instinct, by the traditions of their order for thousands of years, serfs. They never rise above that condition in their native land, and by the inexorable decrees of caste, never can rise. Servile labor to them is their natural and inevitable lot. Hewers of wood and drawers of water they have been since they had a country, and servile laborers they will be to the end of time. Departure from that level with them is never upward; the only change, apparently is from servitude to crime.

The pious anticipations that the influence of Christianity upon the Chinese would be salutary, have proved unsubstantial and vain. Among one hundred and twenty-five thousand of them with a residence here beneath the elevating influences of Christian precept, and example, and with the zealous labors of earnest Christian teachers, and the liberal expenditure of ecclesiastical revenues, we have no evidence of a single genuine conversion to Christianity, or of a single instance of an assimilation with our manners, or habits of thought or life. There are a few, painfully few, professing Christians among them, but the evidence confirms us in asserting that with these the profession is dependent to a great extent upon its paying a profit to the professor. Those Christians who hailed with satisfaction the advent of the Chinese to our shores, with the expectation that they would thus be brought beneath the benign influences of Christianity, cannot fail to have discovered that for every one of them that has professed Christianity, a hundred of our own youth, blighted by the degrading contact of their presence, have been swept into destruction.

Neither is there any possibility that in the future education, religion, or the other influences of our civilization can effect any change in this condition of things. The Chinese in California are all adults. They are not men of families. The family relation does not exist here among them. Not one in a thousand is married; and, in addition, their habits of opium eating are practically destructive of the power of procreation. So that whatever improvement might otherwise be anticipated from instilling into the comparatively unformed and receptive minds of a young and rising generation the educational and religious maxims that control our own race is thus effectually precluded.

Above and beyond these considerations, however, we believe, and the researches of those who have most attentively studied the Chinese character confirm us in the consideration, that the Chinese are incapable of adaption to our institutions. The national intellect of China has become decrepit from sheer age. It has long since passed its prime and is waning into senility. The iron manacles of caste which prevail in that Empire are as cruel and unyielding as those which claim the sudras in Hindostan, to a hereditary state of pauperism and slavery. As an acute thinker has sagaciously observed, the Chinese seem to be antediluvian men renewed. Their code of morals, their forms of worship, and their maxims of life, are those of the remotest antiquity. In this aspect they stand a barrier against which the elevating tendency of a higher civilization exerts itself in vain. And, in an ethnological point of view, there can be no hope that any contact with our people, however long continued, will ever conform them to our institutions, enable them to comprehend or appreciate our form of government, or to assume the duties or discharge the functions of citizens.

During their entire settlement in California, they have never adapted themselves to our habits, modes of dress, or our educational system, have never learned the sanctity of an oath, never desired to become citizens, or to perform the duties of citizenship, never discovered the difference between right and wrong, never ceased the worship of their idol gods, or advanced a step beyond the musty traditions of their native hive. Impregnable to all the influences of our Anglo-Saxon life they remain the same stolid Asiatics that have floated on the rivers and slaved in the fields of China for thirty centuries of time.

In view of all this we inquire, what are the benefits conferred upon us by this isolated and degraded class? The only one ever suggested was "cheap labor." But if cheap labor means white famine it is a fearful benefit. If cheap labor means not only starvation for our own laborers, but a gradual, yet certain, depletion of the resources of our State for the enriching of a semi-civilized foreign country, it is a benefit hitherto unknown to the science of political economy. If cheap labor means servile labor it is a burlesque on the policy of emancipation. And if this kind of cheap labor brings in its train the demoralization consequent upon the enforced idleness of our own race, the moral degradation attendant upon the presence in our midst of the most disgusting licentiousness, and the absolute certainty of pestilence arising from the crowded condition and filthy habits of life of those who perform this so-called cheap labor, it were well for all of us that it should be abolished.

THE "YELLOW PERIL" REVISITED: CAMPAIGN AGAINST THE JAPANESE

The Real Yellow Peril

Before 1882, the anti-Oriental campaign was confined to the Chinese. According to the 1880 census, there were only 148 Japanese in the United States. The passage of the Chinese Exclusion Act of 1882, and the sudden influx of Japanese in the 1880's and 1890's, transformed the anti-Chinese movement into an anti-Japanese campaign.

According to Roger Daniels, in his book The Politics of Prejudice, *the anti-Japanese operation "was in many ways merely a continuation of the long standing agitation against the Chinese." Most of the charges leveled against the Chinese —their resistance to assimilation, low standard of living, hateful customs, and unfair labor competition—were directed against the Japanese as well. The progress made by the homeland under the Young Mikado, and the surprisingly rapid*

Source: [8] Hugh H. Lusk, "The Real Yellow Peril," *The North American Review,* CLXXXVI (May 1, 1907), pp. 375–377.

success of many Japanese-Americans, however, weakened the traditional anti-Oriental arguments and impelled exclusionists to revert to the "Yellow Peril" theme.

The Yellow Peril approach was also enhanced by the growing popularity of racial theories current at the turn of the century. Intellectuals, particularly leading historians, espoused the theory that history had proven the superiority of one dominant race—the Anglo-Saxon. And Orientals were believed to present a special threat to the race's purity. Japan's easy victory over China and Russia revived an old Western prophecy that some successor to the ancient Mongols would again emerge from Asia and attempt to conquer Western civilization. Some Americans reasoned that in the event of such a holocaust, the loyalties of the Japanese in the United States would be with the invaders.

In 1907, an article entitled "The Real Yellow Peril" appeared in the North American Review. *The author of this piece depicted Japan as in the vanguard of a vast Mongolian horde that might conquer the Far East, invade Europe, and launch a "naval war in the Pacific Ocean, and a possible bombardment of American cities on the western coast of this continent. The danger in Japan's recent exploits was in the example it could set for the rest of the Yellow race, and the real Yellow peril was the pressure that population was destined to place upon the Mongolians."*

It is now some years since a note of alarm was sounded in Europe in connection with the future of the Mongolian race. The credit of this warning was given to the German Kaiser, who was supposed by some to have reasons of his own for turning public attention to possible dangers at a distance rather than to actual complications nearer home. It is needless to dwell on these speculations now. The possibilities of fifteen years ago have in this, as in many other things, given place to the experiences of the last three or four, and the question of the future of the peoples of eastern Asia in their relations to the rest of the world has made an immense stride from the realm of abstract discussion towards that of actual world politics.

The evolution of Japan, and her sudden leap into prominence as a naval and military Power, have been the immediate cause of this change; yet it may be doubted whether it has not tended rather to mislead than to enlighten many of the public in this country on some of the larger aspects of the question. To most of us Japan stands today for Mongolia, and her interesting and energetic people for the Mongolian race. Japan's ambitions and projects in the Western Pacific, her designs on Korea, and the covetous eyes she is supposed to have cast on the Philippines; for most people in America these are the really important, as well as the immediately interesting, questions of the Orient today. There is an uneasy feeling abroad that The Yellow Peril may turn out to be real enough, but it is supposed by many that instead of a repetition of the Middle Age invasion of Europe it will take the form of a naval war in the Pacific Ocean, and a possible bombardment of American cities on the western coast of this continent. Looking at the recent history of eastern Asia and the adjacent islands, Japan with her naval, military and industrial activities, seems very naturally, to most people, to embrace everything worth considering—for the present, at any rate—in the political movements of the Mongolian race. This impression, however, is certainly a mistaken one. Only half a century has passed since Japan began to awaken to some perception of the conditions and possibilities of modern civilization; and since then she has accomplished enough in various directions to leave the Caucasian world almost lost in speculation as to what she will do next. From an old-world civilization, easily confounded by our own people with barbarism, they have awakened with a rapidity that was startling to a modern life of commerce and industry, of applied science and liberal politics, of practical economics and advanced national organization, such as a dozen centuries have been hardly sufficient to teach the nations of Europe. The phenomenon is sufficiently startling to make us lose sight of the fact that, while they are undoubtedly a remarkable people, the Japanese are by no means unique in any of the characteristics that have gone in their case to the rapid development of a great national progress. These characteristics are not so much Japanese as Mongolian. The same dogged pursuance of a purpose once taken up; the same remarkable faculty for imitating the arts and learning the methods of other nations that appeal to them as useful; the same capacity for organization, and the same readiness to sacrifice the individual for the advancement of the common object, are to be found in the whole race occupying eastern Asia, as truly, if not yet to our eyes as conspicuously, as in the people of Japan itself.

Should there exist anything that may be looked on as a peril for the civilized world in the awakening of the peoples of Mongolian race, therefore, from the sleep of so many centuries, it is one that is by no means confined to Japan. We might even go farther and say that it is one in which the place of Japan, though prominent, is comparatively a small one, after all. Japan herself, it must be remembered, is but a small kingdom, and her people stand by no means in the front rank of the nations in population. It is true that her islands are crowded, and that her people would be glad of more room for expansion; and this, as all history bears witness, is the primary cause of national aggression. But as yet, at any rate, this need of room for expansion exists on no large scale in the case of Japan. She has already, within the last few years, acquired the large island of Formosa, and she is now engaged in arranging for a still larger outlet for her surplus population by the annexation of the Korean peninsula. It will be years before the new territory thus secured will have been fully occupied; and if it should be found possible, by a friendly arrangement with this country, for her to assume the protectorate of the Philippine Islands, a very considerable time would ceratinly elapse before Japan would feel to any considerable extent the strain of the problem of national expansion.

And in the absence of this there is very little cause to anticipate national aggression on the part of Japan. There is a spirit of unrest abroad among her people, it is true—the aftermath of the great awakening of the last half-century—but there is also a strong perception of proportionate values, characteristic of her public men, and by no means wanting in the nation at large, which rises to the level of that virtue of common sense so long valued as a special possession of their own by the race to which we belong. Under any ordinary circumstances, this quality may be depended on to prevent Japan from doing anything rash in the field of world politics. The Mongolian temperament is essentially a practical one, and neither Japan nor China will be found ready to sacrific much to the merely ideal. It will be found that, even while they assert their claim to equal treatment, they will ask for nothing unreasonable in itself, and even this they will be in no hurry to demand at the cannon's mouth.

It may be asked whether, if this conclusion is correct, we may dismiss "The Yellow Peril" as a mere bogy man, terrible only to children? The answer must be in the negative. There is a real Mongolian peril in existence now; it is one that is growing, and is certain to continue to grow in the near future; it is one also that cannot be too carefully considered and provided against by all nations that value that form of civilization which is essentially Caucasian both in form and spirit. The peril is not, in the first instance, at any rate, one that can be measured by fleets and armies; it does not depend on the ambition of statesmen, or the longing of successful soldiers to achieve further conquests; it is, in fact, a more serious thing than these, and in the long run it may very well be found to embrace these among its incidents. The peril is the oldest and the most natural one that can arise to disturb human arrangements: the problem of population.

California Anti-Alien Bill Campaign

In 1913, the anti-Japanese issue focused on the alien land question. Nativist forces were seeking legislation which would prevent any alien who was not eligible for citizenship from owning land. Since the courts until that time had excluded Chinese and other Orientals from the provisions of the naturalization laws, the Japanese were the obvious targets of alien land legislation. On his second day in office, President Woodrow Wilson received the Japanese ambassador who had come

Source: [9] Franklin Hichborn, *Story of the Session of the California Legislature of 1913* (San Francisco, 1913), pp. 223–224.

*to discuss the proposal then pending in the California legisla-
ture. Wilson promised to see what he and his Secretary of State,
William Jennings Bryan, could do to prevent the legislaton.
Through intermediaries, the Administration contacted the Progressive Party Governor, Hiram Johnson. Johnson and the
Progressive majority in the state legislature, however, were
resigned to the passage of an alien land bill; but they claimed
that they, in fact, sought a law which would satisfy the anti-
Japanese elements, and yet not be too abrasive to the Japanese.
Nevertheless, the land bill that was eventually signed and enacted by Johnson, antagonized the Japanese government and
aggravated racial feelings here. Later, the Progressives ration-
alized that the provisions were, in any case, easy to evade.*

*In the course of the 1913 session of the California legisla-
ture, the chief anti-Japanese land bill introduced was the
Sanford-Shearer law. Senator Sanford had, in the past, proposed numerous pieces of anti-Japanese legislation. As a candidate for reelection in 1910, he had made his stand on the
Oriental question the principal issue. During this campaign,
his organization issued a circular containing a bitter attack on
the opponents to his most recent anti-alien land legislation.*

During the last Legislature, Senator J. B. Sanford introduced
in the Senate a bill to prevent Japanese, Chinese, Hindus and
all other Asiatics from owning or leasing land in California.

This bill, with others, was killed by the "big stick."

If re-elected, Senator Sanford will again introduce this bill
and use every legitimate effort in his power to secure the passage of the same.

An American cannot own land in Japan. He cannot even
lease land unless he marries a Jap woman and becomes a part
of their civilization. If the Japanese think so much of the future
of the little Jap as to preserve their lands for him, why should
we not think enough of Young America to preserve our lands
for the rising generation?

No race of people that cannot become citizens of the United
States should be allowed to gain a foothold in this country.

Several States in the Union have Alien Land laws on their
statute books. Among the first laws Oklahoma placed upon

her statute books was this famous law. Senator Sanford sent to Oklahoma for a copy of it and introduced it in its original form, as it had been tested and proven constitutional.

Statistics show that the number of Japanese, Chinese, Hindus, and Koreans in California exceeds 100,000. Further immigration should be absolutely prohibited.

The amount of land owned, leased, rented, and controlled by Asiatics in California is becoming alarming and amounts to over 200,000 acres of our most fertile lands. The value of the crop products is over 100 million dollars annually. The gradual encroachment of the "little brown men" is fast becoming a problem. The sooner it is handled the easier will it be.

Within the past seven years 93,000 Japs have come into this country, 50,000 of whom have become farmers and farm laborers.

Ten years from now, at the present percentage of increase, the Japs will be in absolute control of the agricultural resources of California and the white people will all be working for the Japs. Every Jap now farming in California is the representative of his male relative in Japan. George Simo, the "Potato King," controls the potato crop of California and is several times a millionaire. There are hundreds of other striking examples.

The Democratic platform endorses the Sanford bill, and Theodore A. Bell says, that if elected Governor, he will sign such a measure if it comes to him for signature.

Let every liberty-loving American citizen put patriotism and love of home above partisan politics and do something for young America by voting for J. B. Sanford, Democratic and Anti-Machine candidate for State Senator-Fourth District.

THE TWILIGHT OF AMERICAN ANTI-SEMITISM

Until the 1880's, anti-Semitism in the United States was sporadic and usually involved attacks upon individuals. With the sharp rise in Jewish immigration, however, Jews became a special target of the American nativists' hate campaign. Since the bulk of the new Jewish immigrants came from eastern Europe, their "strange" dress and customs added to their religious "distinction." Like other immigrant groups, the eastern European Jews were regarded by natives as dirty, undernourished, and impoverished foreigners. And, with the exception of blacks and American Indians, Jews suffered greater persecution in America than almost any other minority. Anti-Semitism was more vicious than the usual anti-foreignism because it contained certain peculiar elements, rooted in the early Middle Ages, which followed Jews wherever they went.

Anti-Semitism had its origin in the bitter religious differences between Christians and Jews; these included the Jewish rejection of the divinity of Christ and the Christian charge that Jews were "Christ Killers." A growing isolation between the two groups resulted in each creating legends about the other. A medieval myth accepted by many Christians was that Jews practiced ritual murder upon helpless Christians to obtain blood for their God. Moreover, it was claimed that Jews were lechers, in league with the devil, and responsible for such calamities as the Black Death.

Another Jewish stereotype that originated in medieval times, and found its way to America, was that of the grasping, greedy Jew. An ancient papal ban on Christians' charging interest had

Sources: [10] Telemachus Thomas Timayenis, *The Original Mr. Jacobs: A Startling Eposé!* (New York, 1888), pp. i–ii, 58–59, 63–64; [11] Timayenis, *The American Jew: An Exposé of His Career Profusely Illustrated* (New York, 1888), pp. 81–85; [12] *Letters of Henry Adams, 1858–1918,* Worthington Ford, ed. 2 vols. (Boston, 1930–1938), vol. 2, pp. 110–111, 338, 620.

left much of the moneylending business to Jews. Although Christian families eventually entered and dominated European banking, a legend arose that there was an international conspiracy among Jewish bankers to gain control of the world's economy.* In the 1890's, American agrarian radicals employed this myth to discredit the gold standard and bankers in general. One representative of agrarian radicalism, Ignatius Donnelly, wrote a novel entitled Caesar's Column, *predicting a world dominated by a Jewish oligarchy.*

During the "Red Scare" of the 1920's, following the Bolshevik Revolution, American nativists applied the international Jewish conspiracy theme to the political scene. The prominence of a few Jews in the new Bolshevik regime and the activity of some Jews in the American socialist movement convinced many in the United States that there existed a Jewish international communist and/or socialist plot to dominate the world. Henry Ford, America's leading industrialist, fearful of Bolshevism and influenced by the current of anti-Semitism in America, enlisted his propaganda organ, The Dearborn Independent, *to discredit American Jews. Growing tired of the international Jewish bankers conspiracy, Ford turned his attention to the anti-Semites' manic fear of an international Jewish plot. After the inception of this "political anti-Semitism," Ford provoked great interest in a* fraudulent *document, concocted by a group of Czarist sympathizers seeking to discredit the Bolsheviks, entitled "The Protocols of the Elders of Zion." The Protocols contained a master plan, supposedly drafted by leading Jews, in the interest of establishing a Jewish dictatorship of the world. Years later, after numerous writers had exposed the document's fraudulence, Ford allegedly tried to make amends for his paper's misdeed. The damage, however, had been done. Despite the denials and apologies, the ideas contained in the Protocols became a permanent part of American nativist thought; and some authorities have asserted that their influence upon European anti-Semitism may have*

* This myth was perpetuated by the non-Jewish latecomers in their competition with Jewish financial institutions in the European banking business. (Ed.)

contributed to the Nazi holocaust that took millions of Jewish lives.

The increased Jewish immigration in the latter part of the nineteenth century, however, resulted in the first wave of significant anti-Semitic literature. In 1888 an obscure writer, Telemachus Thomas Timayenis, produced two of the earliest anti-Semitic tracts published in the United States. The first of these, The Original Mr. Jacobs, *[document 10] warned that powerful Jews would try to prevent the book's sale, and developed the familiar image of the crafty, exploiting, lascivious Jew who, above all, hated Christians. The second work,* The American Jew, *[document 11] dwelled upon the ancient legend of the lecherous Jew who seeks to seduce good Christian girls. The recent reprinting (1970) of* The Original Mr. Jacobs, *under a different title* (The Original Mr. Jew), *by a neo-Nazi group called "The Thunderbolt" underscores the persistence of this type of writing.*

Anti-Semitic writings were not confined to unknowns like Timayenis; bitter but reasoned attacks appeared in the personal observations of one of America's leading intellectuals, Henry Adams [document 12]. Adams revered Norman civilization above all others and emphasized its lack of Jewish influence. Moreover, like most of the Adamses of Massachusetts, he did not feel at home in American industrial society. He feared the emerging power of finance capitalism because he believed that through financial manipulation, Jewish bankers would gain control of the nation. During the free silver debate of the 1880's, his persistent anti-Semitic observations surfaced once again. Adams mocked the arguments of the free silver men by holding that European Jewish bankers, through their control of American finance, would make the final decision in favor of the gold standard. And again, the frustrated Adams once complained to a friend, "We are in the hands of the Jews."

The documents presented below are representative of anti-Semitic writings of the late nineteenth century; these range from the emotional and blatant attacks of a Timayenis to the more reasoned and intellectually acceptable ones of a Henry Adams.

"The Original Mr. Jacobs"

INTRODUCTION

We expect that the Jews will try to boycott "The American Jew," using the same peculiar tactics as in the case of "The Original Mr. Jacobs." They will appoint committees to visit book-dealers, urging them not to handle the book; they will buy up and destroy all copies found exposed for sale; they will bribe, threaten, plead, and try in every possible way to interfere with its sale; they will circulate reports that the book has been "called in," and will spread many other lies,—lies that the Jew knows so well how to disseminate.

But all their efforts toward stopping the sale of "The Original Mr. Jacobs" have been unavailing, for in less than three months this book has achieved a wide-spread circulation. It is, at the present writing, in its twentieth edition, and its sale does not show any signs of abatement.

We have been requested by many prominent men in literary, financial, and commercial circles, to establish a monthly publication, to be called "The Anti-Semite." We have been assured of ample support in this venture. There is certainly enough of patriotism among the masses of the American people to maintain such a publication; and there is, unquestionably, a wide-spread desire to check the diabolical methods of the Jews,— these parasites of the human race.

The periodical we propose to establish, will give a faithful account of the deceits, crimes, and fraudulent transactions of the Jew, in all channels of business. It will be published monthly, at one dollar per year. Efficient correspondents throughout the United States will watch the Jew, and will keep us informed of all his deeds, or rather misdeeds, which will be fearlessly recorded in "The Anti-Semite."

Efforts will not be spared in urging the passage of laws that will afford some protection to the commercial community, and to society in general, from the Jew. Every business-man should support "The Anti-Semite," for this publication will expose dishonesty, and watch over the interests of the business community.

By means of false promises the Jews succeed in gathering from the pockets of the poor, from the depth of woollen stockings and the pockets of old coats, the savings which the faithful wife showed with a happy smile to the husband, who feared that the time was not distant when he would no longer be able to work. With the product of these thefts they buy historic estates, where eminent men of former times rested after having grown old in the service of their country; thereon the degenerate scions of the aristocracy disgrace themselves by bowing to and admiring these thieves and spurious Jew barons, whose coat of arms would be more appropriately impressed upon pigpens.

But how sad to think that these men are nominated ministers and ambassadors, as in the case of Raynal Bischoffsheim and others. A feeling, however, of disappointment has come over the Jews. They seem to say, "Is this all?" In the boxes of fashionable theaters, paid for with the pilfered savings of the poor whom they have reduced to despair, on the balconies of the castles they have stolen, these victors are assailed by the cankerous thoughts which came over the biblical Schelemo on the terraces of his palace and in the alleys of his garden.[1]

THE JEWS' HATRED FOR THE CHRISTIANS

The sentiment that dominates the corrupt and passionate soul of the Jew is his hatred for the Church and its ministers. This hatred is, after all, natural. The vow of the missionary is a permanent mockery at the wealth of the Jew, who is incapable of buying with all his gold what the poorest Christian possesses—faith and hope, sentiments absolutely unknown among the Jews. Religion among the Jews is fidelity to tradition, an attachment to the race to which they belong. But there is not a word in the Hebrew language to express *faith*. The Jewish word *emouna* means constancy, tenacity, but not faith.

---

[1] The Schelemo was a medieval concept of the devil.

Simon, *alias* Lockroy, may insult yonder poor missionary. Dreyfus may raise his voice against those poor sisters of charity who are ever ready to sacrifice their lives upon the field of battle or in the chambers of sickness. There will always remain to them the crucifix they wear around their necks. The fact alone that their sublime virtues and disinterestedness exist is like a thorn in the bed of the vulgar Jew Sybarite who feels himself powerless over these souls.

But if the Jews, these perpetual agitators, have well-nigh succeeded in shaking the foundations of society with the money they have wrongfully acquired, the fact remains that the day is not far distant when a new society will rise that will crush them. The day is near at hand when all their ill-gotten gains will be distributed amongst those who will take part in the mighty struggle now brewing, distributed as formerly lands and fiefs were distributed among the bravest.

In Germany, in Russia, in Austria, in Roumania, in France, even in America, where the movement just begins, all classes, rich and poor, in fact all of Christian origin, agree upon one point—the wisdom of forming an anti-Semitic alliance, an alliance directed against the Jew.

"The American Jew"

THE JEW LECHER

"In all matters pertaining to corruption and pollution, in matters that defile moral character, the Jew stands unequalled."
—THE ORIGINAL MR. JACOBS.

Next to his lust for money, the strongest passion in the Jew is his licentiousness. This, like every other vicious habit of which the Jew is possessed, takes a peculiarly prominent and objectionable form.

The average Jew is disgustingly bawdy in his talk, and interlards his conversation with filthy expressions and obscene words. On the verandas at summer-resorts, in hotel-corridors, in the lobbies of theatres, on steamboats, on railway-cars, and in public places in general, the Jew indulges in this repulsive peculiarity, to the great annoyance and disgust of respectable Christian women and decency-loving Gentile men. This was one of the habits which made him so objectionable at summer-resorts, and has led to his practical exclusion from almost every first-class summer-hotel in the land.

The boldest and most offensive of that class of persons who lounge about the prominent thoroughfares of our principal cities, and are known as "street mashers," are Israelites. Overdressed, with mincing gait and dandified mien, these Jew "mashers" are daily to be seen strutting up and down the leading streets, ogling, with amazing effrontery, every woman who passes them by. Young girls of tender age are especially marked by these Jew "mashers" as their particular prey. Some years ago, in San Francisco, the attention of the police was directed to a band of Jew "mashers," who made a point of following up the girls of a certain public school on their way from the classroom to their homes. These Jew scoundrels, wherever they were unable to make a girl's acquaintance, would follow her up in pairs, talking together in the most disgusting manner, so as to be overheard by the objects of their pursuit. Some of the children's male relatives, assisted by the police, finally succeeded in very effectually disposing of this band of wretches.

Almost any afternoon, in Kearny Street, San Francisco, knots of Jew "mashers" are to be seen hanging around the corners, and ogling the women who pass. Some of these fellows have not merely lascivious propensities in view, but have their sharp and restless eyes open to any possibilities of blackmail that may present themselves. Some years ago, a young married woman who had been foolish enough to allow one of these foppishly dressed Jew scoundrels to make her acquaintance, was so mercilessly blackmailed, although her conduct had in no way passed into the bounds of criminality, that the unfortunate woman was driven into an attempt at suicide. The truth then leaked out; and she and her husband never again lived happily together, and eventually drifted apart.

Upon one occasion, a young lady, while passing the corner of Park and Kearny Streets, was addressed by one of these Jew

Lotharios of the street. Gazing upon the Jew dude with a pitying look, she drew a fifty-cent piece from her pocket, and threw it at his feet, exclaiming,—

"You miserable thing! you don't look as if you were half fed. Go and buy yourself something to eat with that."

The Jew masher gazed for a moment at the coin as it lay on the sidewalk, and then the instincts of his race conquered him. He stooped, picked up the money, and pocketed it. A quick and efficacious way to get rid of the Jew masher is to throw him a little money. It will engross his attention, and secure a release from his importunities.

In Eddy Street, San Francisco, a Jew dentist established himself some time ago in business. One day, while a lady was under the influence of an anaesthetic in the dental chair, this scoundrel, taking advantage of her helpless condition, committed certain improprieties. The lady regained consciousness more quickly than he anticipated, and he was discovered. She went home, and told the whole story to her husband. The latter, arming himself with a stout rawhide, compelled his wife to accompany him to the dental parlors. Arrived there, he laid the lash lustily over the Jew's head and shoulders,—flogged him unmercifully. The Jew coward made no attempt at defence. He simply writhed and squirmed and screamed, like the whipped cur that he was. Finally, lest his humiliation should not already be sufficiently complete, he fell down on his knees before his assailant, grovelling before him, kissing his feet, and imploring him to desist the castigation. Then, still abjectly kneeling, he confessed his attempted crime in terms of sickening servility, and implored the wife's forgiveness. What a disgusting spectacle! But let all Jew lechers be treated likewise.

In another street of San Francisco, within a stone's throw of the famous "Poodle Dog" restaurant, a Jew kept a hair-dressing establishment on a somewhat pretentious scale. In the window of the shop was an immense glass case, under which was a miniature garden most beautifully devised. In the midst of this garden was a quantity of white mice, which were wont to disport themselves in most amusing fashion. The pretty miniature garden and the curious antics of the mice had the effect of drawing numbers of women and girls to the window, where they would stand contemplating the interesting spectacle. The spot upon which they stood was formed of boards in which large holes were pierced. Underneath was the cellar. The Jew barber, as it subsequently transpired, was in the habit of passing a large portion of his time in this cellar, immediately under the woodwork, which, it was proved, had been specially perforated by his orders. This filthy "Peeping Tom" was finally betrayed by a Jew, one of his workmen. The barber had quarrelled with the man, and discharged him; and the latter communicated the story to the police. The Jew was arrested. The story made quite a sensation; and more than one lady in San Francisco, who had been interested in the pretty white mice in the Jew's window, blushed long and deeply as she perused the particulars of his infamous misdemeanor.

Letters of Henry Adams

If the silver-question were a simple matter of money-standard in America, I should advise anyone to buy, of course not bonds but stock, on a silver basis; for, unless the world ends, America is the safest of all now-existing countries; but the money-standard is for the present a very secondary consideration. America is horribly in debt to Europe. The smallest estimate of European capital invested there is £600,000,000 (six hundred million pounds). The common estimate is one thousand millions. A large portion of this—no one can even guess how large—is floating capital, all practically Jew money, and lent practically on call. The owners of this capital have repeatedly and energetically declared that it would be withdrawn if there was even a danger of free coinage of silver. Now, no one doubts,—and every Jew in London has acted on the belief—that America cannot anyway maintain the gold standard. She is insolvent on the gold standard, and must be driven either on to paper or on to silver. The rise in gold has doubled the burden of her debt, and gold is still rising. Therefore, since she must anyway, within a few years, go into insolvency, and

since indubitably a very large political party prefers to throw
her at once into bankruptcy on the gold basis rather than to
make things worse by increasing the debt, the chances are very
great that Europe, partly in self-defense and partly in a wish
to punish and make a terrible example of her, will withdraw
capital enough to force a very severe crisis. Already, stocks
have been let down to the level of the panic of '93. In fact, the
drop was too fast, and the Jew bankers had to try to check
it the other day by helping J. P. Morgan to lend the market
some £20,000,000 of exchange; in other words, they increased our debt on call, or rather on three months' credit, to
that amount. Twenty millions, however, will go a very short
way if Europe really calls her loans; and she may do so any
day.

In this situation an investment is sheer gambling. We are in
the hands of the Jews. They can do what they please with our
values.

But, mind,—when I say that an American investment is a
gamble, I by no means intend to say that European invest-
ments are any better. On the contrary, after the utmost study
that I can give to the subject, I have been able to discover no
possible ground for the values now nominally quoted on the
European bourses.

. . . For three years I have told you that in my opinion
there was only one safe and surely profitable investment, and
that is gold, locked up in one's private safe. There you have no
risk but the burglar. In any other form you have the burglar,
the Jew, the Czar, the socialist, and, above all, the total, ir-
remediable, radical rottenness of our social, industrial, financial and political system.

. . . *Wednesday,* Warsaw. [August 14.] We arrived here
yesterday afternoon, after a tiresome night and day in what
they call an express through a country flatter than Florida, and
less varied. But we had the pleasure of seeing at last the Polish
Jew, and he was a startling revelation even to me, who have
seen *pas mal de Jew.* The country is not bad; on the contrary,
it is a good deal like our plains, more or less sandy, but well
watered. It is the people that make one tired. You would

gratify all your worst instincts if you see a dozen women reaping the grain, and one big, clumsy man standing over them, superintending and doing nothing. With what pleasure should I have called your attention to it, knowing your ferocious and evil nature in regard to my sex! . . . Warsaw is a big, bustling city, like all other cities, only mostly Jew, in which it is peculiar to Poland. I see little to remark in the streets; nothing in the shops. The people are uglier than on Pennsylvania Avenue which is other wise my lowest standard. Like all other cities and places, it is . . . flattened out, and has lost most of its characteristics. The Jew and I are the only curious antiquities in it. . . . The Jew is also a curiosity. He makes me creep.

. . . The winter is nearly over, I am seventy-six years old, and nearly over too. As I go, my thoughts turn towards you and I want to know how you are. Of myself, I have almost nothing to tell. It is quite astonishing how the circle narrows. I think that in reality as many people pass by, and I hear as much as I ever did, but it is no longer a part of me. I am inclined to think it not wholly my fault. The atmosphere really has become a Jew atmosphere. It is curious and evidently good for some people, but it isolates me. I do not know the language, and my friends are as ignorant as I. We are still in power, after a fashion. Our sway over what we call society is undisputed. We keep Jews far away, and the anti-Jew feeling is quite rabid. We are anti-everything and we are wild uplifters; yet we somehow seem to be more Jewish every day. This is not my own diagnosis. I make none. I care not a straw what happens provided the fabric lasts a few months more; but will it do so? I am uneasy about you. I judge you to be worse than we. At least you are making almost as much howl about it.

EUGENICS

Eugenics: A Scientific Basis
for Racial Inferiority

*At the end of the nineteenth century, nativists and racists were
presented with additional arguments for their stance against
free immigration by the study of eugenics. At a time when the
social sciences and history were influenced considerably by the
environmentalists, biologists "advanced dramatic claims for
heredity and even helped to translate them into a political and
social creed." In Europe, building on the work of Gregor
Mendel and August Weismann, Sir Francis Galton had helped
to launch the science of eugenics. The implications of eugenics
—its emphasis upon human inequalities and its warning of the
dangers in the multiplication of the unfit—appealed to nativists and racists in the United States. Here they discovered
further arguments for the adoption of a very selective immigration policy.*

*In the early 1900's, the ideas of the eugenicists gained in-
creasing attention from both intellectuals and the general public. Their theories found their way into the writings of some of
the leading figures of the early twentieth century.*

EUGENICS is the science and the art of being well born. In the
words of Francis Galton, who devised the term, it is the "study
of agencies that may improve or impair the racial qualities of
future generations, either mentally or physically."

The knowledge of the science of Eugenics will sooner or
later develop the art. Knowledge will lead to better men. At
present, though the agencies of charities which perpetuate the

Source: [13] David Starr Jordan, *The Heredity of Richard Roe* (Boston,
1911), pp. 1–2, 4–8.

weak, or war which eliminates the strong, and of an education which makes celibacy a condition of success, we are in a degree of reversing the processes of natural selection. If the fittest do not serve as parents, the next generations will not inherit fitness.

In the present discussion, Richard Roe, a familiar figure in legal practice, serves as a lay figure of heredity, and in tracing his career some of the leading facts and principles of Eugenics are brought under notice.

When Richard Roe was born, "the gate of gifts was closed" to him. It was in fact closed long before that, at the moment of the blending of the two germ cells (ovum and sperm-cell) from the mingling of which his own personality arose. In the instant of conception, the gifts of life are granted. Nothing more comes of itself. Henceforth he must expect nothing new and must devote himself to the development of the heritage he has received from his father and mother. In this he has a lifelong task. He must bring its discordant elements into some sort of harmony. He must form his Ego by the union of these elements. He must soften down their contradictions. He must train his elements of strength to be helpful to some one in some way, that others may be helpful to him. He must give his weak powers exercise, so that their weakness shall not bring him disaster in the competition of life. For it is likely that somewhere, somehow, it will be proved that no chain is stronger than its weakest link. Other powers not too weak, nor over strong, Richard Roe must perforce neglect, because in the hurry of life there is not time for every desirable thing. In these ways the character of Richard Roe's inheritance is steadily changing under his hands. As he grows older, one after another of the careers that might have been his, the men he might have been, vanish from his path forever. On the other hand, by steady usage, a slender thread of capacity has so grown as to become like strong cordage. Thus Richard Roe learns anew the old parable of the talents. The power he hid in a napkin is taken away altogether, while that which is placed at usury is returned a hundredfold. He achieves at last, in greater or less degree, "the higher heredity," the fate that each man must create for himself.

. . . Richard Roe is himself but "an elongation" or continuation of his parents' life, as Erasmus Darwin said a century ago. He was the elongation of two lives, and behind them, of thousands of others, else he could not have individuality and be really himself. But for all that he is a chip off the old blocks. He is made of many chips from many old blocks.

Thus, as man, Richard Roe enters life with a series of possibilities and tendencies granted him by heredity. Each one is held in some fashion in the mystic nucleus of his first germ cell. Let us examine this series. Let us analyze the contents of this pack which he is to carry through life to the gates of the Golden City.

First, from his parents, men and women, Richard Roe has inherited humanity, the parts and organs and feelings of a man. "Hath he not eyes? Hath he not hands, organs, dimensions, senses, affections, passions? fed with the same food, hurt with the same weapons, subject to the same diseases, healed by the same means, warmed and cooled by the same winter and summer" as you or I or any other king or beggar we know of? "If you prick us, do we not bleed? if you tickle us, do we not laugh? if you poison us, do we not die? if you wrong us, shall we not revenge?" All this, the common heritage of Jew or Gentile, goes to the making of Richard Roe. His ancestors on both sides have been human, and that for many and many generations, so that "the knowledge of man runneth not to the contrary." If they had been dogs he would have been a dog like them. Even the prehuman ancestry, dimly seen by the faith of science, had in it the potentialities of manhood else it would not have risen to produce him. Descended for countless ages from man and woman, man born of woman Richard Roe surely is.

We may go farther with certainty. Richard Roe will follow the race type of his parentage. If he is Anglo-Saxon, as his name seems to denote, all Anglo-Saxon by blood, he will be all Anglo-Saxon in quality. To his characters of common humanity we may add those common to the race. He will not be a negro nor Mongolian, and he will have some traits and tendencies not often found in the Latin races of southern Europe. To be sure, Anglo-Saxon is a blend, of course. "Saxon and

Norman and Dane are we." But all other races are likewise blends. The Latin stock has many sources. The Mongolian is no single race, and there are as many sorts of negroes as of chickens or of sheep.

But his friends will know Richard Roe best not by the great mass of human traits nor by his race characteristics: these may be predominant and ineradicable, but they are not distinctive. Many other men on the street show the same proclivities, and from the rest he must be known by his peculiarities, by his specialities and his deficiencies. Within the narrowest type there is room for infinite play in the minor variations. For almost any possible series of these, Richard Roe could find warrant in his ancestry. His combination of them must be his own. That is his individuality. Hue of the eyes, color of the hair, length of the nose, shade of skin, form of ears, size of hands, character of thumb prints, in all these and ten thousand other particulars some allotment must fall to Richard Roe, and this allotment must be all his own.

Nature does not repeat herself,—"almost but never quite." She has "broken the die" in moulding each of his ancestors. She will break the die with him. She will make no servile copy of any of her works. By the law of sex, Richard Roe has twice as many ancestors as his father or mother had. Therefore these could give him anything they had severally received from their own parents. They could give him nothing else. But each one could not give his all, only half at most. The hereditary gifts must be divided in some way, else Richard Roe would be speedily overborne by them. He could not have twice as many qualities as his father. There would be no body left on which to fasten them. The number of traits one man may have cannot be doubled with each succeeding generation. Nature can only double half. Furthermore, any system of division Nature may adopt could not be on the average an equal division. Richard Roe's father might supply half his endowment of inborn characters, his mother furnishing the other half. Nature tries to arrange for some partition like this, but she can never divide evenly, and some qualities will not bear division. Richard Roe's share forms a sort of mosaic, made partly of unchanged characters standing side by side in new combinations,

partly a mixture of characters, in part of characters in perfect
blending, in part of characters dominant and recessive, the one
set evident, the other hidden, to be revived, it may be, in the
next generation.

DARWINIAN IMPERIALISM

*In 1898, the United States decisively defeated Spain in the
Spanish-American War, and stood on the threshold of becoming a leading colonial power. Soon after, a great debate ensued
in the Senate with regard to the wisdom of acquiring and governing overseas possessions, particularly the Philippine Islands.
The proponents of annexation, led by Senator Albert J. Beveridge, found the rationale of Social Darwinism to be a useful
tool in their arguments for expansionism. These Darwinian Expansionists affirmed that, just as the fittest forms of animal life
had demonstrated their superiority through survival, great nations like the United States had proven by their triumph over
weaker states, their right, and even their responsibility to rule
over and civilize others. Beveridge [Document 14] maintained
that Anglo-Saxon mastery of the world had been preordained
by Divine Providence. Ironically, opponents of the annexation
of the Philippines, notably Senator John W. Daniel [Docu-
ment 15], used racial arguments to support their case.*

"The mission of our race"

MR. BEVERIDGE. Mr. President, I address the Senate at this
time because Senators and Members of the House on both
sides have asked that I give to Congress and the country my

Source: [14] *United States Congressional Record*, 56th Cong., 1st
Sess., pp. 704, 708–709, 711; [15] *Ibid.*, 55th Cong., 3rd Sess., pp.
1430–1431.

observations on the Philippines and the Far East, and the conclusions which those observations compel; and because of hurtful resolutions introduced and utterances made in the Senate, every word of which will cost and is costing the lives of American soldiers.

Mr. President, the times call for candor. The Philippines are ours forever, "territory belonging to the United States," as the Constitution calls them. And just beyond the Philippines are China's illimitable markets. We will not retreat from either. We will not repudiate our duty in the archipelago. We will not abandon our opportunity in the Orient. We will not renounce our part in the mission of our race, trustee, under God, of the civilization of the world. And we will move forward to our work, not howling out regrets like slaves whipped to their burdens, but with gratitude for a task worthy of our strength, and thanksgiving to Almighty God that He has marked us as His chosen people, henceforth to lead in the regeneration of the world.

PHILIPPINES COMMAND THE PACIFIC

This island empire is the last land left in all the oceans. If it should prove a mistake to abandon it, the blunder once made would be irretrievable. If it proves a mistake to hold it, the error can be corrected when we will. Every other progressive nation stands ready to relieve us.

But to hold it will be no mistake. Our largest trade henceforth must be with Asia. The Pacific is our ocean. More and more Europe will manufacture the most it needs, secure from its colonies the most it consumes. Where shall we turn for consumers of our surplus? Geography answers the question. China is our natural customer. She is nearer to us than to England, Germany, or Russia, the commercial powers of the present and the future. They have moved nearer to China by securing permanent bases on her borders. The Philippines give us a base at the door of all the East.

Lines of navigation from our ports to the Orient and Australia; from the Isthmian Canal to Asia; from all Oriental ports to Australia, converge at and separate from the Philippines. They are a self-supporting, dividend-paying fleet, per-

manently anchored at a spot selected by the strategy of Providence, commanding the Pacific. And the Pacific is the ocean
of the commerce of the future. Most future wars will be conflicts for commerce. The power that rules the Pacific, therefore,
is the power that rules the world. And, with the Philippines,
that power is and will forever be the American Republic.

. . . But, Senators, it would be better to abandon this combined garden and Gibraltar of the Pacific, and count our blood
and treasure already spent a profitable loss, than to apply any
academic arrangement of self-government to these children.
They are not capable of self-government. How could they be?
They are not of a self-governing race. They are Orientals,
Malays, instructed by Spaniards in the latter's worst estate.

They know nothing of practical government except as they
have witnessed the weak, corrupt, cruel, and capricious rule of
Spain. What magic will anyone employ to dissolve in their
minds and characters those impressions of governors and governed which three centuries of misrule has created? What
alchemy will change the oriental quality of their blood and set
the self-governing currents of the American pouring through
their Malay veins? How shall they, in the twinkling of an eye,
be exhalted to the heights of self-governing peoples which required a thousand years for us to reach, Anglo-Saxon though
we are?

Let men beware how they employ the term "self-government." It is a sacred term. It is the watchword at the door of
the inner temple of liberty, for liberty does not always mean
self-government. Self-government is a method of liberty—the
highest, simplest, best—and it is acquired only after centuries
of study and struggle and experiment and instruction and all
the elements of the progress of man. Self-government is no
base and common thing, to be bestowed on the merely auda-
cious. It is the degree which crowns the graduate of liberty, not
the name of liberty's infant class, who have not yet mastered
the alphabet of freedom. Savage blood, Oriental blood, Malay
blood, Spanish example—are these the elements of self-government?

We must act on the situation as it exists, not as we would
wish it. I have talked with hundreds of these people, getting

their views as to the practical workings of self-government. The great majority simply do not understand any participation in any government whatever. The most enlightened among them declare that self-government will succeed because the employers of labor will compel their employees to vote as their employer wills and that this will insure intelligent voting. I was assured that we could depend upon good men always being in office because the officials who constitute the government will nominate their successors, choose those among the people who will do the voting, and determine how and where elections will be held.

The most ardent advocate of self-government that I met was anxious that I should know that such a government would be tranquil because, as he said, if anyone criticized it, the government would shoot the offender. A few of them have a sort of verbal understanding of the democratic theory, but the above are the examples of the ideas of the practical workings of self-government entertained by the aristocracy, the rich planters and traders, and heavy employers of labor, the men who would run the government.

MAY GOVERN UNDER ANY FORM WE PLEASE

. . . The nation's power to make rules and regulations for the government of its possessions is not confined to any given set of rules or regulations. It is not confined to any particular formula of laws or kind of government or type of administration. Where do Senators find constitutional warrant for any special kind of government in "territory belonging to the United States." The language affirming our power to govern such territory is as broad as the requirements of all possible situations. And there is nothing in the Constitution to limit that comprehensive language, the very reverse is true. For power to administer government anywhere and in any manner the situation demands would have been in Congress if the Constitution had been silent; not merely because it is a power not reserved to the States or people; not merely because it is a power inherent in and an attribute of nationality; not even because it might be inferred from other specific provisions of the Constitution; but because it is the power most necessary for the ruling tendency of our race—the tendency to explore, expand, and grow, to sail new seas and seek new lands, subdue the wilderness, revitalize decaying peoples, and plant civilized and civilizing government over all the globe.

For the makers of the Constitution were of the race that produced Hawkins and Drake, and Raleigh, and Smith, and Winthrop, and Penn. They were of the great exploring, pioneering, colonizing, and governing race who went forth with trade or gain or religious liberty as the immediate occasion for their voyages, but really because they could not help it; because the blood within them commanded them; because their racial tendency is as resistless as the currents of the sea or the process of the suns or any other elemental movement of nature, of which that racial tendency itself is the most majestic. And when they wrote the Constitution they did not mean to negative the most elemental characteristic of their race, of which their own presence in America was an expression and an example. You can interpret a constitution without understanding the race that wrote it. And if our fathers had intended a reversal of the very nature and being of their race, they would have so declared in the most emphatic words our language holds. But they did not, and in the absence of such words the power would remain which is essential to the strongest tendency of our practical race, to govern wherever we are, and to govern by the methods best adapted to the situation. But our fathers were not content with silence, and they wrote in the Constitution the words which affirm this essential and imperial power.

THE WHOLE QUESTION ELEMENTAL

Mr. President, this question is deeper than any question of party politics; deeper than any question of the isolated policy of our country even; deeper than any question of constitutional power. It is elemental. It is racial. God has not been preparing the English-speaking and Teutonic peoples for a thousand years for nothing but vain and idle self-contemplation and self-admiration. No! He has made us the master organizers of the world to establish system where chaos reigns. He has given us the spirit of progress to overwhelm the forces of reaction throughout the earth. He has made us adepts in government that we may administer government among savage and senile peoples. Were it not for such a force as this the world would relapse into barbarism and night. And of all our race He has marked the American people as His chosen nation to finally lead in the regeneration of the world. This is the divine mission of America, and it holds for us all the profit, all the glory, all the happiness possible to man. We are trustees of the world's progress, guardians of its righteous peace. The judgment of the Master is upon us: "Ye have been faithful over a few things; I will make you ruler over many things."

What shall history say of us? Shall it say that we renounced that holy trust, left the savage to his base condition, the wilderness to the reign of waste, deserted duty, abandoned glory, forget our sordid profit even, because we feared our strength and read the charter of our powers with the doubter's eye and the quibbler's mind? Shall it say that, called by events to captain and command the proudest, ablest, purest, race of history in history's noblest work, we declined that great commission? Our fathers would not have had it so. No! They founded no paralytic government, incapable of the simplest acts of administration. They planted no sluggard people, passive while the world's work calls them. They established no reactionary nation. They unfurled no retreating flag.

GOD'S HAND IN ALL

That flag has never paused in its onward march. Who dares halt it now—now, when history's largest events are carrying it forward; now, when we are at last one people, strong enough for any task, great enough for any glory destiny can bestow? How comes it that our first century closes with the process of consolidating the American people into a unit just accomplished, and quick upon the stroke of that great hour presses upon us our world opportunity, world duty, and world glory, which none but a people welded into an indivisible nation can achieve or perform?

"We are asked to annex to the United States a witch's caldron—"

Black spirits and white, red spirits and gray,
Mingle, mingle, mingle, you that mingle may.

We are not only asked to annex the caldron and make it a part of our great, broad, Christian, Anglo-Saxon, American land, but we are asked also to annex the contents and take this brew—mixed races, Chinese, Japanese, Malay Negritos—anybody who has come along in three hundred years, in all of their concatenations and colors: and the travelers who have been there tell us and have written in the books that they are not only of all hues and colors, but there are spotted people there, and, what I have never heard of in any other country, there are striped people there with zebra signs upon them.

This mess of Asiatic pottage, 7,000 miles from the United States, in a land that we can not colonize and can not inhabit, we are told to-day by the fortune of a righteous war waged for liberty, for the ascendency of the Declaration of Independence, for the gift of freedom to an adjoining State, we must take up and annex and combine with our own blood and with our own people, and consecrate them with the oil of American citizenship.

Mr. President, there has never been since time began such a fatuous notion in the breast of a nation. There has never been such condescension from a high ideal and from a noble and manifest destiny. Not only is it a degradation of this American land and of this American race, but the scholars and thinkers of this country, the mighty men who ponder institutions and courses of events, look upon our adoption of these people and our forcible annexation of them as giving the lie to the whole current of American history and repudiating all the great principles of constitutional freedom which we proclaimed at our beginning and which have tended to make us great.

Mr. President, I have no criticism to pronounce upon my

colleagues who differ with me. I have no reproaches for those who see their duty differently. I believe the gentlemen who represented our country in Paris acted honestly and conscientiously. I believe the honorable gentlemen on the other side of the Chamber mean only their country's good; but I am amazed, I am startled, I am thrown away from my ordinary bearings and conception of things to think that such gentlemen and such a body should contemplate the adoption of a treaty that utterly scorns and repudiates our position; that is essentially at war with our institutions; that embodies a country which is no part of the American continent and can not be made so, and that must inevitably take up and work into the destiny of the American people these alien races, or must make us get down from the throne of freedom which we have occupied for one hundred and twenty-five years and condescend with the scrambling nations of the world to get what we can, where we can, and how we can, to the repudiation of our national character and of our settled doctrines and principles.

. . . Not in a hundred years, nay, not in a thousand years, can we lift the Philippine Islands and the mixed races that there inhabit to the level of civilization which this land, God-blessed, possesses. It is easier to let down and to go down than to rise up. We have risen up through the bloody sweat and turmoil of a thousand years of battle and through bitter experiences which have chastened us. *Facilis descensus Averno.* The moment that this treaty is ratified, in some future age, if such shall be the case, the historian will say at that moment commenced the decline of American institutions and of the great career which America had set forth to herself to lead upon this earth.

Any way you go, this Republic will stand; this people will live for hundreds and a thousand of years to come; but I wish that the longevity of this nation might transcend to anything that ever happened before in all the story of time. I would wish that the Declaration of Independence, instead of being belittled, might be carried nearer and closer home to every hearth and hearthstone in all this land; that it might go to the lowly and humble of whatever skin or complexion with the outstretched hand of friendship and with a message of God's love.

I would wish that all might be exalted. But whatever happens, let us not go down. We stand to-day by the bank of a broader and a deeper Rubicon than ever Caesar meditated beside. At our feet we hear the swash of the great Pacific Ocean, and beyond lies the expansionists' dream—Caesar's Rome. Caesar never did wrong without just cause. That is the imperialistic plea, America will not do wrong without a great temptation. That to-day is the emancipationists' plea. For my country I hope that she will ne'er do wrong.

IN THE AFTERMATH OF THE HAYMARKET AFFAIR

The Chicago Haymarket Affair gave nativists an excellent opportunity to press their campaign for excluding undesirable immigrants from the United States. During a meeting held at the Haymarket Square in May 1886, someone threw a bomb that resulted in the death of seven policemen. The police, who on the previous day had killed four strikers, fired into the crowd and killed four persons. The bombing convinced many Americans that the nation's immigration policy was much too liberal. In addition, the industrial strife of the 1880's, growing urban problems, and the rising tide of newcomers prompted politicians and writers to urge a tightening of immigration restrictions.

In the year that followed the Haymarket Affair, newspapers bitterly denounced radical aliens and generally viewed foreigners with suspicion.

"The Red Flag in America"

ANARCHISTIC disturbances that had for some time been growing more and more serious, culminated in riots at Chicago and

Source: [16] *Public Opinion,* May 15, 1886; [17] *Ibid.,* April 30, 1887.

Milwaukee on Tuesday and Wednesday of last week, resulting in numerous casualties. These events have elicited the comments here collated:

Charleston News and Courier (Dem.), May 6.

To have dynamite bombs exploded among a body of two hundred policemen is a novel experience for an American city. Nevertheless, occurring where it did, it should occasion no more surprise than if it had happened in Paris, and much less than if Berlin had been the scene of disturbance. Chicago has had riots before, and the intelligent classes in that city have been anticipating for years just such a terrible tragedy as that of Tuesday night. The working people of Chicago are numbered by hundreds of thousands, and of this vast mass the great majority are not Americans. They are the offscourings of Europe. Many of them have been imported in droves in order to supply the demand for cheap labor. The very best of them have no knowledge of the theory or practical working of our system of government. They are the product of a civilization which divides the people into classes, and in their own country they belong to a class which is allowed no share in the government. Of self-control, the very first element of a freeman, they know nothing, because they have all their lives been accustomed to be controlled by others, and the control being based on force, they habitually look upon all control as tyranny, and have an unreasoning hatred of all government as something hostile to and apart from themselves. The idea that they form part of the Government and share its power and responsibilities, is quite beyond their comprehension. Aggregations of such foreigners are dangerous to any American community. Their presence was not contemplated by the founders of our Government, and there is no special provision in our laws for the exigencies that may arise from the existence of such unassimilated bodies. Our laws do not tolerate the watching of citizens, domiciliary visits, arrests on suspicion and other means used for the management of this class of people in the countries whence they come. We have to wait until they break the laws, and then, in teaching the rioters the necessary lesson that the law is supreme, many innocent persons suffer.

But it can not be helped, and the laws must be enforced at any cost.

· · · · · ·

New York State Sun (Dem.), May 9.

Such foreign savages, with their dynamite bombs and anarchic purposes, are as much apart from the rest of the people of this country as the Apaches of the plains are. Workingmen who are citizens of the Republic and understand its institutions, utterly detest them and their teachings, and would have the law forbid them land on our shores, as they would keep out an invasion of venomous reptiles. But how shall these obnoxious foreigners be kept out? How can they be detected among the mass of immigrants? You cannot always tell that a man is a crazy socialist simply from his looks, and the most careful scrutiny on the part of our foreign consuls would not avail. The restriction of foreign immigration, which the Labor Commissioner says is demanded by "the native and foreign-born citizen, the skilled and the unskilled workman," is a practical question of the greatest difficulty, for nobody, we suppose, is prepared to see all immigration treated as we treat that from China—wholly forbidden. How about a tax of $300 on every immigrant?

· · · · · ·

New York Commercial Advertiser (Rep.), May 6.

These men were criminals and outlaws at home, and in changing their skies they have not changed their minds. Our large tolerance in the matter of free speech and free press has given them opportunities which they lacked at home, and they have abused the privilege after their kind. So long as they contented themselves with vaporings, we Americans, native and naturalized, laughed; but now that they have for the second time taken advantage of labor disturbances and have sought to institute the anarchy and terror which they preach, the American people are in a different mood. The police of Chicago gave expression to that mood when they stood their ground, and with their pistols drove the dynamite-throwers into their kennels. A Chicago jury will doubtless give further expression to the public sentiment when the arrested leaders of the anarchists are put upon their trial for murder. But these measures are directed toward symptoms, merely, and it is time to attack the disease germs themselves.

"Undesirable Immigration"

The probability of extensive immigration from Europe during the present season has elicited press discussion of the necessity for barring out undesirable classes of aliens. Various opinions from representative journals are given below:

"A POSITIVE PERIL."
St. Louis Globe-Democrat (Rep.).

It has been the common habit of all political parties heretofore to offer special inducements for the foreign vote and to make the growth of said vote as easy and extensive as possible; but the time is approaching when the successful party will be the one which shall take a firm stand in favor of the right of Americans to govern America, not in any narrow and unreasonable sense, but in a broadly patriotic and protective spirit, appealing to the best instincts of the true lover of the country. The experiences of the last year have shown plainly that the socialists and anarchists are a positive peril, and that their operations have reached a stage where it is idle any longer to look complacently on them, or to doubt their power of mischief. They are all foreigners, and their ranks are recruited entirely from the European immigration which is pouring in upon us at the rate of about 35,000 a month. There is no such thing as an American anarchist. The men who contend that all property should be confiscated or destroyed, and all the securities of society subverted, were born in other countries and developed under other conditions and influences. The American character has in it no element which can under any circumstances be won to uses so mistaken and pernicious; and in this fact lies the hope of the country for protection against a form of evil that has been permitted to gain a foothold here by reason of a liberality on our part which we have an unquestionable right to abandon, now that it is seen to be a grave and increasing national danger.

"SOCIAL PESTS AND INCENDIARIES."
Philadelphia Telegraph (Ind.).

The events of Chicago, of Milwaukee, of New York, prove that a large percentage of the foreigners to whom we have given welcome are unworthy of it; that they are often idle, vicious socialists and anarchists, social pests and incendiaries, and that, broad as the land is, it is yet too narrow for such as they are. It was not long ago that the consul at Zurich wrote to the New York *Tribune* that scarcely an emigrant ship landed upon our shores that does not bring with it dozens of paupers who are paid to come here, mixed with jail-birds fleeing from justice and readily permitted to escape. Not only that, but the larger part of the emigrants who come here "have been either failures at home, or unfortunate and unlucky men, so-called, who could never prosper anywhere. No small part are adventurers, seeking fortunes, political or otherwise, in a country where they have good reason to believe the most worthless may rise to position." If the statements of this officer of the Federal Government are to be relied upon, it is the offscourings of the Old World that are coming to us—the paupers, anarchists, socialists, and criminals, together with a scant admixture of better materials. All we can hope is that his description of the character of European immigration is a prejudiced one, and that it is better than he thinks. But, be it better or worse, many striking events of the last year or two have demonstrated that no harm could follow some wholesome restrictions of the great alien influx. At least some guarantee of merits entitling a foreigner to the privileges of full citizenship should be exacted. If it be just that the son of native-born American parents shall not exercise the rights of citizenship until he has lived in his country twenty-one years, it is not just that an alien shall exercise the same right in five years. There should be adopted either some means to purify the great tide of immigration, or to check it to some degree.

Henry Cabot Lodge on
Immigration Restriction

Senator Henry Cabot Lodge was a leading advocate of immigration restriction. Born of French and English parents, he readily accepted the Norman racial theory of his mentor, the historian Henry Adams. The New England of the latter part of the nineteenth century, however, was changing rapidly. Like many with his background, Lodge considered himself a member of a displaced class. The Brahmins' dominance of New England was threatened by new leaders, who were the product of a growing industrialism, and by the changing nature of immigration.

Lodge observed that the "nations of Europe which chiefly contributed to the upbuilding of the original colonies . . . [had prior to the 1880's] continued to furnish the chief component parts of the immigration which [had] helped to populate so rapidly the territory of the United States." In the decade preceding 1891, however, the greatest relative increase in immigration had been "from races most alien to the body of American people and from the lowest and most illiterate classes among those races."

After his election to the United States Senate in 1893, Lodge led the fight for a literacy test bill which required that immigrants show a proficiency in the reading and writing of some language. In a March 1896 speech, Lodge insisted that even more important than the need for protecting the American workingman's standard of living was the absolute necessity for preserving the virtues of the Anglo-Saxon race against the hordes of new immigrants.

MR. LODGE. Mr. President, this bill is intended to amend the existing law so as to restrict still further immigration to the United States. Paupers, diseased persons, convicts, and con-

Source: [18] *United States Congressional Record,* 54th Cong., 1st Sess., pp. 6104–6105, 6147–6148.

tract laborers are now excluded. By this bill it is proposed to make a new class of excluded immigrants and add to those which have just been named the totally ignorant.

. . . Two questions arise in connection with this bill. The first is as to the merits of this particular form of restriction; the second as to the general policy of restricting immigration at all. I desire to discuss briefly these two questions in the order in which I have stated them. The smaller question as to the merits of this particular bill comes first. The existing laws of the United States now exclude, as I have said, certain classes of immigrants who, it is universally agreed, would be most undesirable additions to our population. These exclusions have been enforced and the results have been beneficial, but the excluded classes are extremely limited and do not by any means cover all or even any considerable part of the immigrants whose presence here is undesirable or injurious, nor do they have any adequate effect in properly reducing the great body of immigration to this country. There can be no doubt that there is a very earnest desire on the part of the American people to restrict further and much more extensively than has yet been done foreign immigration to the United States. The question before the committee was how this could best be done; that is, by what method the largest number of undesirable immigrants and the smallest possible number of desirable immigrants could be shut out. Three methods of obtaining this further restriction have been widely discussed of late years and in various forms have been brought to the attention of Congress.

. . . The third method was to exclude all immigrants who could neither read nor write, and this is the plan which was adopted by the committee and which is embodied in this bill. In their report the committee have shown by statistics, which have been collected and tabulated with great care, the emigrants who would be affected by this illiteracy test. It is not necessary for me here to do more than summarize the results of the committee's investigation, which have been set forth full in their report. It is found, in the first place, that the illiteracy test will bear most heavily upon the Italians, Russians, Poles, Hungarians, Greeks, and Asiatics, and very lightly, or not at all, upon English-speaking emigrants or Germans, Scandinavians, and French. In other words, the races most affected by the illiteracy test are those whose emigration to this country has begun within the last twenty years and swelled rapidly to enormous proportions, races with which the English-speaking people have never hitherto assimilated, and who are most alien to the great body of the people of the United States. On the other hand, immigrants from the United Kingdom and of those races which are most closely related to the English-speaking people, and who with the English-speaking people themselves founded the American colonies and built up the United States, are affected but little by the proposed test. These races would not be prevented by this law from coming to this country in practically undiminished numbers. These kindred races also are those who alone go to the Western and Southern States, where immigrants are desired, and take up our unoccupied lands. The races which would suffer most seriously by exclusion under the proposed bill furnish the immigrants who do not go to the West or South, where immigration is needed, but who remain on the Atlantic Seaboard, where immigration is not needed and where their presence is most injurious and undesirable.

. . . I now come to the aspect of this question which is graver and more serious than any other. The injury of unrestricted immigration to American wages and American standards of living is sufficiently plain and is bad enough, but the danger which this immigration threatens to the equality of our citizenship is far worse. That which it concerns us to know and that which is more vital to us as a people than all possible questions of tariff or currency is whether the quality of our citizenship is endangered by the present course and character of immigration to the United States. To determine this question intelligently we must look into the history of our race . . .

For practical purposes in considering a question of race and in dealing with the civilized peoples of western Europe and of America there is no such thing as a race of original purity according to the divisions of ethnical science. In considering the practical problems of the present time we can deal only with the artificial races—that is, races like the English-speaking people, the French, or the Germans—who have been

developed as races by the operation during a long period of
time of climatic influences, wars, migrations, conquests, and
industrial development. To the philologist and the ethnologist
it is of great importance to determine the ethnical divisions of
mankind in the earliest historic times. To the scientific modern
historian, to the student of social phenomena, and to the statesman alike the early ethnic divisions are of little consequence,
but the sharply marked race divisions which have been gradually developed by the conditions and events of the last thousand years are absolutely vital. It is by these conditions and
events that the races or nations which to-day govern the world
have been produced, and it is their characteristics which it is
important for us to understand.

. . . During the present century, down to 1875, there have
been three large migrations to this country in addition to the
always steady stream from Great Britain; one came from Ireland about the middle of the century, and somewhat later one
from Germany and one from Scandinavia, in which is included
Sweden, Denmark, and Norway. The Irish, although of a different race stock originally, have been closely associated with
the English-speaking people for nearly a thousand years. They
speak the same language, and during that long period the two
races have lived side by side, and to some extent intermarried.
The Germans and Scandinavians are again people of the same
race stock as the English who founded and built up the colonies. During this century, down to 1875, then, as in the two
which preceded it, there had been scarcely any immigration to
this country, except from kindred or allied races, and no other,
which was sufficiently numerous to have produced any effect
on the national characteristics, or to be taken into account
here. Since 1875, however, there has been a great change.
While the people who for two hundred and fifty years have
been migrating to America have continued to furnish large
numbers of immigrants to the United States, other races of
totally different race origin, with whom the English-speaking
people have never hitherto been assimiliated or brought in
contact, have suddenly begun to immigrate to the United
States in large numbers. Russians, Hungarians, Poles, Bohe-
mians, Italians, Greeks, and even Asiatics, whose immigration

to America was almost unknown twenty years ago, have during the last twenty years poured in in steadily increasing numbers, until now they nearly equal the immigration of those races kindred in blood or speech, or both, by whom the United States has hitherto been built up and the American people formed.

This momentous fact is the one which confronts us to-day, and if continued, it carries with it future consequences far deeper than any other event of our times. It involves, in a word, nothing less than the possibility of a great and perilous change in the very fabric of our race. The English-speaking race, as I have shown, has been made slowly during the centuries. Nothing has happened thus far to radically change it here. In the United States, after allowing for the variations produced by new climatic influences and changed conditions of life and of political institutions, it is still in the great essentials fundamentally the same race. The additions in this country until the present time have been from kindred people or from those with whom we have been long allied and who speak the same language. By those who look at this question superficially we hear it often said that the English-speaking people, especially in America, are a mixture of races. Analysis shows that the actual mixture of blood in the English-speaking race is very small, and that while the English-speaking people are derived through different channels, no doubt, there is among them none the less an overwhelming preponderance of the same race stock, that of the great Germanic tribes who reached from Norway to the Alps. They have been welded together by more than a thousand years of wars, conquests, migrations, and struggles, both at home and abroad, and in so doing they have attained a fixity and definiteness of national character . . .

It being admitted, therefore, that a historic race of fixed type has been developed, it remains to consider what this means, what a race is, and what a change would portend. That which identifies a race and sets it apart from others is not to be found merely or ultimately in its physical appearance, its institutions, its laws, its literature, or even its language. These are in the last analysis only the expression or the evidence of race. The achievements of the intellect pass easily from land to land and from people to people. The telephone, invented but yesterday,

is used to-day in China, in Australia, or in South Africa as
freely as in the United States. The book which the press to-day
gives to the world in English is scattered tomorrow throughout
the earth in every tongue, and the thoughts of the writer become the property of mankind. You can take a Hindoo and
give him the highest education the world can afford. He has a
keen intelligence. He will absorb the learning of Oxford, he
will acquire the manners and habits of England, he will sit in
the British Parliament, but you can not make him an Englishman. Yet he, like his conqueror, is of the great Indo-European
family. But it has taken six thousand years and more to create
the differences which exist between them. You can not efface
those differences made, by education in a single life, because
they do not rest upon the intellect. What, then, is this matter
of race which separates the Englishman from the Hindoo and
the American from the Indian? It is something deeper and
more fundamental than anything which concerns the intellect.
We all know it instinctively, although it is so impalpable that
we can scarcely define it, and yet is so deeply marked that even
the physiological differences between the Negro, the Mongol
and the Caucasian are not more persistent or more obvious.
When we speak of a race, then, we do not mean its expressions
in art or in language, or its achievements in knowledge. We
mean the moral and intellectual characters, which in their association make the soul of a race, and which represent the
product of all its past, the inheritance of all its ancestors, and
the motives of all its conduct. The men of each race possess an
indestructible stock of ideas, traditions, sentiment, modes of
thought, an unconscious inheritance from their ancestors, upon
which argument has no effect. What makes a race are their
mental and, above all, their moral characteristics, the slow
growth and accumulation of centuries of toil and conflict.
These are the qualities which determine their social efficiency
as a people, which make one race rise and another fall, which
we draw out of a dim past through many generations of ancestors . . .

    . . . Such achievements as M. LeBon credits us with are
due to the qualities of the American people, whom he, as a
man of science looking below the surface, rightly describes as

homogeneous. Those qualities are moral far more than intellectual, and it is on the moral qualities of the English-speaking race that our history, our victories, and all our future rest. There is only one way in which you can lower those qualities or weaken those characteristics, and that is by breeding them out. If a lower race mixes with a higher in sufficient numbers, history teaches us that the lower race will prevail. The lower race will absorb the higher, not the higher the lower, when the two strains approach equality in numbers. In other words, there is a limit to the capacity of any race for assimilating and elevating an inferior race, and when you begin to pour in in unlimited numbers people of alien or lower races of less social efficiency and less moral force, you are running the most frightful risk that any people can run. The lowering of a great race means not only its own decline but that of human civilization. M. LeBon sees no danger to us in immigration, and his reason for this view is one of the most interesting things he says. He declares that the people of the United States will never be injured by immigration, because the moment they see the peril the great race instinct will assert itself and shut the immigration out. The reports of the Treasury for the last fifteen years show that the peril is at hand. I trust that the prediction of science is true and that the unerring instinct of the race will shut the danger out, as it closed the door upon the coming of the Chinese.

Mr. President, more precious even than forms of government are the mental and moral qualities which make what we call our race. While those stand unimpaired all is safe. When those decline all is imperiled. They are exposed to but a single danger, and that is by changing the quality of our race and citizenship through the wholesale infusion of races whose traditions and inheritances, whose thoughts and whose beliefs are wholly alien to ours and with whom we have never assimilated or even been associated in the past. The danger has begun. It is small as yet, comparatively speaking, but it is large enough to warn us to act while there is yet time and while it can be done easily and efficiently. There lies the peril at the portals of our land, there is pressing in the tide of unrestricted immigration. The time has certainly come, if not to stop, at least to check, to sift, and to restrict those immigrants. In careless strength, with generous hand, we have kept our gates wide open to all the world. If we do not close them, we should at least place sentinels beside them to challenge those who would pass through. The gates which admit men to the United States and to citizenship in the great Republic should no longer be left unguarded.

PART 7

Racist Persistence: From the "Great Depression" to the End of the Warren Court

INTRODUCTION

After World War I, Negroes were once again bitterly disappointed by their unchanging status, after contributing their efforts to a national cause. It was true that many blacks had found jobs both in the expanding southern textile and northern automobile industries, but they still were barred from many unions. Black business enterprises grew but not at the same rate as the nation's economy. Most Negroes who had left the South for the northern urban areas found little improvement in their lot. Those who remained in the rural South were among the chief victims of the farm depression of the 1920's. And when the Great Depression of 1929 struck, no group suffered more than the nation's Negroes.

The New Deal was to bring an important change in the black man's political life. His long affiliation with the Republican party had begun to weaken even before the 1932 election. Like many poor whites, Negroes identified themselves with Franklin D. Roosevelt's Administration and, in increasing numbers, shifted their alliance to the Democratic party. Although most New Deal relief and public assistance programs operated within a framework of segregation, blacks felt generally they had benefited from them. Moreover, many blacks obtained important posts in the New Deal agencies, and a number of the Administration's liberals had commendable records in the area of civil rights. And, in general, Negro leaders were encouraged by a feeling that change and reform were in the air. Nonetheless, the status of the black man in American life remained fundamentally unchanged; Jim Crow and racism persisted in all parts of the country.

Nor did the black man's enormous contribution to the World War II crusade for the "Four Freedoms" basically alter his destiny. During that war, approximately one million Negroes served in the armed forces, and almost one-half million were sent overseas. Their efforts to end discrimination in the military service often met with stern opposition resulting in serious race riots at prominent military bases in the United States. Although work training programs and the creation of a fair employment practices commission helped to broaden job opportunities for many Negroes in wartime plants, especially in the iron, steel, and aircraft industries, the black man still experienced discrimination and a lack of promotional mobility wherever he went. Moreover, the sudden upsurge of black migration into northern urban areas heightened racial tensions and led to several serious uprisings, notably the Detroit riot of 1943.

The most significant effect of the war on the black man's destiny was that it served to encourage those Negro leaders who retained the belief that through black activism, rather than white liberal aid, would true equality be achieved. The black man continued to receive some bastioning from governmental programs and policies: e.g., the Truman Administration's efforts to integrate the armed forces, the Presidential program of fair employment in the federal services, and advances in the integration of public housing. Of greater importance to the Negro, however, was the vigor and militancy displayed by black organizations in the fight for equality. In 1954, the N.A.A.C.P.'s struggle to end the "separate but equal" doctrine finally achieved success in the landmark decision of the Supreme Court case, *Brown v. Board of Education of Topeka.*

During the 1960's black activism became so prevalent a phenomenon that the years have been called the decade of the "Black Revolution." Negroes were becoming increasingly intolerant of their status and were outraged by the violence perpetrated on members of their race. In the northern cities, new Negro leaders emerged with programs intended to alleviate the problems of ghetto life. The growing pervasiveness of black political involvement was demonstrated in the increasing number of registered Negro voters, the weight carried by the black vote in the 1960 Presidential election, the passage of the Civil Rights Acts of 1960 and 1964, the fruits of Martin Luther King's work and the rise of Negro militancy.

Aside from the fate of the Negro, the treatment of Japanese-Americans during World War II represents one of the darkest chapters in American history. The Japanese people in America deemed the Immigration Act of 1924 the ultimate indignity in a long series of affronts which they had experienced while in this country. They felt that they were the particular target of the law's restrictions. Although the quota system in the legislation discriminated against southern and eastern Europeans, Japan was not assigned any quota at all (the Chinese had already been excluded since 1882). And all the favorite arguments against Oriental immigration continued to haunt the Japanese. As relations between Japan and the United States deteriorated in the 1930's, there was a growing anxiety among Americans that the Nisei (born in America), and particularly the Issei (born in Japan), were a potential "fifth column" in the event of war.

The Japanese attack on Pearl Harbor appeared to blatantly confirm the warnings of the anti-Japanese elements in the United States. On February 19, 1942, President Roosevelt signed Executive Order 9066, the infamous "relocation" Proclamation, authorizing the Secretary of War to designate military areas which were to be emptied of all persons and to provide for the "residents of any such area who are excluded therefrom." Thus, the evacuation and relocation of over 110,000 Japanese-Americans into these designated areas was set in motion.

The relocation centers stretched from California to Arkansas. Despite attempts to disguise their true nature, the new "homes" were manifestly concentration camps. This policy engendered the economic ruin of many of the victims, seriously disrupted normal family life, and demeaned an entire segment of the nation's population. For the first time in the nation's history, race was the single factor used to determine whether an American would be incarcerated or remain free. In this ignoble relocation program, racism and nativism became one.

Not all Japanese-Americans, however, submitted meekly to the order. Two young Nisei challenged the legality of the policy. Both were arrested, tried, and pronounced guilty for their refusal to comply; and their convictions were upheld by Supreme Court decisions. Eventually, however, in the Endo case of 1944, the Court reversed its position. And, with the end of the war in sight, the government finally revoked the relocation order.

In the 1970's, racism has become the cause of this nation's greatest domestic conflict. America's ability to survive as a democracy, and to remain a haven of freedom, may depend largely upon its ability to solve this crucial problem. Our history has revealed that the United States has evolved from a unique capacity, however precarious at times, to absorb a wide variety of racial and ethnic groups into its life style. And in the light of America's experience, it becomes manifest that racism is totally destructive to the nation's ideological and moral integrity, as well as being a call to violence.

THEIR BIRTHRIGHT VIOLATED: JAPANESE-AMERICANS IN AN AGE OF GLOBAL CONFLICT

The hysteria which followed the attack on Pearl Harbor gave nativists their long-awaited opportunity to take decisive action against Japanese-Americans. The vast majority of Americans had no contact with their fellow Japanese citizens. However, they harbored the popular stereotypes generally associated with the Orientals. Therefore, after December 7, 1941, few Americans challenged the charges made by newspapers, politicians, and organizations that Japanese-Americans were a threat to this nation's security. Men like Attorney General Earl Warren of California and columnist Walter Lippman joined with the American Legion, labor unions, and nativist associations to

Sources: [1] Senator Thomas Stewart, A Jap is a Jap, *United States Congressional Record*, Vol. LXXXVIII, 77th Cong., 2d Sess., pp. 1682–1683; [2] Congressman John Rankin, *Ibid.*, This is a Race War, February 18, 1942, pp. 1419–1420; *Ibid.*, Concentration Camps For Japanese, February 23, 1942, pp. A768–A769; *Ibid.*, Our Golden Opportunity, March 10, 1942, p. A931; *Ibid.*, Labeling of Blood Banks, May 28, 1942, p. A1985.

demand that action be taken against this new "yellow peril."

Congressmen added their voices to the bitter racial attack upon the Japanese-American community. Ironically, the congressional representatives from the Pacific Coast, the dwelling place of the greatest concentration of native-born Americans of Japanese descent, did not lead the fight on the floor of Congress for evacuation. Instead, they allowed the most outspoken southern bigots on Capitol Hill to spearhead the effort to segregate the Japanese-American element and to broadcast anti-Japanese racism. Motivated by what can only be explained as a deep hatred and distrust of anyone or anything not 100 percent American, Senator Thomas Stewart [Document 1] and Congressman John Rankin [Document 2] of Mississippi threw their support for evacuation behind their Pacific Coast colleagues.

Thus, amid the fear that permeated the American scene of a possible "fifth column" in America, and the racial hysteria that characterized anti-Japanese rhetoric, President Franklin D. Roosevelt, on February 19, 1942, signed the "relocation" order. The far-reaching consequence of this drastic policy was the renunciation of their American citizenship by over nine thousand Nisei in the post-war years.

"A Jap is a Jap"

Senator Thomas Stewart of Mississippi

MR. STEWART. Mr. President, I think the time has arrived when we should deal sternly with the Japanese in this country. If we do not, we may come to grief. I have, therefore, introduced a bill which has for its purposes the incarceration of all Japanese in the United States and its Territories.

There are within this country, especially in the States on the west coast and in some of our island possessions such as Hawaii, many thousands of Japanese who were born on American soil, and for that reason, under the first clause of the fourteenth amendment of the Constitution of the United States, claim citizenship. The first clause of the fourteenth amendment provides that all persons born in the United States are citizens of the United States, provided they are subject to the jurisdiction thereof.

It is my belief that Japanese born on American soil should not be allowed citizenship within the meaning of the fourteenth amendment, because they are not "subject to the jurisdiction" in the sense that the amendment intends. Their parents could not have become naturalized under the laws of the United States, and it seems absurd to claim that those whose parents could not themselves become naturalized should become citizens by the mere accident of birth on American soil. Furthermore, under the Japanese law, every person whose father is Japanese is a subject of the Emperor and a citizen of Japan. We have, therefore, the question of dual citizenship to contend with if we permit American citizenship by reason of birth on American soil.

America is at war and will have to fight to the bitter end. The Japanese are among our worst enemies. They are cowardly and immoral. They are different from Americans in every conceivable way, and no Japanese who ever lived anywhere should have a right to claim American citizenship. A Jap is a Jap anywhere you find him, and his taking the oath of allegiance to this country would not help, even if he should be permitted to do so. They do not believe in God and have no respect for an oath. They have been plotting for years against the Americas and their democracies.

It is my belief that one Jap at large in this country or its possessions is a threat to the defense program of America.

I introduced the bill to which I have referred last Thursday, February 19, and on Saturday morning thereafter I was delighted to read in the newspapers that the President of the United States had issued an Executive order giving full wartime authority to remove any and all persons, even American citizens, from any area he might wish. We are given to understand that this action is aimed principally at the Japanese. This is a wise step. Many Japs live near our oil-reserve properties, naval bases, and factories which manufacture defense materials.

. . . The presence of Japanese in America is inimical to the interests of the people. We should oust them from our land, and now is the opportune time. They do not share the views of Americans; our social, political, and religious views are as different and as far apart as is the East from the West. In fact, this is a case of "never the twain shall meet." Their customs are not our customs, and ours can never be theirs. They retain allegiance to Japan, and we must deal with them accordingly.

"This is a Race War"

Congressman John Rankin of Mississippi

MR. RANKIN of Mississippi. Mr. Chairman, we are going to have to run the Japanese out of Hawaii or they are going to run us out. The sooner the American people understand that fact the better off we are going to be.

I know the Hawaiian Islands. I know the Pacific coast where these Japanese reside. Even though they may be the third or fourth generation of Japanese, we cannot trust them. I know that those areas are teeming with Japanese spies and fifth columnists. Once a Jap always a Jap. You cannot change him. You cannot make a silk purse out of a sow's ear.

When I went to Hawaii in 1937 on a committee to investigate the proposition of statehood for Hawaii, we found the Japanese were 100 percent for it. They wanted a State they could control. They knew they had the balance of power in Hawaii. They were denouncing what was called the Rankin bill. That was a bill I had introduced at the request of President Roosevelt to give him the right to appoint the Governor of Hawaii from the continental United States. We found that the elective officers in Hawaii were all afraid of these Japanese because of their political power. They constituted about

40 percent of the voting strength of the Hawaiian Islands. In our investigation I drew out and exposed the dual citizenship, under which, while claiming protection of the American flag, the Hawaiian-born Japanese admitted allegiance to the Japanese Empire.

Some of them who had voted in our elections the year before were then being drafted into the Japanese Army and Navy. Some were volunteering. We found throughout Hawaii, Shinto temples where these Japanese worshipped the Emperor of Japan. Some of those temples exist in California, Oregon, Washington, and probably Alaska. When we came back I refused to sign the report recommending statehood for Hawaii. Those Army and Navy officers told me that the island was literally teeming with Japanese spies. They pointed to the oil tanks and said, "Every one of them is in danger at any time a movement is made by Japan against these islands." The officer in charge of the air force in Hawaii at that time heard my statement that we needed the strongest air force in the world. He said:

For God's sake give us more of it in Hawaii.

This is a race war, as far as the Pacific side of this conflict is concerned, and we might as well understand it. The white man's civilization has come into conflict with Japanese barbarism. Christianity has come in conflict with Shintoism, atheism, and infidelity. One of them must be destroyed. You cannot regenerate a Jap, convert him, change him, and make him the same as a white man any more than you can reverse the laws of nature, or, as the Bible says:

Bind the sweet influences of Pleiades or loose the bands of Orion.

This is a question we have to settle now, and we might as well understand it. I am for catching every Japanese in America, Alaska, and Hawaii now and putting him in concentration camps and shipping them back to Asia as soon as possible. If they own property in this country, after the war we can pay them for it, but we must ship them back to the Orient, where they belong. Until that is done, we will never have peace on the Pacific, and we will never have any safety in Hawaii, Alaska, Washington, or California.

MR. BLAND. Mr. Chairman, will the gentleman yield?

MR. RANKIN of Mississippi. I yield to the gentleman from Virginia.

MR. BLAND. We found also that they had their own schools, in addition.

MR. RANKIN of Mississippi. Yes; I was coming to that. The gentleman from Virginia [Mr. BLAND] was a member of that committee, and he saw what was going on. He and I discussed it at the time, along with the gentleman from North Carolina [Mr. KERR], who now sits before me. I said then that we had to get rid of those Japs or they would get rid of us. There can be no compromise.

I spoke in practically every high school in Honolulu, practically everyone on the island of Oahu, and they told me there that just as soon as those schools were out in the afternoon the Japanese children, and children of Japanese descent, would go directly to a Japanese-language school. The distinguished gentleman from North Carolina [Mr. KERR], who was a very able member of that delegation, will vouch for that statement.

MR. NORRELL. Mr. Chairman, will the gentleman yield?

MR. RANKIN of Mississippi. I yield.

MR. NORRELL. Does not the gentleman think we should have an amendment in this bill providing for the deportation of Japanese from Hawaii in place of an investigation?

MR. RANKIN of Mississippi. Yes; that is what I want. We must get rid of the Japs in Hawaii or they will get rid of us.

This is not a new proposition with me. I agreed with Richmond P. Hobson when he called the Japs "the yellow peril" more than 25 years ago.

Right after the World War, if you remember, the Japanese sneaked into Mexico and tried to secure a naval base in Magdalena Bay in Lower California. I have seen the very spot where they tried to establish that base, and would have done so if we had not blocked them.

We are at war. We are at war with Japan, the most ruthless and damnable enemy that ever insulted this country, and I am in favor of treating it as war and stopping all this interracial nonsense by which we have been petting the Japanese for the last quarter of a century.

MR. RANDOLPH. Mr. Chairman, will the gentleman yield?

MR. RANKIN of Mississippi. I yield.

MR. RANDOLPH. Mr. Chairman, I rise to vindicate the courage with which the gentleman from Mississippi speaks.

MR. RANKIN of Mississippi. I thank the gentleman from West Virginia.

MR. RANDOLPH. I should like to say that many Members of this House, including the gentleman now addressing the Committee [Mr. RANDOLPH], have suggested that the Civilian Conservation Corps camps now vacant be used to take care of the thousands and thousands of Japanese who are a menace on the west coast.

MR. RANKIN of Mississippi. Certainly! I do not care where you put them, so long as you put them in concentration camps. I now yield to the gentleman from Washington [Mr. COFFEE].

MR. COFFEE of Washington. I just wanted to add to what the gentleman has said about schools in Hawaii: That in the State of Washington the Japanese-Americans attend Japanese schools and study the Japanese culture daily following their attendance at the public schools. The American Legion and the Veterans of Foreign Wars have taken the same stand as the gentleman from Mississippi.

MR. RANKIN of Mississippi. And another thing, they go to the Shinto temples and practice the Shinto religion, in which they worship the Emperor of Japan as god. Do not forget that.

MR. COFFEE of Washington. That is correct.

MR. RANKIN of Mississippi. Do not forget that once a Japanese always a Japanese. I say it is of vital importance that we get rid of every Japanese whether in Hawaii or on the mainland. They violate every sacred promise, every canon of honor and decency. This was evidenced in their diplomacy and in their bombing of Hawaii. These Japs who had been there for generations were making signs, if you please, guiding the Japanese planes to the objects of their iniquity in order that they might destroy our naval vessels, murder our soldiers and sailors, and blow to pieces the helpless women and children of Hawaii.

Damn them! Let us get rid of them now!

"Concentration Camps for Japanese"

I want to renew my insistence that the Japanese in this country, in Alaska, and in Hawaii be placed in concentration camps at once.

. . . Mr. Speaker, this morning's paper carried the following Associated Press story with reference to the Civil Liberties Union:

CIVIL LIBERTIES UNION PROTESTS REMOVAL ORDER

. . . This Civil Liberties Union has long been regarded by many as a communistic and un-American organization. Recently the head of this Civil Liberties Union is quoted as having stated that "the unhappy people of Japan are our brothers."

Well, so far as I am concerned, I am ready to become "our brothers' keeper" for the duration of this emergency by putting them every one in concentration camps until the war is over, then shipping them back to Asia and never permitting another one to come to this country to live.

I wonder how it sounds to our boys in the service who are suffering their lives for this country to read where this Civil Liberties Union is protesting against our trying to protect the American people from these treacherous Japs. It is about time the Government looked into this Civil Liberties Union, and put a stop to its attempts to stir up race trouble along the Atlantic seaboard, here in Washington, and throughout the Southern States. It would be interesting to know how many of its members belong to an organization that is dedicated to the overthrow of this Government.

It is well known that Hawaiian-born Japanese, who claim the protection of the American flag, were giving information to Japan by radio, telephone, flashlight, and other signals prior to and during the Pearl Harbor attack, and have been doing so since—just as these American-born Japs are now doing along the Pacific coast.

Unless we drive the Japanese entirely out of Hawaii, they are going to drive us out. While the Germans and Italians are attacking us in front, these treacherous Japs, who have sponged on our generosity for their very existence, are now driving the dagger in our backs, and at the same time their racial cohorts are undermining and sabotaging us up and down the Pacific coast and throughout the Hawaiian Islands.

We should round up and confine every German and every Italian in this country about whose loyalty there is the slightest question. We cannot afford to take chances with them. And when it comes to the Japanese, we should make it unanimous. Once a Jap, always a Jap. We cannot afford to trust any of them. The leopard cannot change his spots.

You will note also that these American- or Hawaiian-born Japs are using their alleged American citizenship to help destroy this country.

This is war. Our country, our homes, our civilization, our way of life are threatened on every hand. We cannot afford to take chances.

The Civil Liberties Union says the President's action in going after these Japs is "unprecedented and founded on no specific evidence of need."

How much more "specific evidence of need" does the Civil Liberties Union want us to have than Pearl Harbor and the revelations that have been uncovered relative to these Japs since the Pearl Harbor attack? As for such action being unprecedented, let me remind these newcomers to our shores that Andrew Jackson was accused of acting without precedent on a similar occasion more than a hundred years ago, when he moved certain Indian tribes in order to avoid further trouble. We should follow Andrew Jackson's example now.

Japanese fifth columnists have been stirring race trouble in this country for a long time. I am told that they have been so successful among the Negroes in Harlem, New York, that the city authorities have entirely lost control and have called upon the State of New York to help maintain law and order. They are working through such organizations as this Civil Liberties Union and associations for the advancement of the colored races. In my opinion, they are behind this drive to try to stir up trouble between the whites and the Negroes here in Washington by trying to force Negroes into hotels, restaurants, picture shows, and other public places. They know that, if they can start race riots in Washington and throughout the country, it will aid them in their nefarious designs against the people of the United States.

A news item from Tokyo on November 29, 1941, under the heading "Japs see United States color problem," we find the following striking statement from Yoshichi Nagatani, who is referred to by the Japanese press as a "prominent business man and expert on America," in which he is quoted as saying:

When it becomes plain that America is going on the rocks, 20,000,000 Negroes, 10,000,000 Americans with Axis antecedents, 10,000,000 unemployed, and 5,000,000 members of labor unions, and numerous Communists will rise in revolt and create chaos.

Nagatani goes on to refer to President Roosevelt as a "buffoon," and predicts that the first Japanese victory "will result in confusion throughout the United States."

Remember this statement was published just 8 days before the Japanese attack on Pearl Harbor. I do not know who led this Japanese spy to believe that all the American Negroes could be deluded into such a trap. If these agitators will let the Negroes alone, we will have no trouble with them. The white people of the South who have always been the Negroes best friends, and who know the Negro problem, will have no trouble with the colored race if these fifth columnists and the flannel-mouthed agitators throughout the country will let them alone.

It is silly and stupid for the Japs, or any other enemy, to expect support from the patriotic laboring men and women of this Nation, and so far as their Communist cohorts are concerned, it is high time that everyone of them who agitates trouble of any kind in this country was taken in hand.

It is being argued in some quarters that we do not have the constitutional right to handle the Japanese who are born in this country. They take the position that these Japanese are American citizens and entitled to the same rights as are the descendants of the signers of the Declaration of Independence. I most emphatically deny that assertion. These Japanese are not citizens of the United States and never can be.

. . . Mr. Speaker, it is my contention that since these Japanese could not become citizens of this country but remain citizens of Japan, their legal status was that of visitors to our shores and their children became subjects of Japan and not citizens of the United States, and that their children's children assumed the same status.

The truth of the business is that these facts have been recognized by Japan from the beginning, and by these Japanese themselves. When these children are born their names are registered with the Japanese consul, who sends them in to Tokyo where they are registered as Japanese citizens entitled to all rights as such, just the same as if they had been born on Japanese soil. They never can become Americans. There is a racial and a religious difference they can never overcome. They are pagan in their philosophy, atheistic in their beliefs, alien in their allegiance, and antagonistic to everything for which we stand.

This is one of the most momentous questions that has confronted our people in a thousand years, and I for one am in favor of meeting it squarely and deciding it in our favor by declaring that no Japanese can ever become a citizen of the United States but that they are aliens in our midst and should be deported at the earliest opportunity.

Let us save America for Americans!

"Our Golden Opportunity"

. . . Here is a statement written by the daughter of an officer in our Navy which I hope you will all take time to read. It points out very forcefully the seriousness of the situation. It reads as follows:

All Japanese—American born and aliens—must be placed in concentration camps at once. There must be no half measures. Any one of them may jeopardize the lives and safety of hundreds, especially in Hawaii and in California and their fifth column may cause us to lose these places and Alaska to Japan. The sexes must be kept absolutely separate. Only in concentration camps can they be later exchanged for our people now imprisoned in Japan.

It is unthinkable that Japan is allowing any white people freedom there. Why should we allow them freedom here? Many of the present half measures now being taken are worse than useless. They lull our people into a false sense of security. A few hundred Japs rounded up from Terminal Island only gives warning to the rest of them to be careful or to go in hiding into the mountains or escape to Mexico. I believe that the majority of their main spies have gone to South America or to sea already, but have left means for reaccess to this country and have an underground railway well disciplined for mass action when they choose to strike. Singapore has fallen. They may strike soon. Having all alien Japanese register and carry identification cards, having them turn in all radios, cameras, and firearms and having the Army empowered to remove some of them living near vital areas en masse will not end this terrible danger. With each commanding Army officer there will be varying degrees of surveillance and pressure will bear on him to spare certain groups because of agricultural needs. Among those not taken into custody or removed there will be a huge fifth column left to cause us losses only to be recovered by heavy fighting.

Undoubtedly cruel "bushido" methods are being used in Japan to get secret information from individuals and rubber-hose beatings as they used on reporters and other white people long before December 7. So far, we have no Japanese prisoners of war. They have 1,100 sailors and marines from Wake Island as well as 1,200 civilian workmen from there alone. They claim the capture of 200 allied merchant ships and the men aboard are now prisoners. Americans are now being put to work for Japan. Many from Manila, etc., are in their hands. The Japanese are treating American prisoners better than they do the British and Dutch mainly because of the several hundred thousand Japanese in our midst. We must not let this valuable asset escape gradually over the border or by sea, but must use them as the hostages they really are for the good treatment and final exchange for Americans. Our only hope to have a semblance of fair treatment for our people imprisoned there is to keep all those of Japanese ancestry here where they are confined and can do no harm.

We can rid America of this pyramiding danger now. We must insist on keeping the sexes separate, or they will use this internment time as an incubating period and in 5 years each family may emerge with five more children. Unconfined, in one generation we will have five times and in two generations, 25 times as many Japanese to cope with. This is our golden opportunity to rid the United States of them for good. The Japanese will be glad to go while Japan is successful and Japan will welcome them and release Americans in exchange. Many Japanese left Hawaii and California to live in Japan again during our depression years and they know the going will be more than hard for them here from now on. Among the thousands of aliens and the American-born Japanese, who have all been exposed to propaganda teaching at their language schools for years, too many have an important part assigned them for mass destruction and murder in a surprise attack to paralyze us that would make Pearl Harbor pale by comparison. These fifth columnists cannot be weeded out, but all must be confined for our self-preservation.

Nothing short of every Japanese—American-born or not—in concentration camps with the sexes absolutely separate will give any real measure of security. Every day's delay may cost us heavily in loss of life and property and lose us our outposts of Hawaii and Alaska and our west coast States. Immediate action is imperative.

"Labeling of Blood Banks"

Mr. Speaker, one of the most vicious movements that has yet been instituted by the crackpots, the Communists, and parlor pinks of this country is that of trying to browbeat the American Red Cross into taking the labels off the blood bank they are building up for our wounded boys in the service so that it will not show whether it is Negro blood or white blood.

That seems to be one of the schemes of these fellow travelers to try to mongrelize this Nation.

They are not so much interested in its effect upon our wounded boys as they are in carrying out their Communist program.

Thank God, the Red Cross has stood its ground and refused to permit this outfit to have Negro blood pumped into the veins of our wounded white men on the various fronts.

That is no discrimination against the Negroes. I am not sure that it would not be as detrimental to a Negro to pump the blood of some other race into his veins as it would be to pump Negro blood or Japanese blood into the veins of white men.

Being unable to browbeat the Red Cross into submission, they are now bringing pressure to bear upon the O. C. D. to try to get them to take the labels off the blood they are storing up for the civilians of this country when a disaster occurs. They seem to have some crackpot alien doctors advising them that it makes no difference what race this blood comes from. I suppose that these doctors and their fellow travelers would contend that it would be all right to fill our soldiers full of Japanese blood.

They had better remember that there is still a Congress of the United States, and that Congress represents the American people, and that the American people through their Congress are not going to permit such outrages against our wounded boys at the front, or against our men, women, and children who are injured in local disasters.

One of the papers that has been urging or advocating taking these labels off this blood is a New York tabloid known as PM. In its edition of Friday, May 22, it quotes one of these doctors as saying that "whether the blood comes from Negro or white makes no difference whatsoever."

I am calling this to the attention of Congress now, so that each and every one of you may know what is going on. I am going to demand that the O. C. D. label this blood it is storing up to be used on the men, women, and children of this country just as the Red Cross is doing that to be used in treating our injured men in the armed forces.

THEIR BIRTHRIGHT DEMANDED: FROM CIVIL RIGHTS TO BLACK POWER

Global Conflict and the Solidification of Segregation

While the United States was fighting the racist regime of Nazi Germany and proclaiming as its war aims the "Four Freedoms," the American system of legal and de facto segregation was flourishing. Provoked by this hypocrisy, racial tensions developed to the breaking point. As a result, the nation witnessed in Detroit, on June 20, 1943, the most serious race riot in its history.

In response to growing black dissatisfaction in wartime America, Theodore G. Bilbo, Mississippi Senator and infamous segregationist, delivered a scathing attack on the country's integrationists before his state's legislative body. In what was a preview of his book, Take Your Choice: Separation or Mongrelization *(1947), he warned of the impending danger as-*

Source: [3] *Address by Senator Bilbo Before Mississippi Legislature. United States Congressional Record.,* 78th Cong., 2d Sess., pp. A1795–A1802.

sociated with A. Philip Randolph's proposed march on Washington to "Let the Negro Masses Speak," and verbally assaulted the federal Anti-Poll Tax Bill as "unconstitutional." Furthermore, he reiterated the historical theme of amalgamation by asking rhetorically, "How can anyone be a party to encouraging white girls into the arms of Negro soldiers at a canteen while singing 'Let Me Call You Sweetheart'?"

As he addressed a receptive Mississippi audience, Bilbo asserted that the southern states were outvoted in Congress and, thus, could not seek help from the Federal Government. Therefore, in order to successfully handle the race problem in the future, he demanded that the South "draw the color line tighter and tighter, and any white man or woman who [dared] to cross that line . . . be promptly and forever ostracized."

. . . The anti-poll tax bill, which would make unlawful by Federal statute, the requirement for the payment of a poll tax as a prerequisite to voting in a primary or other election for national officers, is clearly unconstitutional.

. . . Nothing is more closely shown by the debates in the Constitutional Convention than the intention of the founding fathers that each State should have the power to fix the qualifications of the electors within its borders. The power to fix such qualifications was one which the States zealously guarded.

. . . Nowhere in the Constitution is Congress given the power to strike down or add to the qualifications for electors as set up by the sovereign States nor is the Congress given the power to define the qualifications or prerequisites for electors. The decisions of the United States Supreme Court are unanimous in holding that the poll tax laws are constitutional and non-discriminatory. The tax applies equally to whites and Negroes and the proceeds are generally used for educational purposes.

Regardless of what any of us may think of the poll tax as such and regardless of whether or not we are in favor of its abolition by our State—just here let me say that for the holding of our white party primaries I have long contended that the poll tax should be abolished—nevertheless, the Congress has no power under the Federal Constitution to pass this bill outlawing the tax. Such a law would be an unconstitutional, unwarranted interference with the rights of the sovereign States and would destroy our dual system of constitutional government.

Section 241 of the Mississippi Constitution provides that a qualified elector must have lived in the State 2 years and the election district of his county 1 year next preceding the ensuing election; Section 244 provides for the educational test. Now, if the Congress succeeds in abolishing the poll tax, then the precedent will be set for the abolition by the Congress of any or all of our franchise laws and our ballots in Mississippi, and in all the other 47 States, will be at the mercy of the Federal Government. Constitutional government, as we have known it for over 150 years, would then no longer exist and the rights of the sovereign States would be destroyed.

In the face of these facts, you may rightly ask: Who are the advocates of this infamous unconstitutional bill? Why are the forces behind this piece of legislation so strong that we will have to resort to a filibuster to bring about its defeat in the Senate? You will recall that during the last Congress a similar bill was killed by a filibuster during the closing days of the session, in which I spoke 4 days, but the bill was revived and passed by the House of Representatives last May 25. It is now on the Senate Calendar and may be brought up for consideration at any time.

There are various individuals and organizations sponsoring this bill, but the main pressure groups behind it are Negro organizations. They are able to wield this power because the Negro vote in some nine northern States constitutes something of a balance-of-power between the white Democratic and Republican Parties. And these groups are determined to make an all-out effort to secure passage of this anti-poll tax bill because the enactment of this piece of legislation is one of the steps— the entering wedge—toward the fulfillment of the "full equality" program which the Negro leaders have launched in this time of war. While I am prepared to speak and filibuster this damnable bill for 8 months to kill it, yet I warn you that if our colleagues in the Senate ever succeed in invoking the cloture rule, which stops debate, the bill will pass.

Thus, the poll tax bill brings the entire race question before the American people. Because of this implication and because of conditions existing in Washington, of which city I am now mayor ex-officio by virtue of the chairmanship of the Senate Committee on the District of Columbia, I wish to discuss with you this grave race problem fully and frankly. In the interest of our Nation, our Southland and our own State of Mississippi, I shall be forced to make startling revelations to you. Such action I have decided is absolutely necessary at this time.

. . . The so-called leaders of the Negro race have deliberately chosen this time of war to launch their program of full equality of the races in this country. The March-on-Washington movement, a Negro group headed by A. Philip Randolph, president of the Brotherhood of Sleeping Car Porters, carried their demands to the White House in June 1941. Thousands of Negroes threatened to march in mass upon Washington in what they termed "protest of discrimination in Government employment and in the war industries." After conferences with the Negro leaders, President Roosevelt issued Executive Order 8802 and the march on Washington was called off. This order, issued June 25, 1941, provided that:

"There shall be no discrimination in the employment of workers in defense industries or Government because of race, creed, color, or national origin."

The order also established the Committee on Fair Employment Practices to carry this policy into effect. There is nothing in Executive Order 8802 about abolishing segregation and ordering the mixing of the races. However, as a result of the order there is today no segregation in the United States Government offices in Washington.

In the Federal offices in Washington, whites and Negroes work in the same rooms, the same offices, eat together at the same cafeterias, use the same rest rooms and recreational facilities. White girls may be assigned as secretaries to Negro men, and Negro girls may be sent to the offices of white officials. I remember one occasion when a Government official, a man from Atlanta, Ga., called me and asked my advice on a certain matter. He said that upon his request for stenographers the Civil Service had sent him colored girls. In many bureaus and departments, the mixing of the races has gone so far that southern girls, going to the capital city to work, have returned to their homes. Others, who for various reasons must remain there to work, find such conditions almost unbearable.

So far Executive Order No. 8802 has not been successfully enforced in the war industries in the South. Perhaps the attempt to do so in the Mobile shipyards, which resulted in a race riot, was sufficient warning.

The March-on-Washington group proposes to abolish segregation completely throughout the United States, and to bring about the full political, economic, and social equality of the races. So that you will have no doubts about their demands, I wish to read you excerpts from an article, "Why Should We March," by A. Philip Randolph, head of the movement, appearing in the November 1942 *Survey Graphic*.

". . . What are the reasons for this state of mind? The answer is: discrimination, segregation, Jim Crow . . .

"It is to meet this situation squarely with direct action that the March-on-Washington movement launched its present program of protest mass meetings. . . . Meetings of such magnitude were unprecedented among Negroes. . . .

"The March-on-Washington movement is essentially a movement of the people . . . the plan of a protest march has not been abandoned. Its purpose would be to demonstrate that American Negroes are in deadly earnest, and all out for their full rights. No power on earth can cause them today to abandon their fight to wipe out every vestige of second-class citizenship and the dual standards that plague them. . . .

"By fighting for their rights now, American Negroes are helping to make America a moral and spiritual arsenal of democracy. Their fight against the poll tax, against lynch law, segregation, and Jim Crow, their fight for economic, political, and social equality, thus becomes part of the global war for freedom."

This is the kind of propaganda being fed to the Negro masses. It is the contention of these Negro leaders that segregation is in itself discrimination. This question has been before the United States Supreme Court on a number of occasions and the Court has held that segregation is not discrimination as long as adequate accommodations are provided for both races.

The theory that segregation is discrimination is adhered to by the Negro judge, William H. Hastie. Hastie resigned from his post as civilian aide to the Secretary of War because of his disagreement with the War Department over its policy of segregation in the armed forces. In a speech before some 20,000 Negroes in Detroit in June 1943, Hastie declared that there is a terrific waste of energy and man-hours by the segregation of Negroes into their own Army groups and by denying Negro officers the right to command Army groups composed in part, or entirely, of white men.

At this same mass meeting, there was also a speech made by Roy Wilkins, assistant secretary of the National Association for the Advancement of Colored People. This association is another of the Negro organizations leading in this fight for full equality of the races. Wilkins declared:

"We refuse to listen to the weak-kneed of both races who tell us not to raise controversies during the war. We believe, on the contrary, that we are doing a patriotic duty in raising them."

. . . The race situation has for some time been tense in Washington. Negroes already compose 30 to 40 percent of the population of the Capital City, and efforts are being made by their leaders to get as many Negroes as possible on the Government pay rolls. If suffrage should be granted in the District of Columbia, the Negroes would soon have control of the city and the alleys would be completely outvoting the avenues.

On the 7th of February 1944, a Negro attorney, John P. Davis, carried his 5-year-old son to a white school in Washington and attempted to enroll him. Davis had already been told that the child would not be accepted, but he carried out his plans to make the attempt to enroll him in order that he may bring a test case challenging the dual school system in Washington.

In February the C.I.O. opened a canteen in Washington for service men and women. Immediately a storm of southern protest was sounded for it was unbelievable that newspaper accounts of the opening of the canteen could be true. However, these accounts did paint a true picture of the activities. On opening night there were some 200 service men and women present. There were about an equal number of white and Negro soldiers who attended and white girls and Negro girls served as hostesses to those soldiers in equal numbers. Can you picture such social affairs taking place in our Nation's Capital? In speaking of the opening of the canteen, Congressman McKenzie of Louisiana, asked:

"How can anyone be a party to encouraging white girls into the arms of Negro soldiers at a canteen while singing 'Let Me Call You Sweetheart'?"

The sponsors of this mingling of the whites and Negroes in social equality declared that the "plan was proving successful." And Joseph Phillips, president of the C.I.O., Washington Industrial Union Council, said that his organization was proud to sponsor the "first effective non-Jim Crow canteen in Washington." He added that "when people come to our dances they dance with whomever they choose."

Have we reached the place in this country when we are going to permit our white girls to attend social functions with Negro soldiers? If we do permit such, can we profess to be surprised at what the results may be? No possible good, but much harm, can come to both races by activities of this kind. Are our soldiers and sailors fighting to save this Nation, or are they fighting so that we may become a mongrelized people? Practicing social equality of the races is certainly the surest way to destroy the culture of the white race.

We condemn such activities as are being carried on at this canteen and we also condemn those in high authority who sponsor or attend or endorse such activities.

We in the Southland, being fully aware of the attempts to break down segregation and implant social equality of the races throughout the Nation are ready to do some plain talking. The Negro leaders have brought this issue of race relations before us in this time of war; they have stated their demands so we have no alternative but to tell them where we stand.

We in Mississippi are justly proud of the harmonious relations existing here among the races. Our population is almost equally divided and we are glad to have peaceful, law-abiding Negroes within our midst. We ask no Negro to leave our State; at the same time we ask no discontented Negro to remain.

Brown v. Board of Education and the Dissenting "Declaration of Constitutional Principles"

With the 1954 landmark decision of Brown v. Board of Education of Topeka, *the Supreme Court of the United States, fifty-eight years after the adoption of the "separate but equal" doctrine contained in* Plessy v. Ferguson *(1896), declared segregation in public schools unconstitutional. According to the opinion of the Court, the inherent inequality of racial separation denied blacks the protection guaranteed by the Fourteenth Amendment—"even though the physical facilities and other 'tangible' factors of white and Negro schools may be equal." In addition, the Court on May 31, 1955, announced that the integration of schools must proceed with "all deliberate speed."*

In response to the new attitude on the part of the Federal Judiciary, representatives from eleven "Jim Crow" states issued a "Declaration of Constitutional Principles." In this manifesto [Document 4] of March 12, 1956, southern Senators and Congressmen declared that "the gravity of the situation following the decision of the Supreme Court in the so-called segregation cases" necessitated a pledge to "use all lawful means to bring about a reversal of this decision . . . and to prevent the use of force in its implementation." Furthermore, in an attempt to intimidate integrationists, they appealed to their constituents "not to be provoked by agitators and troublemakers *[civil rights workers]* invading their states." *

Although the Brown v. Board of Education *decision was*

Sources: [4] "The Decision of the Supreme Court in the School Cases—Declaration of Constitutional Principles," *United States Congressional Record* 84th Cong., 2nd Sess., pp. 4459–4462.
* Editor's italics.

concerned primarily with segregated educational facilities, it became the precedent for the Court's subsequent desegregation rulings.

DECLARATION OF CONSTITUTIONAL PRINCIPLES

The unwarranted decision of the Supreme Court in the public school cases is now bearing the fruit always produced when men substitute naked power for established law.

The Founding Fathers gave us a Constitution of checks and balances because they realized the inescapable lesson of history that no man or group of men can be safely entrusted with unlimited power. They framed this Constitution with its provisions for change by amendment in order to secure the fundamentals of governments against the dangers of temporary popular passion or the personal predilections of public officeholders.

We regard the decision of the Supreme Court in the school cases as a clear abuse of judicial power. It climaxes a trend in the Federal Judiciary undertaking to legislate, in derogation of the authority of Congress, and to encroach upon the reserved rights of the States and the people.

The original Constitution does not mention education. Neither does the 14th amendment nor any other amendment. The debates preceding the submission of the 14th amendment clearly show that there was no intent that it should affect the system of education maintained by the States.

The very Congress which proposed the amendment subsequently provided for segregated schools in the District of Columbia.

When the amendment was adopted in 1868, there were 37 States of the Union. Every one of the 26 States that had any substantial racial differences among its people, either approved the operation of segregated schools already in existence or subsequently established such schools by action of the same lawmaking body which considered the 14th amendment.

As admitted by the Supreme Court in the public school case *(Brown v. Board of Education),* the doctrine of separate but equal schools "apparently originated in *Roberts v. City of Bos-*

ton (1849), upholding school segregation against attack as being violative of a State constitutional guarantee of equality." This constitutional doctrine began in the North, not in the South, and it was followed not only in Massachusetts, but in Connecticut, New York, Illinois, Indiana, Michigan, Minnesota, New Jersey, Ohio, Pennsylvania and other northern States until they, exercising their rights as States through the constitutional processes of local self-government, changed their school systems.

In the case of *Plessy v. Ferguson* in 1896 the Supreme Court expressly declared that under the 14th amendment no person was denied any of his rights if the States provided separate but equal public facilities. This decision has been followed in many other cases. It is notable that the Supreme Court, speaking through Chief Justice Taft, a former President of the United States, unanimously declared in 1927 in *Lum v. Rice* that the "separate but equal" principle is "within the discretion of the State in regulating its public schools and does not conflict with the 14th amendment."

This interpretation, restated time and again, became a part of the life of the people of many of the States and confirmed their habits, customs, traditions, and way of life. It is founded on elemental humanity and common sense, for parents should not be deprived by Government of the right to direct the lives and education of their own children.

Though there has been no constitutional amendment or act of Congress changing this established legal principle almost a century old, the Supreme Court of the United States, with no legal basis for such action, undertook to exercise their naked judicial power and substituted their personal political and social ideas for the established law of the land.

This unwarranted exercise of power by the Court, contrary to the Constitution, is creating chaos and confusion in the States principally affected. It is destroying the amicable relations between the white and Negro races that have been created through 90 years of patient effort by the good people of both races. It has planted hatred and suspicion where there has been heretofore friendship and understanding.

Without regard to the consent of the governed, outside agitators are threatening immediate and revolutionary changes in our public-school systems. If done, this is certain to destroy the system of public education in some of the States.

With the gravest concern for the explosive and dangerous condition created by this decision and inflamed by outside meddlers:

We reaffirm our reliance on the Constitution as the fundamental law of the land.

We decry the Supreme Court's encroachments on rights reserved to the States and to the people, contrary to established law, and to the Constitution.

We commend the motives of those States which have declared the intention to resist forced integration by any lawful means.

We appeal to the States and people who are not directly affected by these decisions to consider the constitutional principles involved against the time when they too, on issues vital to them, may be the victims of judicial encroachment.

Even though we constitute a minority in the present Congress, we have full faith that a majority of the American people believe in the dual system of government which has enabled us to achieve our greatness and will in time demand that the reserved rights of the States and of the people be made secure against judicial usurpation.

We pledge ourselves to use all lawful means to bring about a reversal of this decision which is contrary to the Constitution and to prevent the use of force in its implementation.

In this trying period, as we all seek to right this wrong, we appeal to our people not to be provoked by the agitators and troublemakers invading our States and to scrupulously refrain from disorder and lawless acts.

Catholics Need Not Apply: The Presidential Election of 1960

In 1960, for the second time in the nation's history, an Irish-Catholic was nominated by the Democratic party for the office of President. In response to the selection of John F. Kennedy, anti-Catholic hate groups, who deeply resented the attempt by a "religious outsider" to control the White House, organized a campaign to discourage Protestant voters from electing a Catholic President. The handbill printed on the next page is only one example of the thousands that were distributed during the Presidential campaign.

BEFORE YOU VOTE CATHOLIC FOR PUBLIC OFFICE.. THINK AHe ad

— Consider what the Popes have said —

What will happen if the Pope eventually "takes over" in the U. S. A., through Catholic politicians, as he has already taken over in Spain, Italy, Colombia and many other Catholic dominated countries?

(Below is a direct quotation of one of the "infallible" Popes)

"You ask, if the Pope were Lord of this land and you were in a minority, what would he do to you? That, we say, would entirely depend upon circumstances. If it would benefit the cause of Catholicism, he would tolerate you; if expedient, he would imprison or banish you, probably he might hang you. But, be assured of one thing, he would never tolerate you for the sake of your glorious principles of civil and religious liberty." - Pope Pius IX

It's a FACT . . . in Colombia, South America, which is a Roman Catholic stronghold, during the past 10 years alone . . . .

> 66 Protestant Churches have been destroyed
> 200 Protestant schools have been closed
> 115 Protestant Christians have been murdered

What kind of a plan does the church of Rome have in order to penetrate into our democratic government and others. What are Roman Catholics commanded to do?

"They must penetrate, wherever possible, in the administration of civil affairs . . . All Catholics should do all in their power to cause the Constitution of States and Legislation to be modeled on the principles of the true (Catholic) Church." . . . . Encyclical of Pope Leo XIII

No man can serve two masters — Holy Bible

For additional information write:
CITIZENS COMMITTEE
P. O. Box 197, Limerick, Pa.

SO BEFORE YOU VOTE . . . THINK AHEAD
"God grants liberty only to those who love it, and are always ready to guard and defend it." - Webster
(Help Distribute — 150 Copies $2.00)

The National Renaissance Party and the Resurgence of Nazism

The issue of police brutality reached its peak in New York City, when in 1967, groups representing several of the city's minorities demanded a Police Civilian Review Board. In an attempt to racially polarize the population, the neo-Nazi National Renaissance Party, a New York City-based hate group, distributed literature attacking the alleged Jewish-Negro conspiracy to "dictate and control police policy." The leaflet on the next page is indicative of the organization's ideology.

Cops Grab Rapist Attacking Girl in Midtown Hallway

Bandits Shoot 2; Both Rape Girl
GLADEWATER, TEX.

Choir Singer Raped In Annunciation School
By WALTER GOLD

National Renaissance Party
10 WEST 90th STREET
New York 24, N. Y.

REDS SUPPORT THEIR
PUBLICATIONS, CAN THE
RIGHT-WING DO
AS WELL?

Bride-to-Be Choked Unconscious, Raped

How come everytime a police officer attempts to protect people by arresting, or if necessary, shooting a negro criminal, we suddenly witness an uproar among liberal action groups, the slanted newspapers and black agitators demanding an "investigation" and the establishment of a "Civilian Review Board"?

If a policeman has to shoot a black criminal, he is called a "murderer" by these same black agitation groups. The newspapers with their pro-negro attitude, make it look like the negro criminal shot by the police was some kind of innocent victim of "police brutality". Just what is a policeman supposed to do in order to stop the rising black crime rate? Is he supposed to look the other way everytime a white woman is raped? Is he supposed to turn his head and walk away while white men, women and children are robbed, assaulted, stabbed and murdered on the streets and in the subways? The answer is YES, according to the civil rights agitation groups!

WHAT IS A "CIVILIAN REVIEW BOARD"?

The real motive behind all the shouts of so-called "police brutality" by civil rights groups is to establish "Civilian Review Boards" which will investigate the police and discipline any policeman whom the board feels is guilty of "police brutality" and discrimination against negroes and other "minorities". The purpose of the "Review Boards" is to place a group of liberal, pro-negro agitators over the heads of the police that will dictate and control police policy.

In order to control the streets and be free to do as they please, the black agitation groups must first remove the major obstacle in their path.... THE POLICE! The "civil rights" groups are out to CONTROL THE POLICE Departments with the establishment of the "Civilian Review Board". If you think things are bad now, just wait until your police DO NOT DARE PROTECT YOU or your women and children for fear of losing their jobs or of being accused of "discrimination" by the "Civilian Review Board".

POLITICIANS DON'T CARE!

The politicians do not care about the white people, who are the majority, because the politicians depend on the minority vote to keep them in office. White people divide themselves up as "republicans" and "democrats." The negroes and Jews do not divide themselves up. They vote together (united) as a solid bloc vote. When all the votes have been cast, the republican votes and the democratic votes just about come up EVEN... AND with whomever the negroes and Jews cast their vote, that person is going to WIN THE ELECTION! That is why the politicians do as the negroes want! That is why politicians don't care about the white people. Politicians are greedy opportunists who want to stay in office and in order to do so they must kiss the foot of every negro they can find!

WHITE PEOPLE! UNITE AND FIGHT BACK! PROTECT OUR WOMEN!
For further information write:
NATIONAL RENAISSANCE PARTY
Read; Subscribe: 10 West 90th Street   New York 24, N.Y. $3.00 per 12 issues

NATIONAL RENAISSANCE BULLETIN

The Emergence of Black Anti-Semitism

In 1968, New York City witnessed the largest and longest teacher strike in the history of the nation. Although it began as a protest against the firing of teachers, the work stoppage soon took on the overtones of a racial conflict between blacks and whites—especially Jews. Thus, in an attempt to intimidate the Jewish teachers who comprised a majority of the teaching staff, black anti-Semites began to preach the anti-Jewish rhetoric of the past one hundred years. The flyer reprinted below, which refers to teachers as "Middle East murderers of colored people" and "bloodsucking exploiters," was one of several placed in school letter boxes and distributed to students emerging from schools with a predominantly black student body. Ironically, whereas the Neo-Nazi Renaissance Party had referred to a Jewish-Negro conspiracy in 1967, only one year later black extremists were issuing bitter anti-Semitic propaganda.

Copy of flyer distributed to students emerging from Theodore Roosevelt H.S., Bronx, at dismissal time.

If African-American History and culture is to be taught to our black children it must be done by African-Americans who identify with and who understand the problem. It is impossible for the Middle East murderers of colored people [Arabs] to possibly bring to this important task the insight, the concern, the exposing of the truth that is a *must* if the years of brainwashing and self-hatred that has been taught to our black children by these bloodsucking exploiters and murderers is to be overcome.

The idea behind this program is beautiful, but when the money changers heard about it, they took over, as is their custom in the black community. If African-American History and Culture is important to our children to raise their esteem of themselves, then the only persons who can do the job are

African-American brothers and sisters, and *not* the so-called liberal Jewish friend.

We know now from his tricky deceitful maneuvers that he is really our enemy and he is responsible for the serious educational retardation of our black children.

We call on all concerned black teachers, parents, and friends to write to the Board of Education, to the Mayor, to the State Commissioner of Education to protest the take over of this crucial program by people who are unfit by tradition and by inclination to do even an adequate job.

The black community must unite itself around the need to run our own schools and to control our own neighborhoods without *Whitey* being anywhere on the scene. We want to make it crystal clear to you outsiders and you missionaries, the natives are on the move!! Look out! Watch out! That backfire you hear might be your number has come up. Get out, stay out, Stay off, Shut up, Get off our backs, *or your relatives in the Middle East will be finding themselves giving benefits to raise money to help you get out from under the terrible weight of an enraged black community.*

The Sophistication of Racism—
"Desegregation: fact and hokum"

Not all racist utterances are or have been blatant, overt or maniacal. Many of them have been written by intelligent, sophisticated and generally well-informed members of the "intelligentsia." These arguments are often cohesively and persuasively expressed. Nonetheless, however well-documented and logical these expositions may appear, the underlying racist ideology is apparent to the trained reader.

One of the most subtle and coherent (and, consequently, one of the most dangerous) of these utterances is contained in a pamphlet entitled Desegregation: fact and hokum *by Henry E. Garrett, Ph.D.*

Source: [8] Henry E. Garrett, Ph.D., *Desegregation: fact and hokum* (Richmond, Virginia, 1965?), pp. 5–24.

Dr. Garrett headed the Columbia University Department of Psychology for sixteen years; he was visiting professor at a number of fine American universities, and is and has been a member or leader of many eminent psychological associations.

His pamphlet, published and distributed by an organization known as The Patrick Henry Group of Richmond, Virginia, is an example of the very sophisticated and well-reasoned racist statement.

The second attempt at "reconstruction" in the South dates from May 17, 1954, but the preparations for it long antedated the Supreme Court decision. The storm had been brewing for more than 30 years and had been steadily gathering force. This was shown in the increased barrage of northern criticism which should have been warning enough, but the fact is that the reaction of the white southerner to the desegregation decision was one of puzzlement rather than of anger or annoyance. Many speculated on what was behind the decision and many doubted that it need be taken seriously. Time and time again I was told that the Supreme Court's action was "political" (an attempt to influence the Negro vote in northern cities), or directed toward placating Mr. Nehru and the new black African nations, or toward convincing Khrushchev of our kindly intentions, or of improving our international "image." Very few indeed believed that segregation was immoral or inhuman, or that the '54 decision was based on valid legal and scientific grounds.

RUDE AWAKENING

The first rude awakening in the South began with the NAACP-inspired suits in the Federal Courts, and culminated in the punitive invasion of Little Rock in 1957. The use of paratroopers with fixed bayonets to keep eight Negro children in a white school brought home to many southerners for the first time the strength and fanaticism behind the new reconstruction. Southerners knew that paratroopers had not been brought in to quell the frequent bloody strikes in New York's waterfront and elsewhere in the nation. But in Little Rock where there were no deaths and little real disorder, the army was dramatically flown in to force a handful of Negro children into a school where they were unwanted and unwelcome. The Little Rock affair will go down in history as a cruel exhibition of the use of naked Federal power against civilians. It was perhaps the most tyrannical government action since the first reconstruction.

WISHFUL THINKING

Many white southerners believed and still believe that the drive for "integration" will spend itself as they cannot conceive of an integrated white-black society. A good many are apathetic or uninterested because they have no children, or have them in private schools, and fatuously believe that desegregation will not affect them. Others are more concerned with loss of business than in the fate of their children. Some have joined the various humanitarian groups for what they hope are moral reasons. Many ministers of religion fall in the last category. The real affection of the white southerner for many of his Negro neighbors makes him hesitate to take economic or other counter-measures against them; and this very kindness has been exploited to the hilt by the NAACP.

The highly articulate mulattoes and near-whites of the NAACP want complete social integration because of its presumed prestige value. They look down on the darker Negroes and are generally shunned by the whites. Thus they hang between heaven and earth. What the dark-skinned Negro wants is hard to say, though my guess is that he would gladly settle for a better job, a better home and a newer car. In 1944, Myrdal [1] reported that economic improvement, not social mixing, was the Negro's goal and the same is probably true today.[2] But what the Negro would say as reported by the NAACP is quite another matter.

SOCIAL SECURITY

The white southerner has always looked after the Negro— given him work, fed him, nursed him when sick and gotten

---

[1] *An American Dilemma,* 1944, New York: Harper & Bros.
[2] When the Belgians left, many Congolese came with baskets to get their "independence."

him out of jail when drunk. Several perceptive northerners have remarked to me that the paternalism of the white southerner was a kind of personal social security system for the Negro—far more humane than the government welfare bureau.

The border states, where the Negro population is small, have desegregated a number of their schools and the Washington, D.C., schools, having been desegregated in 1954, have now resegregated, they are nearly all-Negro again. The whites have left the city. After 8 years, the amount of desegregation in the states of the old Confederacy is minuscule, though the Civil Rights Act is expected to alter this situation. There is still little organized opposition to desegregation in the South, except in Mississippi, Alabama and Louisiana. Here a solid phalanx of white public opinion faces the compulsive reformers. The strong opposition of the individual white is the main enemy of social integration; and is the reason why it will not come soon, if at all. Someone has said that integration is that period between the coming of the first Negro and the departure of the last white. The Negroes may not be sure what they want. But the mass of white southerners is certain what it doesn't want, and won't have, social intermixing of Negroes and whites.

TWO

Segregation is, in many respects, a unique American institution. After the Civil War, the South was left with the problem of what to do with its former slaves and freed Negroes. Most of the blacks were illiterate and many were exceedingly primitive. The abolitionist, as seems to be characteristic of the professional reformer, considered his work done once slavery was destroyed, and settled down, full of self-righteousness, in his northern home where there were no Negroes and no race problem. Segregation in the South was first self-protective. Unless some social barriers had been erected, and if miscegenation had been general, the South would have degenerated into a Puerto Rico, its material destroyed by war, and its European heritage ruined by mongrelism. It is likely that all but a handful of diehards in the North approved of segregation, at least grudgingly, when first instituted.

MERIT IN SEGREGATION

Segregation has in actuality worked quite well and would have worked out better, if the "separate but equal" principle had been adhered to more rigidly. Segregation forced him [the Negro] on his own initiative to build his own stores, churches, restaurants and banks; it built up a closely knit Negro society. At the same time, it permitted close friendships with whites in a sort of Big Brother relationship. The sensitive white who professes horror at segregation is thinking of himself, not of the dark-skinned Negro who is far less sensitive and may welcome it. When one protests that segregation has caused the Negro's backwardness, he is really saying that the Negro must be "integrated" into white society in order to progress: that he cannot move forward when he associates only with his own kind.

IT WAS DYING

Many of the trivial but galling restrictions under segregation had died out long before 1954: they simply fell because their utility had ended. In Richmond, Virginia, for example, when many Negroes worked in the tobacco factories, there was good reason why they should sit in a designated part of the street car on returning from work. As work in the tobacco factories became cleaner over the years, segregated sitting served no real purpose and was being abandoned.

WHY THE PROTEST

Desegregation of schools is protested by the white southerner because it requires a social intermingling hitherto unknown in this region. In many rural areas, the school building is the center of community and social activities; P. T. A. meetings, concerts, lectures, dances. In the North where the Negroes are fewer in number, the social problem is often acute but less massive. Hotels, restaurants, swimming pools are mostly segregated North and South, and any attempt to desegregate in either part of the country nearly always leads to tension and often to open strife. But it is abundantly clear that general social intermingling is the avowed purpose of the NAACP and of the national government, aided by the TV and the northern press, which makes almost a fetish of playing up mixed Negro and white groups. Pressure for social integration regardless of personal preferences is a disservice to both Negro and white. It has already led to outright riots in Chicago, Philadelphia, Rochester, San Francisco, and in other cities.

THREE

Up to World War I, it is probable that American scientists generally believed the Negro to be less intelligent and more indolent than the white and to be lacking in traits of honesty and reliability. And this judgment was concurred in by most white Americans.

Many social scientists today do not accept these one-time common-sense judgments. Instead, they hold that racial differences are only skin deep (a "paint job"); that whereas the black African differs from the white European in the breadth and depth of his culture, there are no inherited factors to account for these differences; that all races are potentially equal in mental potential and differ only in their opportunity for expression. Often times, the social scientist will include motivation as a cause of racial differences, together with discrimination and prejudice.

EQUALITARIANISM

The view that except for environmental pressures all races are equal has been called the "equalitarian dogma." It has spread through our colleges and schools and is widely acclaimed by sincere humanitarians, social reformers, crusaders, sentimentalists and—ostensibly—by politicians. Many ministers of religion, convinced that the concept of the "equality of man" is in keeping with the ideals of Christian brotherhood have joined the social scientists. Last, but by no means least, the Communists and their allies vigorously uphold the equalitarian dogma. Today, perhaps 20 per cent of scientists are in general agreement with equalitarianism, 10–15 per cent are strongly opposed, and the rest are neutral, uninterested or inclined to the "kind" side. But the man in the street, unenlightened by social science, is puzzled and quite unconvinced. He continues to trust the evidence of his eyes and ears.

CHIEF SUPPORT

Equalitarianism—or egalitarianism as it is sometimes called —finds its chief support in two clearly identifiable sources: the alleged scientific groups which have "proved" equality, and the religious groups which accept this proof and, on the basis of it, assert that belief in racial differences implies superiority and inferiority and is unchristian and blameworthy. Each camp supplements the other. The social scientists turn to moral platitudes and denunciation when their evidence is feeble, and the religious fall back on "science" to bolster their own moral preachments. From these two directions, the American people have for more than 30 years been subjected to a barrage of propaganda unrivalled in its intensity and self-righteousness.

Today in most colleges and universities departments of psychology, anthropology, sociology and even genetics, the equalitarian dogma is installed as a major premise. Young scientists jeopardize their careers by challenging the dogma and may be silenced by strong disapproval, or even dismissal. Many college students have been indoctrinated and parrot the equalitarian arguments with competent familiarity with the evidence, shifting from the scientific to the moral position as the occasion requires. The northern press and most of the slick magazines, together with the radio and TV, confidently proclaim equalitarianism.

FOUR

The shift from a general belief in native racial differences to acceptance of the no-difference formula has provided the basis (and the justification) for the second attempt at reconstruction in the South. There are at least five sources, I believe, which have initiated and directed the propaganda barrage which prepared the way for legal and social pressures. Let us examine these in order.

By far the most potent assault on the belief in native differences from the scientific side has come from the work of Franz

Boas and his followers. Boas may be described as the "father of the equalitarian movement."

Franz Boas (1858–1942) was born in Minden, Germany, and educated at Heidelberg, Bonn and Kiel. He came to this country in 1886 and from 1899 to 1936 was professor of anthropology at Columbia University. In his early years, Boas' main concern was physical anthropology, but in his later years he turned to "cultural or social" anthropology, and the study of primitive languages. In the first edition of his book, *The Mind of Primitive Man* (1911, revised 1938) Boas accepted the idea of different races, and held that since races (for example, Negro and white) differ in structure, they probably differ in mental traits. (It may be noted that races also differ in physiological, metabolic and biochemical characteristics.) In the 1938 edition of *The Mind,* Boas dropped out this statement having, as his disciple, [Otto] Klineburg wrote, "changed his mind."

NO NEGRO GREATS

On page 268 of *The Mind,* Boas wrote ". . . it seemed barely possible that *perhaps* (italics mine) the race (Negro) would not produce *quite so many* (italics mine) men of highest genius as other races, while there was nothing at all that could be interpreted as suggesting any material difference in the mental capacity of the bulk of the Negro population as compared with the bulk of the white population." As Boas had made no comparison of the "bulk" of the two populations, this statement is little more than a wishful guess. Furthermore, as regards men of genius, could Boas have truthfully said that the black African has produced *any* men *at all* to compare with the best of European whites: to compare, for instance, with Aristotle, Virgil, Thomas, Aquinas, Galileo, Voltaire, Goethe, Shakespeare or Newton? There is considerable evidence that Boas' devotion to the equalitarian dogma in his later years was motivated, at least in part, by strong political and ideological convictions. But it is hard to document this. Suffice it to say several of Boas' colleagues have been charged with Communist sympathies and one (Wetfish) was dropped from Columbia ostensibly for tenure reasons. In a public

speech, Wetfish charged the American army with using germ
warfare in Korea. The storm of protest from alumni and friends
of Columbia probably contributed to her ouster.

ABSURD STATEMENTS

Otto Klineberg, a social psychologist, is a disarming writer
and a thorough believer in culture as the "cause" of racial differences. In the UNESCO publication, *The Race Question in
Modern Science* (1956), Klineberg concludes his chapter on
Race and Psychology with the words: "The scientist knows of
no relation between race and psychology" (p. 84). I have com-
mented elsewhere on the sweeping character of this statement
in view of the feeble data presented in support of it. As it
stands, and without great qualification, the sentence is absurd.

BUNKUM

The equalitarian rarely offers objective measurements recognized as valid for judging the comparative abilities of various
groups of people. Rather, he resorts to three techniques which
should be looked for and guarded against by the unwary. First,
he uses bluff and positive statements, rhetorical questions and
glittering generalities. (For example, "Everyone knows there
are no race differences: look at Ralph Bunche.") If challenged,
the equalitarian falls back on evasion and ridicule. Favorite
epithets are bigot and racist, the latter meaning almost nothing.
Finally when pushed to the wall, he becomes emotional with
dark threats of what happened to Hitler.

NOSE COUNTING

Another technique frequently used by the equalitarian is
that of nose-counting. Many persons have read the UNESCO
pronouncements on race (1950 and 1952) but few have looked
into the qualifications of those who endorsed them nor have
they examined the objections voiced by many who refused to
sign. In a meeting some time ago, the American Anthropological Association passed the following resolution: "The American Anthropological Association repudiates statements now
appearing in the United States that Negroes are biologically
and in innate ability inferior to whites . . ." The vote of the

committee drawing up the resolution was 192 to 0. Much has been made of the unanimity of this vote but little of the fact that the Association lists some 1500 members, and that many of those voting were not experts on Negro-white differences in mental traits in the United States. Moreover, the resolution goes on to say that no citizen should be deprived of his voting rights because of race—a view which everyone can endorse. If voting were restricted to those who had intelligent opinions on a candidate or the issues, the electorate would be sharply reduced; and New York would be sparsely represented.[9]

THE FACTS

The view presented here is that psychological tests offer the most valid (because quantitative) data on Negro-white differences in mental ability in this country. The best recent survey of the comparative standing of American Negroes and American whites will be found in A. M. Shuey's *"The Testing of Negro Intelligence"* (1958, J. P. Bell, Lynchburg, Va.). This book covers 44 years, from 1913 to 1957, and analyzes some 240 studies. Comparisons are made of preschool children, grade and high school pupils, college students, the gifted and retarded, soldiers, delinquents, racial hybrids and migrants. Relevant conclusions are as follows:

1. The I.Q.'s of American Negroes, on the average, fall 15 to 20 points below those of comparable whites.
2. Negro overlap of white median I.Q.'s ranges from 10 per cent to 20 per cent—equality would require 50 per cent. The importance of overlap has been greatly exaggerated by equalitarians. To argue that overlap means no difference is as silly as to argue that because some women are taller than the average man there is no height advantage in the male. Or that because the insane overlap the normal of almost every test, everyone is normal (or insane).
3. About 6 times as many whites as Negroes fall in the "gifted

[9] A good example of how to settle an issue by nose-counting is that of the first-grade class which was given a kitten. As no one knew the sex of the little animal, the children voted on it. Female won, as there were more girls than boys in the class!

child" category; and about six times as many Negroes as
white fall below I.Q. 70, that is, in the feeble-minded group.
These differences follow, of course, from the fact of the
large mean difference.

4. Negro-white differences in test score occur in all types of
   mental tests, but the Negro lag is greatest in measures of
   an abstract nature (for example, problems involving reasoning, deduction and comprehension).

5. Differences between Negroes and whites increase with age,
   being largest at the upper age levels.

6. Large differences in favor of whites appear even when
   socio-economic factors are equated.

It is clear that the evidence from mental tests does not favor
the equalitarian dogma; in fact, just the opposite.

FIVE

Undoubtedly Hitler's cruelties and the absurd racial superiority theories of the Nazis set up a favorable climate for
the proponents of the equalitarian dogma. Hitler was a true
"racist," as is anyone who believes in the general superiority in
intelligence and character of some group (usually his own).
Racism uses such trems as "nordic Supremacy" and "Chosen
People."

MORE BUNKUM

It is easy for the equalitarian to argue that acceptance of the
fact of racial differences is the forerunner of racial superiority
notions with resultant discrimination, prejudice and persecution. But the argument is fallacious. Recognition of differences
between men and women, children and adults, normal and
insane, or normal and feeble-minded does not lead to persecution: but to the contrary. Recognition of the excellence of
many Negroes in sports and entertainment has if anything improved the feeling of the white majority toward Negroes generally. Hitler's persecution of the Jews has greatly oversensi-
tized the American Jew toward anything that smacks of racial
exclusion. The preoccupation of the Jews with racial matters
is evident in the activity of the various Jewish organizations

today. These groups aggressively support equalitarianism which they accept as scientifically proven. Ironically enough, the Jews who usually draw the racial line at the marriage altar stand to lose very little by so-called "integration."

SIX

The loudly proclaimed struggle for freedom and self-determination of the peoples of Africa has aroused the sympathy of many Americans and has strengthened the emotional appeal in the idea that all men are equally endowed at birth.

But emotionally founded beliefs can be deceptive. Apologists for the Africans speak as though the period of European colonialism was all suppression and exploitation of the black man, who was "insufficiently prepared" by the white man for life in the 20th century.

But why did the white man have to "prepare" the black man in the first place?

BLACK HISTORY

The African has had self-government (of a tribal sort) throughout most of his history, the colonial period being relatively short—only 80 years in the Belgian Congo. During this long period, we find not the fantasy of the happy savage free of modern tensions, but the reality of a miserable creature tormented by disease and by human and animal enemies, living a life of indescribable squalor. Murder of blacks by blacks was common, as were mutilation and extermination of one tribe by another.

Slavery and cannibalism were general.

It is true that several kingdoms in West Africa, during the middle ages, attained briefly a relatively high level of civilization, but these "magnificent civilizations" as the equalitarian calls them were hardly the equal of the then flourishing cultures in Europe and the Near East. The so-called "great university" at Timbuctu was a large mosque with a few teachers.

Moreover, this university was Arabic and Moslem, not Negro.

Linton [10] writes that these West African states were advanced in arts and crafts, but were not "literate." Garn [11] has said that there was no real civilization south of the Sahara. In short, the black African did not construct a system of writing an alphabet, built no bridges or terraces, did not discover the principle of the wheel, had no literature (only folk lore) and no science. The historian, Toynbee, has said that of the 21 great civilizations of the past, not one was Negro. For thousands of years before the coming of the Belgians, the Congolese made little apparent effort to grow into the 20th century: how could the Belgians pull them in, in the short space of 80 years? One may well wonder whether in the light of African history, the black African is capable of self-government. Recent events in the Congo confirm this gloomy outlook.

SEVEN

On May 17, 1954, the Supreme Court of the United States handed down its decision on desegregation of schools. This decree was hailed by equalitarians who rightly regarded it as a great victory for their cause. Ministers of religion and religious folk jumped on the band wagon, and even southern preachers who had lived contentedly under segregation found the moral pressure too much and came out for unrestrained brotherhood without discrimination. Public figures in the North called on the South to obey as "the law of the land" a mandate that for 60 years previously had been just the opposite.

REWRITING HISTORY

A historian, A. H. Kelley [12] has given us an account of how the history of the 14th amendment was rewritten to make it more palatable to the Supreme Court.

At the behest of the NAACP, Kelley was assigned the task of selecting, slanting and editing the accounts of the adoption of the 14th amendment so that it could be construed as opposing segregated schools. Kelley's story is a frank recital of a de-

---

10 Linton, Ralph. The Tree of Culture. 1955, N.Y., Knopf.
11 Garn, S. M. Personal Communication, March 1962.
12 Kelley, A. H., U. S. News and World Report, Feb. 5, 1962, 86–88.

ception which in a saner time and with a less emotional subject
would have led to his being discredited by his colleagues.

DIRTY HANDS

It has been argued that the Supreme Court relied on modern
social theory rather than legal precedent. This is probably true
—at least to a large extent—and hence it is important for us
to examine the credentials of the social scientists referred to in
the Court's decision. Of the 8 listed by the Court as references
in the decision, none had a national reputation; one had 18
citations of membership in communist-front organizations, another 10. Two were Negroes. Obviously, the Court's authorities did not come before the American people without bias and
with clean hands.

Perhaps the Court's reference to "generally Myrdal" has
been the most severally criticized. Gunnar Myrdal, a Swedish
"social economist" (his own description), is the author of *An
American Dilemma,* a book published in 1944 with the help of
a grant from the Carnegie Corporation. The book is in two
volumes which together total about 1500 pages. Myrdal is no
admirer of the American system or form of government. He
speaks, for instance, of the "cult of the constitution" which he
says has been able to "block the popular will." Again he writes
that there is an anarchistic tendency in American legal circles
"to desire to regulate human behavior tyrannically by means
of formal laws." The Court agreed with the first statement, but
missed the second. Myrdal was aided by 70-odd social scientists many of them well-known radicals with long communist-
front records. Throughout the two volumes the equalitarian
dogma is assumed to be true.

EIGHT

It is certain that the Communists have aided in the acceptance and spread of equalitarianism although the extent and
method of their help is difficult to assess. Equalitarianism is
good Marxist doctrine, not likely to change with gyrations in
the Kremlin "line." Moreover, the forceful application of the
dogma foments tension and bitterness on which the Communists thrive. Communists and their front-men have served the

cause of equalitarianism well: in government, entertainment, radio, the press and television. Many non-Communists, stung by the claims of the Communists of "brotherhood," loudly champion equalitarianism.

WEIGHT OF THE EVIDENCE

The weight of the evidence strongly favors the view that racial differences in mental ability are real and are probably genetic. No effort should be spared to give the Negro better training, to upgrade him in his job, to provide technical and professional education. But unless the equalitarian dogma is discredited and abandoned, it will lead inevitably to social integration, intermarriage, amalgamation of white and Negro, and to a general deterioration in American standards of culture and intelligence. This is not a pleasant prospect, and is the reason why the South is refusing again to be reconstructed. Social segregation will continue to be maintained in the South without legal support, as it has been maintained all along in the North. Most white Americans whose contact with the Negro is direct and personal, realize (if they do not express) the great gulf between the two races. They know intuitively that we can ill afford any retrogression in the world today. And racial amalgamation might just be the difference between survival and destruction.

THE LEGACY OF THE PAST: RACISM IN PRESENT-DAY AMERICA

The printing presses of racist organizations continue to spill out their materials. In the 1970's, they repeat many of the old familiar arguments: the need for African colonization, the inherent inferiority of blacks, the dangers of miscegenation and "Jewish money power." In addition, recent extremist literature claims the existence of a black-Jewish-liberal-Communist conspiracy to amalgamate the races and establish totalitarian control of the United States. And anti-Catholic feeling, usually associated with the nineteenth century, is still evident.

While most of the literature emanates from the South, many of its sources can be found in cities from coast to coast. Thus, no area and no minority group today is immune to racist propaganda. And currently, Mexican-Americans and Puerto Ricans are among the prime targets of the nation's bigots. One other unfortunate development of the 1970's is the practice of racism by one of its leading victims—the blacks. Apparently, the lessons taught by racial extremists have been adopted by some blacks who have produced their own brand of hate literature. Thus, in areas of large black-Jewish concentrations (New York City), where there is close daily contact, some blacks utilize the timeworn American custom of anti-Semitism to vent their frustrations on Jewish landlords, teachers and shopkeepers.

Due to the blatant and unsophisticated nature of the racial assaults of the seventies, detailed explanations of the following documents are unnecessary. These bitter racist publications of contemporary America literally shout out their story, and so are presented without comment.

Had enough, Whitey?

Now that you've had a good, hard look at the wonders of the colored brother, Honky, how much longer are you just going to sit there with your thumb up your behind?

The grand experiment has fizzled. Higher education and Negroes do not mix. The moist-eyed, color-blind equalitarians, of course, will never admit that a government grant, a little interracial sex, and a lot of wishful thinking won't convert a Negro into a valuable and useful citizen. After all, that great savant and Negro chemist, George Washington Carver, after only thirty years in the laboratory discovered that smashed-up peanuts make mighty good peanut-butter sandwiches. And besides, what about the Rights of Man, Equal Opportunity, and Human Dignite-e-e?

If you're getting a little tired of these insane, racially destructive cliches, regardless of the straight face with which they're shoved at you, maybe there's some hope for you yet.

Gangs of subhuman blacks have been acting like lobotomized, antisocial chimpanzees at schools all over America long enough now. They are disrupting studies, wrecking campuses, and catastrophically lowering the prestige of American universities in the eyes of the world.

You can abandon all hope that Tricky Dick or any of the other Party politicians, left or right, will straighten out the mess. The gutless, self-interested System will NEVER face the truth and take the radical measures necessary to solve the racial problem in America. For there is only one realistic, long-term solution—only one FINAL SOLUTION—and that is to make this an all-White America. The time to start building toward this goal is NOW.

In addition to the Jews, the masochistic, self-hating liberals, and the cowardly compromisers, there are certainly White men and women at your school with healthy convictions and the courage to back up those convictions. The National Socialist Liberation Front, the student-activist arm of the National Socialist White People's Party, has a program of action for White students in American universities.

If you are proud of your racial heritage, vitally concerned about the future of your own people, and too mad to be intimidated into silence any longer, write TODAY for free information. (Send a stamped, self-addressed envelope.)

 NATIONAL SOCIALIST WHITE PEOPLE'S PARTY
2507 N. Franklin Road   Arlington, Virginia   22201

THE REAL PROBLEM IN D C...

... is not police brutality or White racism, for certainly no other police force has been more restricted in its handling of criminals, and nowhere else have White liberals so totally capitulated to Black demands.

The problem in D.C. is not a scarcity of welfare handouts, because money to the unemployed and unemployable flows more freely here than in any other American city.

The problem in Washington is not a shortage of jobs. Not since FDR's CCC days have so many jobs been artificially created.

The problem in our Nation's Capital is not poor education. Only three other cities in the country spend more to educate each pupil.

The real problem in D.C. is not poor administration by the city council, although dim-witted Walter Washington and his sly Jewish cohort Gilbert Hahn have admittedly done everything in their power to make D.C. unfit for habitation.

The real problem in D.C. is Niggers!

Wherever Negroes go they breed immorality, filth, and disorder. Neither federal handouts nor restrictions on the police nor jobs nor higher education will improve the Negro mentality.

The only way to treat a cancer is to cut it out by the roots. The only way to cure the Negro problem is to make this an all-White America.

If you're sick and tired of unsafe streets in the Nation's Capital, of footing the bill for the biggest handout program in history, and of the phony excuses for America's problems which are fed you by the press, contact us; we've got some answers:

NATIONAL SOCIALIST WHITE PEOPLE'S PARTY
2507 N. Franklin Road   Arlington Virginia   22201

WHITE POWER MESSAGE—CALL 528—4361

UPTIGHT About School...
...or just about the Niggers??

Have you "had it" with Black animals following you home to beat you up, or pushing your head in the toilet when you go to the john, or "holding" your lunch money for you?

Are you "up to here" with Black bastards who steal your clothes, your wallets, your pocketbooks?

Are you really uptight because White girls have to submit to being "felt up" in the halls by crowds of grinning Black monkeys?

If you're uptight about any of these things, you've probably noticed that whenever a White student tries to do anything about it he gets shafted.

On the other hand, the Blacks can get away with whatever they want, because they stick together and because the gutless school administration is afraid to oppose them.

Conditions in schools have become so rotten that trying to get an education has become a laugh. Who can learn anything caged up with a bunch of cannibals?

They've been telling us for years that niggers are "equal." What a bunch of crap! An administration that believes that is really out of it. As long as they stick together and we don't, we're screwed. But when we learn to stick together, there's nothing we can't accomplish. Let's start learning!

The only way we'll ever have control of our schools again is to ORGANIZE and then throw the Black scum out into the streets.

Students! Support White self-determination in this school. Join the National Socialist Liberation Front, an organization of students for a White America.

For information, write:

 NATIONAL SOCIALIST LIBERATION FRONT
2507 N. Franklin Road, Arlington, Virginia 22201

YOUTH
CAMPS

SCOUT CAMPS

How would you like it if your exquisitely formed White child was no longer White? Pink cheeks no longer pink? Blue eyes no longer blue, lovely hair no longer lovely?

It's sensitive mind no longer sensitive but ape like? It's beautiful body no longer beautiful but black and evil smelling?

A few drops of negro blood in your child's veins and it could have a coal black negro baby.

The blood in your White child is the most precious thing on earth (civilizations are built upon it)and many evil minded men know this to be a fact. They have organized into groups to "get" this blood away from you.

Some foolish Christians tell you it is God's will -- as if God who aims at the beautiful, the good, and intelligent, would want to destroy and dirty his loveliest gifts.

These evil men have organized child movements and camps to further their evil designs. Some of these camps are Jewish, some Christian, some political, some union. All pose as democracy in action and the object of all is to get your White child's blood.

People only go after what is better than they have and never hunt something inferior to what they possess.

Remember it is always grown people " adults " who operate these camps. Adults with a queer bent who could never prey upon a grown person but must have the tender, innocent, unsuspecting mind of your child with which to do their evil work.

Scientists claim that such adults who are unduly attracted to White children and wish to mix them with negroes are suffering from a Freudian Complex that gives them a sex thrill at the very thought of mating your lovely child with the evil ape like body of the negro.

This act of mating is not done at the camps but your child's mind is poisoned with false social and religious ideas at its most susceptible stage so that the act of marriage can be accomplished later. They must steal your child's mind before they can steal its body.

This should be warning enough. You know where your treasure is. Protect it. To keep your child from negroes it will be necessary to keep it away from all youth movements - - with especial emphasis on those that pose as religious or political or democratic.

Don't let the devil with the angle's wings carry away your Lovely. It is only the lovely they want and what a howl these hyenas can make of race discrimination when they can't get your lamb in their fangs.

Remember all youth movements have for their special feature the mixing of negroes with your White child and if it were not for the beauty of the White child none of these camps would be in existence.

Boy camps condition your boy to bring home a negro buddy for your little daughter. Girl camps condition your daughter to bring home a negro pal for your White boy. Don't let them get by with it.

Here is just a few with sweet sounding names. The spider's web to catch the unsuspecting fly -- in this case your pretty White cherub.

YMCA, YWCA, Labor Union Camp, Chicago Community Conference, Youth Congress, Young Adult Councils, Youth For Christ, Young Civic Councils, Political Action Volunteers, Youth For Democracy, Jewish Welfare Group, Scout Camps For Boys, Scout Camps For Girls.

These are just a few. A lot of these camps change their names when they are found out, but they continue to operate under new names and their object is to destroy the civilized world for Communism by mating your White Innocent with the loathsome negro.

© W. Wolfe

Negro Blood Destroyed the Civilization of Egypt, India, Phoenicia, Carthage, Greece and Rome.

It will Destroy America!

5¢ per copy   THE WHITE SENTINEL   50 for $1.00
P.O. BOX 9013
FT. LAUDERDALE FLA.

AIN'T WORKING ON NO RAILROAD"

I ain't working on no Railroad,
I won't work for twice de pay,
I works for Mr. Johnson,
On de Federal give-a-way.

You ain't seen me dig no taters,
You ain't seen me rend no lard,
'Cause I gets 'em both for nuttin,
With my commissary card.

Ain't no early in de mawnin',
So I lays in bed til late,
'Cause early in the mawnin',
Ain't no time to demonstrate.

Sometimes I lays on de sidewalk,
Sometimes I lays in de door,
An when I feels rambunctious,
I burns up a liquor store.

Den dey catch me by de feet,
and drags me off to county jail,
But I'se out next mawnin,
On N-double A-CP bail.

Den Mr. King gets on de air,
He says dey is mean to me,
So we makes up a song,
An calls it "Police Brutality".

Den Mr. Johnson says,
"Turn him loose, let him be,
I done got him registered,
He gwine vote for me"

I once thought white folks was smart,
But now I think their brains has went,
Dey gwine wake up one mawnin,
And us'ns will be President!

United Klans of America, Inc.
Realm of Indiana,
Post Office Box 426
Greenwood, Indiana 46142

SONS OF LIBERTY

BOX 1896·HOLLYWOOD, CA.

11/70

Dear Patriot:

Enclosed you will find our latest book lists.

The Sons of Liberty is the oldest patriotic organization in America founded by Samuel Adams in 1768.

In recent years we have been active in publishing suppressed books and booklets on the race issue and distributing our hard hitting <u>SONS OF LIBERTY NEWSLETTER</u>. In the last three years we have published: Judaism in Music, Proof of Negro Inferiority, The Jews, Jewish Press Control, Adam Weishaupt: A Human Devil, The Five Races of Europe, The Whiteman's Guidebook, A Gallery of Jewish Types, Judaism and Bolshevism, Riddle of the Jews Success, and many other booklets on Race and religion.

Through our efforts thousands of books long suppressed by the jews have been distributed throughout America. We are a non-profit political organization and all our money goes back into the fight for the preservation of the White Race and Western Civilization.

Our latest project has been to print and distribute thousands of copies of the PROTOCOLS and BEHIND COMMUNISM at cost plus postage. (Protocols: 73 pages, 10 for $1.50; Behind Communism: 100 pages, 10 for $2.50) We have also started a service to supply patriots with NEW books at up to 60% discount. (Special titles we list each month) A list of our book specials is printed on the back of this letter.

In the past five months we have distributed 5,000 Protocols, 3,500 Behind Communism, 1,000 Bible Speaks to America and numerous other books, booklets and newsletters.

In the coming year we hope to distribute at least 50,000 protocols and many thousands of other books specially printed for mass distribution. Will you stand with us in our fight for the survival of the White Race and Western Civilization? Your book orders and contributions make it possible for us to keep on the firing line and to expand our work.

We hope to hear from you soon.

For the White Race,

Dr. James K. Warner
National Leader, Sons of Liberty

Are You An Anti-Semite?

IF you are a Christian believing in the divinity of Jesus Christ crucified, — **You are a potential antisemite.**
You will be so classified by the leaders of the Anti-Defamation League, which is a branch of the powerful Jewish Order of the B'NAI BRITH.

IF you believe in the unity of action of the Christian world, regardless of denomination, race or color, — **You are an antisemite.**

IF as an American you believe in and proclaim the unadulterated essence of the Constitution, the sovereignty of the American nation, its independence, freedom and liberty, — **You are an antisemite.**

IF you believe and say that America is a Christian nation, — **You are an antisemite, a dangerous one.**

IF you believe in Patriotism, loyalty to America, if you pledge allegience to none but the American flag and are devoted to the service of your country, — **You are an antisemite.**

IF you oppose INTERNATIONALISM, COMMUNISM under all its forms, variations, transformations, disguises and masks and trace it every time to its source, — **You are an antisemite.**

IF you show Communism behind Socialism, Fabianism, Fascism, Zionism, Collectivism, Public ownership, nationalization of the country's natural and industrial resources, — **You are an antisemite.**

IF you voice opposition to the tortures and bloody massacres of Christians, namely Catholics of the Roman and Russian-Greek Orthodox faith, as exemplified in Russia, Spain, Mexico, Hungary, Poland, Czecho Slovakia, Armenia, China, Korea, — **You are an antisemite.**

IF you decry the monstrous injustice and crimes committed against the Arabs by the Zionist Jewish power in Palestine with the sanction of our present Administration, — **You are an antisemite.**

IF you believe in the need of Christian education of Christian American children and demand that the Bible and the Lord's prayer be re-introduced in all American schools, — **You are an antisemite**

IF you object to the discriminatory treatment meted out to American Junior high school students who, in Santa Ana, California were refused the use of a school room in their school building after hours to hold their Bible reading club, —**You are an antisemite.**

IF you are justly revolted and indignant at the order given by the Zionist Anna M. Rosenberg, Under-Secretary of Defense, to suppress crosses marking the graves of young Christian Americans sacrificed on the battlefields. — **You are an antisemite.**

IF you believe in the protection of children to save them from delinquency and criminality and vehemently oppose the existence and maintenance of **"national rings of perversion of young children"** as revealed, last August, at the trial of the abominable GUZIK case in Phoenix, Arizona, — **You are an antisemite.**

IF you oppose the atheistic, godless educational program of the National Education Association, its dictatorship exercised through the system of Progressive Education, — **You are an antisemite.**

IF in politics, you oppose corruption, bribery, blackmail and the control of the White House, the Administration Congress, and political parties by the Jewish hierarchy, — **You are an antisemite.**

IF you oppose and expose the **Internationalism** of the ideologies of WORLD GOVERNMENT, UNITED NATIONS, WORLD FEDERALISM, ATLANTIC UNION, all destroyers of patriotism through wars, revolutions, and slavery, — **You are an antisemite.**

IF you dare attack the power and tyranny of the Labor Union Bosses, — **You are an antisemite.**

IF you denounce the control exercised over the F.B.I. by the Anti-Defamation League, the persecution of loyal Christian patriots contrasted with the protection and immunity granted to spies and Communists of all kinds in the U. S. — **You are an antisemite.**

IF you condemn treason and "turn your back" on traitors of the Alger Hiss variety and other followers of Judas Iscariot, — **You are an antisemite.**

IF you speak of and denounce the "Invisible and Secret Government" in the United States as exposed in Congress and the Press, — **You are an antisemite.**

IF you oppose the butchery of young boys in Korea and elsewhere to impose upon peoples the rules of the international United Nations under the U.N. international flag, — **You are an antisemite.**

IF you dare oppose the tyranny and despotism of International Finance as did Father Coughlin, the late Congressman Louis T. McFadden, the late Senator Schall, — **You are an antisemite.**

IF you believe that the revelations made by Disraeli in his book Coningsby on world control by Jewish power are sustained by historical facts, — **You are an antisemite.**

IF you believe that the diabolical, Machiavellian plans of statesmanship formulated in the Protocols of the Elders of Zion are being gradually applied for the attainment of world domination, — **You are an antisemite.**

Search your own heart and mind and give yourself the answers to the above questions in the glowing light of **truth.** Gird yourself with fearlessness and indomitable courage, then, if to be a Christian patriotic American causes you to be stigmatized by the name "antisemite", be justly proud of this title which is not a term of odium but has now become the trade mark of fearless Christian American Patriotism opposed to Communist Internationalism.

If you can ignore the aspersions cast upon your character, your reputation in the columns of a controlled Press, if you calmly defy the Whispering drives started against you, if you can withstand persecution, smear, false accusations, even jail and torture such as the 33 Christian Patriots had to endure in the "SEDITION Case" of 1942 because they were accused of antisemitism, **then be proud of** being also called antisemites. **This term applied to you is evidence that you are working loyally and faithfully in the service of your Christian Faith and Country.**

For Christ and Country
KEEP AMERICA COMMITTEE
P. O. BOX 3094, LOS ANGELES 54, CALIF.
E. W. Courtois, Secretary

December, 1951
Reprinted May, 1954.

NATIONAL CITIZENS UNION
156 FIFTH AVENUE, NEW YORK, N.Y. 10011

ELIZABETH SHEPHERD
Founder and Director

P.O. Box 2055, Grand Central Stat
New York 17, N.Y.

May 22, 1964

Dear Members and fellow Patriots:

It's on. It will not be stopped. Those who choose to live only in freedom are making plans for

1,000,000 Caucasians to

MARCH ON WASHINGTON

July 4, 1964

THESE ARE THE PEOPLE who are weary of writing to their Congressmen protesting disarmament, civil rights legislation, the income tax, foreign aid, prayer bans, government by executive order, and all other sovietizing measures, and who are beginning to realize that even if all of these measures were defeated this year they would all appear again next year, under a different guise, unless the source of these evils is curbed. THESE ARE THE PEOPLE who know that life in a free country is not to be wasted away writing and writing and writing to their Congressmen. THESE ARE THE PEOPLE WHO WANT VILLANY BROUGHT UNDER CONTROL.

For all members of the National Citizens Union who will be able to make this trip, the following is a review of our purpose, and the reasons:

The source of these evils is the Jewish community, and the sovietizing of this land, and other civilized nations, cannot be ended until Jewish activities are restricted by an Amendment to the Constitution. Below is a partial list of Jewish abuses of this nation's freedom, stated here as reasons for seeking this amendment:

1) They have broken down all concepts by which intellectual progress is achieved, and have destroyed the carefully developed political and judicial structure of this nation.

2) They have displaced the best scholars in our universities, condemning them to silence or the alternative of professional ruin through smear, while depriving us of important knowledge.

3) They have ended religious freedom in America by forbidding Christian ministers to quote on radio and television, and even in their own churches, what Christ said about the Jews, or Scriptural bases for separation of the races.

4) They have kept their own religious book, the Talmud, secret from non-Jews, though it is the basis of the religion they practice in this country. The Talmud teaches that non-Jews are not human beings, and can be deceived, robbed and degraded, and that the best Gentiles must be killed. It teaches that all property belongs to the Jews, who can seize it without scruples.

5) They are the leaders of all organizations aiming to achieve total integration of White Christians and Negroes, with the avowed aim of destroying the White race.

6) They have entered this country illegally in large numbers, defying the laws they then expect to protect them after they have arrived.

7) They use their freedom to organize, then advocate measures designed to destroy the freedom of White Christians--to enforce integration with Negroes, to dictate to the Christian churches, to send our substance overseas, to set up a dictatorship in our government, and so on.

8) They send money out of the United States in large sums to Jews in other parts of the world, then recommend restricting provisions for soldiers' families overseas in order to prevent the outflow of the American dollar.

) They hold an excessive number of high posts (appointive) in government, but a low percentage f them are found among the soldiers on the fighting front.

10) They center their efforts on those areas in our society through which all the rest of society can be controlled, as in publishing, news, law, public relations, finance and government.

11) They have been proven to be the leaders of syndicates for crime, prostitution and abortion, and the publishers and purveyors of unspeakable immoralities sold in "respectable" book stores as literature or new psychological knowledge.

12) They protest against "anti-Semitism" yet use their influence as a group to win political support for Israel against Arab (Semitic) nations.

13) They have purposely misrepresented our earlier patriots in order to further their own goals in the name of these patriots. Their persecution of today's patriots is a matter of record.

14) Their part in setting up Soviet control in Russia, their murder of millions of Christians and other peoples since 1917, and their favoritism toward Soviet Russia and soviet-style governments is well established. Their numbers in our government have brought about the slaughter of Christian leaders in South Vietnam, Laos, the Middle East, and all countries where their communistic goals have been challenged.

THE FOLLOWING AMENDMENT IS THEREFORE PROPOSED:

Congress shall pass such laws as it deems necessary to restrict the power of Jews, without regard to the limitations on freedom of speech, press, religion and commerce as such laws mi might incur to them. Such laws should:

    a) Forbid Jews to run for elective office or hold appointive office in any local or state government, or the Federal government.
    b) Forbid Jews to own or be employed by banks or other financial concerns.
    c) Forbid Jews to own or be employed by any concern that publishes, or any concern that produces news and entertainment.
    d) Forbid Jews to teach in schools and colleges attended by non-Jews.
    e) Forbid Jews to organize as Jews.
    f) Forbid Jews to obtain passage from the U.S. to any other White Christian nation.

While Fourth of July celebrations used to be joyous occasions, this one will be a solemn proclamation to the world that we will not relax until we can be assured that this villany will not again consume our culture and destroy justice in THIS LAND OR ANY OTHER CIVILIZED NATION.

Hoping to see you in Washington, I am

                          Yours for a free America,

                          Elizabeth Shepherd

THE NEGRO PROBLEM IS A SEXUAL PROBLEM

Close That Bedroom

Copies Available $2
FROM —

TRUTH SEEKER CO., BOX, 2R
NEW YORK 3, N.Y.

THIS LEAFLET: 1 COPY, 1¢; 100, $

You will notice a woman's hand closing that bedroom door.

One might ask, "Where, for Pete's sake, is her husband at a time like this?"

Well, in this mixed up land, like as not the husband is on the other side of that door helping the Negro.

Perhaps you have not noticed before that it is the white man rather than the white woman who is leading the fight for Negro rights in white society. Men make up our courts, occupy our pulpits, lead our political parties, manage the armed forces, boss our schools, in each of which the Negro's advancement is a great crusade. We see these white men on TV, hear them on the radio and read their stuff in the press urging and extolling the social (and therefore inevitably the sexual) integration of the races. That invisible white man behind that door demanding entrance for the Negro might even be named Nixon or Warren or Peale or Pike or Eisenhower, but for the fact, perhaps, that white men of prominence insulate themselves from social contacts with Negroes and thus never offer their own women and children as pawns on the altars of miscegenation and debased standards. Rather, these white leaders proffer freely and with a great show of religion and liberalism the little man's womenfolk and progeny as being exactly what the Negro needs to uplift him in school, in college, in swimming pools and, it would appear, in dark alleys, too. These are to serve as bait for the Negro's patronage in the voting booth and confessional.

The point is that this surrender of our racial heritage was originated and is being actively promoted by white men.

The white woman's attitude toward the Black is different. She is instinctively aware that this trumped up demand that the Negro be admitted to white people's parlors is a sly invitation to him that he go a step further into the bedroom where her sex and her kind are the bait in the political and religious trap, the appeal for votes, the lamb on the altar stone. We can rest assured that the American white woman, unlike the renegade white leader, wants no amalgamation of the races, now or ever.

CLOSE THAT BEDROOM DOOR is a stirring appeal to the white woman to stand and fight. It tells the story of woman's long struggle for civil rights of her own. It covers sex and the Negro in slave days as never before. It is crowded with little known facts about the African in America. It is an important book!

But the proposition has not until now been presented to the white woman as a sexual campaign with interbreeding the aim. All through the North and the West she is told that this is simply a campaign for justice and civil rights long denied to an oppressed minority. Thus is she brain-washed, beaten over the head endlessly with that vicious sophistry, "all men are created equal," a cliche which the slave-owning planter Thomas Jefferson never meant for a moment. Only thus is the white woman induced to take the Negro by the hand.

It boils down to this: if the white race is to last another 200 years in America we must look to our women for action—political action. Woman suffrage in this country is only 37 years old, Negro suffrage 87. The Negro is thought now to carry the balance of power; they say he will elect our next President!

But what political power lies in the hands of 50 million white women! When scores of them are being raped daily by Negroes! When their bright children in school are being down-graded to the level of the Negro mentality! When it has become unsafe to go abroad at night, even with a male escort!

Close

That

Bedroom

Door!

by

Patricia

Schuyler